T0301364

Governance, Regulation and Innovation

Governance, Regulation and Innovation

Theory and Evidence from Firms and Nations

Edited by

Mehmet Ugur

University of Greenwich, UK

Edward Elgar

Cheltenham, UK • Northampton, MA, USA

Published by
Edward Elgar Publishing Limited
The Lypiatts
15 Lansdown Road
Cheltenham
Glos GL50 2JA
UK

Edward Elgar Publishing, Inc.
William Pratt House
9 Dewey Court
Northampton
Massachusetts 01060
USA

A catalogue record for this book
is available from the British Library

Library of Congress Control Number: 2013936183

This book is available electronically in the ElgarOnline.com
Economics Subject Collection, E-ISBN 978 1 78254 066 3

ISBN 978 1 78254 065 6

Typeset by Servis Filmsetting Ltd, Stockport, Cheshire
Printed and bound in Great Britain by T.J. International Ltd, Padstow

Contents

Contributors

Andrea Conte is an Economist at the European Commission, Joint Research Centre, Institute for Prospective Technological Studies, Seville (Spain). He holds a MSc and PhD in Economics from CORIPE (2003) and the Economics Department of the University of Turin, Italy (2007). He was a visiting research fellow at the CNR (Italian National Research Council), ISTAT (Italian National Statistical Office), Rome, Italy; ILO (International Labour Organization), Geneva, Switzerland; and Birkbeck College, London, UK. He was Senior Research Fellow at the Max Planck Institute of Economics, Jena, Germany from 2005 to 2007. He joined the European Commission in 2008 in the Directorate General – Economic & Financial Affairs (ECFIN), Brussels, Belgium before moving to the Joint Research Centre, Seville (Spain). He is a specialist in innovation, public finance and regional policy, and has authored or co-authored a number of articles on these issues.

Pelin Demirel is Lecturer in Industrial Economics at Nottingham University Business School, UK since 2008. Her research interests span various areas related to innovation and industry dynamics; in particular, the drivers of environmental innovations in developed and developing countries, the role of external finance in supporting clean-technology innovations and the implications of R&D for firm performance. Her main publications appear in *Research Policy, Regional Studies, Ecological Economics, Industry and Innovation, World Economy* and *Strategic Change*. Her research has been funded by the ESRC Innogen Centre, British Academy and University of Nottingham Researchers' Funds. She currently participates in various research projects investigating the firm level drivers of environmental innovations in the UK, the relationships between innovation and growth among Chinese start-up firms, industry dynamics in the UK's clean-tech sector and the motivating factors for environmental protection in Turkey.

Peter-Jan Engelen is Associate Professor of Corporate Finance and Corporate Governance at Utrecht University, the Netherlands. He is doing research on comparative corporate governance, the impact of institutions on corporate finance, financial crime, and investment under uncertainty (real options applications on R&D and sustainable energy solutions). He has published in several journals including the *Journal of Banking and Finance, Research Policy, Technovation, Journal of Business Finance & Accounting, Review of Law and Economics, European Journal of Law & Economics*, and *Journal of Business Ethics*.

G. Scott Erickson is Professor of Marketing in the School of Business at Ithaca College, Ithaca, NY where he has also served as Associate Dean and as Chair of the Marketing/Law Department. He holds a PhD from Lehigh University, Masters degrees from Thunderbird and Southern Methodist University, and a BA from Haverford College. He served as Fulbright Research Chair at The Monieson Centre at Queen's Business School, Kingston, ON in 2010/2011. He has published widely on intellectual property, intellectual capital, knowledge management, and competitive intelligence. His latest book with Helen N. Rothberg, *Intelligence in Action*, was published by Palgrave Macmillan in fall 2012 and was launched with a keynote presentation at the 13th European Conference on Knowledge Management in Cartagena, Spain.

Marc van Essen is Assistant Professor at the Sonoco International Business Department at the Moore School of Business, University of South Carolina. His primary research interests cover comparative corporate governance, institution-based view of business strategy, and meta-analytic research methods, with particular focus on ownership concentration and identity. His work has been published or is forthcoming in: *Academy of Management Journal, Asia Pacific Journal of Management, Journal of Banking and Finance, Journal of International Business Studies, Journal of Management*, and *Organization Science*.

Nawar Hashem is Lecturer in Financial Markets at Damascus University, Syria. He holds a PhD in Business from the University of Greenwich. His doctoral thesis is on industry concentration and stock returns, using data on publicly listed companies in the UK. Previously, he has worked as part-time lecturer and part-time research fellow at the University of Greenwich. His main research interests lie in the areas of asset pricing, industrial economics, innovation and risk, governance quality, and corporate governance.

Freddy Huet is Assistant Professor in Economics at the University of La Reunion (Reunion Island). He holds a PhD in Economics from the Department of Economics, University of Paris I (2006). His field of research is contract economics, organizational choices and the performance of public-private partnership agreements with applications in the water and waste industries. He has authored and co-authored articles and has worked on projects for the Ministry of Environment on these issues.

Effie Kesidou is Lecturer in Applied Economics at the University of Leeds and holds a PhD in Economics from Eindhoven University of Technology, Eindhoven Centre for Innovation Studies, the Netherlands (2007). Previously, she was employed as a Lecturer at the University of Nottingham and as a Research Associate at the Centre for Enterprise, Manchester Metropolitan University, UK. Her research interests lie in the areas of environmental innovations, economics of innovation, economic development and the software industry. She has received funding from the Netherlands Organisation for Scientific Research (NWO) and the University of Nottingham. She has published her work in journals of international excellence, such as *Research Policy, Ecological Economics, World Development, European Journal of Development Research,* and *Industry and Innovation.*

Simon Porcher is Research Fellow at Université Paris 5 and Sorbonne Business School. He holds a PhD in Management from Université Paris I Panthéon-Sorbonne. He authored and co-authored a number of scientific articles and book chapters on the motivations behind organizational choices for the provision of public services and on the link between these choices and performance. He has also published several articles and book chapters on industrial policy, stakeholder theory and the informal economy. He serves as a reviewer for several economic journals. He is an expert for the influential French think tank Terra Nova.

Eshref Trushin is Senior Teaching Fellow at Durham University Business School, Department of Economics and Finance. Previously, he has worked as chief and senior economist at BearingPoint-USAID Central Asia Economic Reform Project (2003–05 and 2006–07); and as consultant for the World Bank's Development Economics Research Group (2002). Before moving to Durham, he worked as lecturer in International Business and Economics at the University of Greenwich. His research is on economics of innovation, pharmaceutical R&D, and econometric policy evaluation.

Mehmet Ugur is Professor of Economics and Institutions at the University of Greenwich Business School. His research is on the interactions between economic governance, corporate governance and economic performance in terms of economic growth, innovation, employment, income distribution and EU public policy. He is research coordinator for the Department of International Business and Economics and convenor of the Master's program in Business and Financial Economics. He has led and managed research projects funded by the European Commission, the Department for International Development (DFID), and the Economic and Social

Research Council (ESRC). He is also Co-convenor for the Cochrane and Campbell Collaborations Economics Methods Group (CCEMG) and the coordinator of the Centre for Economic Performance, Governance and Regulation (CEPGR). He is the author of several books and journal articles on the relationship between governance quality and economic, corporate and public policy performance.

Preface

Innovation is a major driver of productivity and long-run growth. However, fostering innovation is a complex policy issue because factors that affect firm incentives to innovate are varied and do not necessarily work in tandem. On the one hand, the level of competition bears upon pre- and post-innovation profits and may encourage or discourage innovation depending on the overall effect. Similarly, firm- and country-specific factors such as corporate governance, economic governance institutions, regulatory frameworks, and macroeconomic variables may also encourage or deter innovation as they create different incentives and constraints that affect the innovative effort differently. Furthermore, market structure and firm/country characteristics are likely to interact and create complementary or offsetting effects that call for careful consideration of policy choices.

This volume aims to disentangle the complex relationship between innovation and its potential determinants, paying special attention to the roles of governance and regulatory frameworks and the ways in which the latter interact with the market structure. Its findings call for careful policy choice and design. One general conclusion is that innovation may be associated with deadweight losses due to a positive relationship between market power and innovation – especially when market power is initially high. Another conclusion is that regulation is not necessarily harmful for innovation, especially when regulation imposes standards that firms, left to their own devices, may not be willing to comply with. The third conclusion is that the quality of economic governance institutions matters for innovation, on its own and in interaction with the market structure. Finally, corporate governance rules also matter but not necessarily in line with the predictions of the agency theory – which takes the level of product-market competition as given. Hence, this volume suggests that policy-makers must tread carefully through a long menu of policy alternatives, paying attention to the costs and benefits of innovation and to the quality of governance institutions and regulatory frameworks.

Acknowledgements

I would like to thank two reviewers who read and commented on the book proposal and the draft chapters that accompanied it. Their comments have made a significant contribution to the quality of the outcome. I would also like to thank the contributors for their splendid cooperation and their generosity in putting up with my editorial intrusions. I dedicate this book to Sema, Deniz and Suha Ugur, who provided unqualified support and encouragement while I was working on this project.

Mehmet Ugur

Abbreviations

AMECO	Annual Macro-Economic Database – EU Commission
BERD	business expenditures on research and development
CEO	chief executive officer
CG	corporate governance
CSR	corporate social responsibility
DEA	data envelopment analysis
DEFRA	Department for Environment, Food and Rural Affairs
DGS	Direction générale de la santé – Directorate General for Health – France
DOJ	Department of Justice – USA
ECORD	eco-innovation research and development
EGI	economic governance institutions
EMAS	European Union's Environmental Management and Audit Scheme
EMS	environmental management systems
EOP	end-of-pipeline pollution control technologies
EPO	European Patent Office
ERAWATCH	European research database – EU Commission
EU	European Union
FDI	foreign direct investment
GDP	gross domestic product
GGDC-ICOP	Groningen Growth and Development Centre – International Comparisons of Output and Productivity database
GIS	geo-referring information system
GLS	generalized least-squares estimator
HHI	Herfindahl-Hirschman index
IC	intellectual capital
ICRG	International Country Risk Guide database
ICT	information and communications technology
IFEN	Institut français de l'environnement – French Environment Institute
INSEE	Institut national de la statistique et des études

	économiques –National Institute of Statistics and Economic Studies – France
INT	integrated cleaner production technologies
IP	intellectual property
ISO	International Organization for Standardization
JPO	Japan Patent Office
LABREF	Labour Market Reforms database – EU Commission
MICREF	microeconomic reforms database – EU Commission
MSTI	Main Science and Technology Indicators database – OECD
NIS	national innovation system
OECD	Organisation for Economic Cooperation and Development
OLS	ordinary least-squares
PCSE	panel-corrected standard errors
PMR	product-market regulation database – OECD
PMRP	public sector presence in product markets – OECD
PPP	public-private partnership
R&D	research and development
REGIMP	indicator of sectoral regulation database – OECD
REGREF	regulatory environment indicators for network industries – OECD
SEC	Securities & Exchange Commission
SIC	Standard Industrial Classification code
SOA	Sarbanes-Oxley Act
SWIID	Standardized World Income Inequality Database
TFP	total factor productivity
TRIPs	Trade-Related Intellectual Property Rights Agreement
UK	United Kingdom
UNDP	United Nations Development Programme
USA	United States of America
USPTO	United States Patent and Trademark Office
WDI	World Development Indicators database
WTO	World Trade Organization

1. Governance, regulation and innovation: new perspectives and evidence

Mehmet Ugur

INTRODUCTION

For a long time, determinants of innovation were studied with an exclusive focus on market structure, industry characteristics, technology choice, and appropriability of innovation profits. This institution-free approach can be traced back to Schumpeter's (1934, 1942) seminal work, which argued that large firms and concentrated market structures promote innovation. Arrow (1962) takes issue with the Schumpeterian hypothesis and demonstrates that a monopoly shielded against competition has less incentive to innovate compared to firms within a perfectly competitive market. According to Gilbert (2006), we are still far from a general theory of the relationship between innovation and market structure as industry characteristics, the nature of technological competition and the distinction between product and process innovation emerge as confounding factors. Yet, recent empirical work informed by Aghion et al. (2002a, 2005) demonstrate that the relationship between market structure and innovation is likely to be non-linear, with competition fostering innovation at low levels of competition but reducing innovation when the initial level of competition is already high (Peneder, 2012).

Although the quality of governance institutions does not feature in this debate, protection of intellectual property does. Indeed, together with product-market competition, protection of intellectual property determines the extent to which innovators can appropriate the returns on innovation. Hence, the relationship between institutional factors and innovation is implicit in the debate, but the latter has unfolded without due attention to the ways in which the wider institutional framework (including economic and corporate governance institutions) interact with market structure and other factors to affect innovation incentives and outcomes.

Two strands in the literature represent a departure from this institution-free view of innovation: the national innovation systems (NIS) approach and the work on the relationship between corporate governance and firm performance. In the pioneering work on NIS (Freeman, 1987; Lundvall, 1988; Dosi et al., 1988; Nelson, 1993), innovation is analysed within a national environment that consists of government incentives for innovation, intellectual property protection, support for education, trade policies, competition and industrial policies, and economic culture. Although it lacks a fully fledged institutional perspective, the NIS literature has been influential in shifting the attention towards the relationship between innovation and the national environment, which is an amalgam of policy and institutional factors that affect the costs and incentives faced by economic actors.

However, the NIS literature has been criticized on two grounds. First, the work has remained mainly normative, indeed practical (see Erickson's contribution in chapter 10). Secondly, its normative quality has led to a strong policy uptake of its research outcomes, but its focus on the 'right' environmental factors that make countries or regions more innovative has created taxonomies rather than specific hypotheses that can be tested rigorously. This weakness is evident in the ways in which the 'optimal' NIS examples pointed out by this literature have changed over time, from the Japanese model in the 1990s to more varied models associated with emerging innovators such as China, India or Brazil.

In contrast, the literature on the relationship between corporate governance draws on the agency theory or the theory of contracting to derive and test hypotheses about how corporate governance dimensions affect firm performance, including innovation. This literature tends to take the level of product-market competition as given and investigates the ways in which corporate governance rules may encourage or hinder innovation by resolving/minimizing the agency problem or facilitating contracting. Pioneering works include Hill and Snell (1988), Baysinger and Hoskisson (1990) and Baysinger et al. (1991) on the relationship between board independence and innovation; Jensen (1988), Shleifer and Summers (1988) and Stein (1988) on the relationship between anti-takeover defences and innovation; and Graves (1988) and Hill et al. (1988) on institutional ownership and innovation. Extensive reviews of this literature are provided in Belloc (2012) and Sapra et al. (2009), with further reviews in chapters 3 and 4 of this volume by Engelen and van Essen and Hashem and Ugur, respectively.

Most of the corporate governance (CG) literature tends to overlook the effects of market structure on innovation and how the latter may interact with governance with complementary or offsetting effects. Notable exceptions include Aghion et al. (1999, 2002b) who examine the interactions between CG dimensions and innovation, and some recent work by Sapra et al. (2009) and Atanassov (2012) who include market structure as a control variable.

The few studies on the relationship between macro-level governance institutions and innovation also tend to overlook the interaction between market structure and governance. For example, Keefer and Knack (1997: 591) report that firms tend to invest less in new technologies if the rule of law is weak and the risk of 'expropriation' is high. This finding is supported by Clarke (2001), Lundvall et al. (2002), Dakhli and de Clercq (2004), and Giménez and Sanaú (2007) who report that innovation performance tends to be lower in countries where the risk of expropriation is higher and the rule of law is weaker. More recently, Tebaldi and Elmslie (2013) demonstrate that institutional quality in general encourages innovation by facilitating patent registration, diffusion of ideas, enforcement of property rights and reducing the uncertainty of new projects. Yet, none of these studies investigates the interactions between economic governance institutions and market structure.

The key rationale for this book (and for the conference that preceded it in September 2011 at the University of Greenwich) has been to develop the case for: (i) according a central role to governance as a potential determinant of innovation; and (ii) analysing the effects of governance dimensions on innovation in conjunction with the effects of the market structure. This rationale can be justified easily. Investment in innovation is costly and associated with uncertain returns. Furthermore, investment in innovation projects is characterized by indivisibilities and economies of scale. Third, it may be difficult to ascertain the quality of the innovation projects due to asymmetric information between innovators on the one hand and creditors or shareholders on the other. Finally, innovation projects may have spill-over effects and/or the results of innovation may be subject to partial non-excludability (Jones and Williams, 1998; Aghion and Howitt, 1992; Mansfield, 1985; Jaffe, 1986; Acs et al., 1994).

Hence, at a given level of product-market competition, innovation performance at the firm or national levels would depend on the extent to which governance institutions are effective in fostering innovation as a result of encouraging risk taking, resolving or minimizing collective action problems, mitigating market failures, and aligning the interests of different actors such as managers, shareholders, employees, and policy makers. Similarly, at a given level of governance quality, innovation performance also depends on the degree of competition, which determines the levels of pre- and post-innovations profits that can be appropriated by innovators. Given these dynamics, it is necessary to investigate not only the partial effects of governance and market structure on innovation but also the ways in which both dimensions interact and with what consequences for innovation.

ECONOMIC GOVERNANCE, CORPORATE GOVERNANCE AND INNOVATION

Our contribution in this book is empirical, but informed by seminal work on the economics of innovation and recent developments in the economics of governance institutions. According to North (1990, 1994), a country's institutional environment constrains actor's choices and behaviour, and as such hinders or supports economic performance in general and innovation in particular. Governance institutions can be considered as the 'rules of the game' and consist of both formal and informal institutions. Formal institutions include written rules, regulations, laws and contracts; whereas informal institutions consist of norms, values and trust that a society has developed and internalized over time.

As Dixit (2009) has indicated, governance institutions affect economic outcomes in general because good governance is necessary for securing three essential prerequisites for market economies: (i) security of property rights; (ii) enforcement of contracts; and (iii) resolution of collective action problems. The relevance of these prerequisites for innovation is evident. Institutions that secure property rights foster innovation by enabling innovators to appropriate post-innovation profits (Acemoglu, 2006). In addition, governance institutions that secure contract enforceability reduce transaction costs and foster innovation by enabling firms to choose advanced technologies that tend to prevail in contract-intensive sectors (Acemoglu et al., 2007). Finally, institutions that minimize or resolve collective action problems also foster innovation because they facilitate internalization of the externalities associated with innovation, hence enabling countries or firms to avoid prisoner's dilemmas in the management of common pool resources such as knowledge.

Given these relationships between governance institutions and innovation, what remains to be explained is the combination of economic governance institutions, corporate governance rules and regulation within a single project. The normative explanation is the following: we aim to make a case for analysing innovation in the light of formal and informal governance institutions that affect the costs and incentives faced by economic actors. Therefore, we have cast the net wide and included both country-level economic governance and firm-level corporate governance dimensions. The country-level governance dimension, in turn, is defined widely to include both general institutional indicators such as rule of law, accountability, control of corruption and bureaucratic efficiency; and more specific rules codified in product-market or industry regulations.

Yet, we have not let our normative preferences dominate the choice of governance dimensions in our analyses. In his address to the 121st meeting of the American Economic Association in San Francisco, Avinash Dixit (2009) has indicated that 'good economic governance underpins the whole Smithian process whereby individuals specialize in different tasks and then transact with one another to achieve the full economic potential of the society'. Furthermore, governance is not a disciplinary field per se, but 'an organizing concept for many fields' in social sciences and as such 'offers a unique opportunity for the social sciences to have a meeting point . . . after their separation over a century ago.' This perspective clearly implies that regulation is a subset of economic governance as it also 'underpins the Smithian process' and affects the cost and incentive structures faced by economic agents.

What about corporate governance? Is it justified to include the latter within a book that aims to make the case for more systematic analysis of the relationship between governance and innovation? Again, we draw on Dixit (2009), who considers corporate governance as the 'more popular cousin' of economic governance and provides useful insights into the relationship between the two. Dixit (2009: 8, 11, 12) distinguishes between formal and informal governance institutions. Whereas the former include constitutions, the legislature, the judiciary and regulatory agencies, the latter include private and social institutions that reduce transaction costs. Corporate governance rules adopted by firms (with or without a macro-level governance framework) can be considered as a subset of the informal governance institutions that internalize contracts and hence convert contract enforcement into an agency problem in corporate governance. Therefore, our inclusion of corporate governance as a subset of the governance framework is justified.

GOVERNANCE, REGULATION AND INNOVATION: NEW PERSPECTIVES

Given the rationale indicated above, contributors to this book endeavour to address the following questions: does governance affect innovation effort at country or firm levels? How do governance and market structure interact and affect innovation? Stated more specifically, do market structure and governance dimensions have complementary or offsetting effects on innovation? Do these interaction effects differ between economic/corporate governance and regulation? If good governance fosters innovation, how does the innovation effort affect policy reform aiming to enhance governance? Similarly, if regulation affects innovation, how does investment in innovation affect regulatory outcomes?

Although the contributions in this book are embedded within relevant theoretical frameworks, their answers to these questions are essentially empirical. In other words, we let the data 'speak', making sure that our data analysis methods are appropriate and our models are informed by relevant theoretical perspectives on innovation, governance institutions, agency and contracting problems, regulation, competition, and policy reform. Seven of the eight main chapters are based on unique datasets that allow for investigating not only the relationship between governance widely defined and innovation, but also the interactions between the two. Two of the empirical chapters also examine the effects of investment in innovation on the probability of policy reform in 27 members of the European Union (EU) and on regulatory outcomes in public-private partnerships in the French water industry. Finally, one chapter takes a normative approach to develop the case for enhanced governance of intellectual capital – an emerging but less-easy-to-govern process of innovation compared to processes analysed in intellectual property or national innovation systems literature.

The book is organized in three parts. In Part I, we present four chapters that investigate the relationship between innovation and governance, including country-level economic governance and firm-level corporate governance dimensions. Part II also includes four chapters, which focus on the relationship between regulation and innovation. Finally, we devote Part III to one chapter on governance of intellectual capital and a concluding chapter that summarizes the main findings and discusses their research and policy implications.

In Chapter 2, Ugur begins with the observation that the existing literature tends to investigate two potential determinants of innovation (market structure and governance institutions) separately. In addition, the policy discourse tends to be based on the assumption that competition and innovation go hand in hand, with little or no attention to whether the competition-innovation relationship could be non-linear or how market structures and governance may interact and produce complementary or offsetting effects on innovation. Given this observation, Ugur argues that it is necessary to verify if product-market competition is conducive to innovation or whether innovation entails deadweight losses associated with market power as a driver of innovation. He also argues that it is necessary to pay attention not only to the partial effects of governance and market structure, but also to the interactions between the two to see if such interactions produce complementary or offsetting effects.

The chapter by Ugur is based on a panel dataset on patenting activity in 24 OECD countries from 1988–2007. Following an extensive literature review, the chapter proposes a model in which the relationship between market power and innovation is non-linear and governance affects innovation both directly and indirectly through interactions with market power. The case for the model is based on theoretical and empirical insights from institutional economics (Acemoglu, 2006; Acemoglu et al., 2007; Dixit, 2009) and economics of innovation (Aghion et al., 1999, 2002a, 2002b and 2005). Ugur utilizes a generalized least-squares (GLS) estimator with panel-corrected standard errors (PCEs), which allows for error structures that are heteroskedastic and contemporaneously correlated across panels (Beck and Katz, 1995; Egger, 2002). This method is reported to be efficient when the number of time periods is close to the number of cases (countries) (Chen et al., 2009) – and this property matches the structure of the dataset used, which contains observations for 24 countries over 20 years.

One finding reported by Ugur is that the non-linear relationship between market power and innovation that is established at the firm level also holds at the national level. Another finding is that the non-linear relationship is U-shaped in the full sample, but it has an inverted-U shape in countries with higher-than-average levels of per-capita GDP, economic openness and governance quality scores. Ugur explains the difference by arguing that markets in the latter countries are contested more heavily (i.e., market power in these countries is usually lower than the sample average) and therefore the Schumpeterian hypothesis tends to hold – i.e., innovation is driven by increased market power when the initial level of the latter is relatively low.

Ugur also provides novel evidence on the relationship between governance and innovation. He reports that the governance score (a composite index derived from five governance indicators that include bureaucracy quality, control of corruption, investment profile, law and order, and government stability) is related positively to patenting activity in the full sample and in the split samples. Although similar findings are already reported in the literature, Ugur argues that the existing findings may suffer from model misspecification bias. He demonstrates that market power interacts with governance and has an offsetting effect on the relationship between governance and innovation, leading to smaller marginal effects overall. In addition, the interaction between governance and market power also modifies the marginal effects of market power on innovation, having a complementary effect until the turning point of the U-shaped curve but an offsetting effect thereafter. Hence, Ugur establishes that both partial and the marginal effects (i.e., the sum of partial and interactive effects) of governance or market power on innovation may be biased if both variables and the interaction between them are not included in the model.

Ugur also reports a range of significant relationships between innovation and other country characteristics. For example, income inequality and economic openness are related negatively to patenting activity. On the other hand, per-capita GDP, depth of the stock market and military expenditures as percentage of GDP are related positively to patenting activity. The relationship between labour share in national income and patenting activity is also positive but it is significant only in some estimations. These findings are robust to sample selection and standardization of the standard errors.

Chapter 3 by Peter-Jan Engelen and Marc van Essen focuses on the recent financial crisis and addresses a highly topical question: how do country-level economic governance institutions and corporate governance characteristics of the firms affect the rate of curtailment in research and development (R&D) expenditures by European firms during the financial crisis of 2007–09? To address this question, Engelen and van Essen assemble a dataset for 411 firms from 16 European countries from 2006 to 2009. They estimate a model in which economic and corporate governance influences the management's R&D investment decisions directly and indirectly as a result of interaction between the two dimensions of governance. The model is derived from a number of hypotheses that authors distil from existing theoretical and empirical work.

Engelen and van Essen make three contributions to the evidence in this volume and the wider literature, two of which are novel. First, they provide evidence on the relationship between two governance dimensions and R&D effort during the crisis by taking into account both country- and firm-level data. Earlier studies have focused only on firm-level factors (Munari et al., 2010) or combined only industry-level data with country-level data (Barbosa and Faria, 2011). Secondly, they provide evidence on both partial and combined effects of different governance dimensions, taking into account the interactions between the two. Although the interaction between country-level economic governance and firm-level corporate governance has been investigated in other studies on firm performance, the study by Engelen and van Essen is the first that investigates the interaction in the context of innovation performance. Finally, the authors focus on the recent financial crisis and complement the literature that investigates the relationship between governance and innovation in European firms during normal times (Honoré et al., 2011; Munari et al., 2010).

Engelen and van Essen report that firms with large institutional owners or under government ownership tend to curtail R&D investment more than other firms during the crisis. This finding is interpreted as evidence of institutional investors' short time horizons, which induce preference for short-term gains as opposed to long-term commitment. This finding is in line with the wider corporate governance literature, which report that institutional investors engage in high trading volumes around the announcements of quarterly earnings (Kim et al., 1997; Lang and McNichols, 1997; and Potter, 1992). Firms under government ownership may be induced to curtail R&D investment as a result of fiscal deterioration. Neither board size nor CEO duality or board independence has a significant effect on R&D curtailment during crisis times.

With respect to country-level governance institutions, Engelen and van Essen report that firms in countries that rely mainly on equity finance tend to curtail R&D spending more than others in countries that rely mainly on bank finance. The authors explain this finding by indicating that banks in Europe have opted for coordination with distressed firms rather than shutting down the credit lines. This finding is also supported by findings on the interaction effects, which indicate that market-based financial systems tend to augment the adverse effect of institutional ownership on R&D effort whereas the interaction between bank-based regimes and creditor rights is associated with higher R&D effort (i.e., less R&D curtailment).

In chapter 4, Hashem and Ugur focus on the relationship between corporate governance and R&D expenditures by US-listed firms. Utilizing a panel dataset for more than 1,500 firms from 2004–10, the authors investigate the partial and interactive effects of corporate governance on R&D intensity (R&D/sales ratio) by controlling for non-linear effects from market concentration. The joint analysis is justified on the grounds that both corporate governance and market structure affect R&D effort by influencing the incentives of the managers to invest in risky innovation projects. Corporate governance may enhance the R&D effort if it exerts discipline on managers and/or mitigates the agency problem by aligning managerial and shareholder interests. Similarly, market concentration also affects the R&D effort depending on the extent to which it causes managerial slack and/or affects the levels of pre- and post-innovation profits. Therefore, one needs to take account of interactions between the two. Paying attention to interactions between corporate governance and market structure is also necessary from an empirical perspective: partial effects from estimations that exclude the interaction term would be inaccurate due to model misspecification bias.

The authors utilize a two-way cluster-robust estimation method that yields standard errors that are robust to cross-sectional and time-series dependence between the error terms and the independent variables. They control for non-linear relationship between market concentration and R&D intensity by utilizing an industry-based Herfindahl-Hirschman Index and its square. Their corporate governance indicators capture four dimensions: board independence and board diversity; ownership structure (insider and institutional ownership); anti-merger defences; and shareholders' rights.

They report that board independence is related positively to R&D intensity and that market concentration acts as a complement that strengthens the positive relationship. All other CG indicators (number of women directors on the board, percentage of shares owned by insiders and institutional investors, and percentage of vote required to approve mergers or amend company charters) are related negatively to R&D intensity. In addition, market concentration tends to have a substitution effect when it is interacted with these CG indicators. They also report that the relationship between market concentration and innovation has a U-shape, implying that an increase in market concentration is associated with lower R&D intensity when the initial level of concentration is low; but the change is positive when the initial level of concentration is high. These results are robust to other measures of R&D effort (R&D expenditures and R&D expenditures per employee) and to inclusion of firm-characteristics such as firm size, age, returns on assets, Tobin's Q, and the ratio of long-term debt to capital as control variables.

Hashem and Ugur's findings confirm the non-linear relationship between competition and innovation analysed by Aghion et al. (1999, 2002a, 2002b and 2005). They also provide novel evidence on the significance of interactions between market concentration and corporate governance indicators, after controlling for a wide range of firm characteristics. Their findings indicate that the effect of corporate governance rules is mediated through market concentration and the effect of market concentration is mediated through corporate governance rules.

The last chapter in Part I is by Andrea Conte, who addresses the relationship between governance and innovation from a different angle. Conte is interested in the determinants of policy reforms that are likely to enhance a country's innovation performance. In other words, his dependent variable is not innovation effort *per se*, but the extent of policy reforms that the European Union (EU) and its member states consider as necessary for better governance of the knowledge economy and better performance in terms of innovation. The policy reforms are placed within five policy areas related to innovation: allocation of public resources for innovation, support for private-sector R&D, supply of researchers, projection of intellectual property rights and technology transfer.

Conte's research is highly topical and policy-relevant as it provides new evidence on what factors tend to increase the probability of policy reforms by EU member states in the context of the Lisbon Agenda and the Europe 2020 strategy. The analysis is based on a rich panel dataset from the European Commission's database on microeconomic reforms (MICREF) and estimates a probit model, in which the dependent variable is the reform performance of 27 EU member states in the five policy areas from 2004 to 2008. The time frame is determined by data availability for 27 member states. In the model, the probability of reform depends on two clusters of variables: (i) innovation and education-related performance indicators (which include business and government R&D expenditures as percentage of GDP, patenting activity, human resources in science and technology sectors, and public expenditure on education); and (ii) a set of macroeconomic variables that include per-capita GDP, government debt, tax burden and a measure of the business cycle.

The findings by Conte indicate that there are both convergence and divergence between EU member states with respect to the relationship between past innovation performance and undertaking of policy reforms that would encourage innovation in the future. Convergence is evident in policy areas related to governance of innovation inputs such as government and business R&D expenditures and expenditures on education. In these policy areas, countries with lower performance in the preceding year tend to have a higher probability of introducing reforms in the current year in order to enhance future performance. These findings indicate that the Lisbon Strategy, through its targets and monitoring mechanisms, has been effective in closing the gap between low- and high-performing member states in terms of building the governance structures necessary to support innovation.

However, the evidence indicates that the Lisbon Strategy is also associated with divergence between EU member states in policy areas related to governance of the 'inventive stock' reflected in the number of patents per-capita, technology trade and protection of intellectual property rights. In these areas, the current reform effort is positively related to past performance, indicating that the governance gap between high- and low-performing member states is widening. Hence, the findings by Conte indicate that the type of past innovation performance is an important predictor of policy reforms that would eventually affect the quality of the governance structures closely related to both innovation inputs such as R&D and education expenditures and innovation outcomes such as technology transfer and intellectual property.

In Part II, we have four chapters on the relationship between regulation and innovation. In chapter 6, Demirel and Kesidou utilize a dataset of 289

UK firms that responded to a survey conducted by the UK's Department for Environment, Food and Rural Affairs (DEFRA) in 2005 and 2006. The survey provides a valuable source of information on eco-innovation expenditures by UK firms, with good coverage across manufacturing industries. It also allows for exploring the determinants of different types of eco-innovation investments in: (i) end-of-pipeline pollution control technologies (EOP); (ii) integrated cleaner production technologies (INT); and (iii) eco-innovation research and development activities (ECORD). The authors provide a review of the related literature and articulate a conceptual framework that relates eco-innovation investments to two sets of factors: the environmental regulation framework and the internal firm-specific motivations. The environmental regulation framework provides for two types of regulation: prescriptive regulations that require compliance with environmental protection standards, and incentive-based regulations that entail environmental taxes and subsidies. So far as the internal firm-specific motivations are concerned, Demirel and Kesidou investigate the effects of organizational capabilities, efficiency considerations and corporate social responsibility (CSR) considerations.

One novelty in this chapter is that the authors also distinguish between three types of environmental innovation expenditures. The distinction is based on the extent to which the innovation type affects the range of products produced and processes used by innovating firms. Expenditures on EOP technologies are considered at the lower end of the impact spectrum as manufacturing firms apply EOP solutions mainly to treat, handle, measure or dispose of emissions and wastes from production. At the high end of the impact spectrum, we have ECORD expenditures that enable firms to improve products and processes by devising solutions for cleaner production and consumption. Environmental R&D has a higher technological impact because (a) it enhances absorptive capacity and (b) the scope of environmental R&D is not limited only to process innovations but also covers product innovations. Finally, integrated cleaner production technologies (INT) are considered to have a medium innovation impact as they help modify production processes but fall short of inducing significant product innovation.

Demirel and Kesidou utilize a Tobit regression methodology and report a rich set of findings. Their estimation results enable the reader to find out not only about the marginal effect of environmental regulation on the probability of a firm being an innovator, but also about decomposed effects on: (i) the probability that regulation induces the firm to undertake investments in eco-innovations; and (ii) the conditional mean level of eco-innovation expenditures that the firm undertakes.

With regards to environmental regulation frameworks, their results indicate that prescriptive regulatory instruments are effective in driving two types of eco-innovation: EOP innovation at the lower end of the impact spectrum and ECORD innovation at the higher end of the impact spectrum. In contrast, incentive-based regulatory instruments such as environmental taxes fail to motivate any of the three eco-innovations considered, with the exception of marginal effect on the probability of innovation by existing innovators in the middle of the impact spectrum. In addition, Demirel and Kesidou report that prescriptive regulations increase the probability of eco-innovation not only by existing innovators but also by firms that are new to eco-innovation. This is in contrast to incentive-based regulation that induces only existing innovators to innovate (i.e., picks up winners) – and only in the case of medium-impact innovation investments in integrated technologies.

These findings expand the existing evidence base not only by providing evidence on the relationship between regulation and different types of eco-innovation, but also by distinguishing the marginal effects on non-innovators as well as existing innovators. Hence, the authors report not only a U-type relationship between prescriptive regulations and eco-innovations, whereby prescriptive regulatory rules tend to have significant effects on the low and high ends of the eco-innovation spectrum. They also report that prescriptive regulation tends to have stronger effects on the probability of non-innovators taking a decision to innovate compared to its effects on the innovation efforts of firms that are already innovators.

Demirel and Kesidou also report interesting findings on other determinants of eco-innovation. For example, efficiency considerations tend to be significant in driving eco-innovation expenditures whereas CSR considerations are insignificant. The impact of environmental management systems (for example the effect of subscribing to ISO 14001) is reported to be positive and significant with respect to EOP and ECORD innovations. The decomposed marginal effects suggest that subscription to ISO 14001 standards is effective in motivating firms to start investing in EOP and has a significant but smaller effect on increasing the EOP investments of those firms that already invest in EOP. In the case of ECORD, ISO 14001 is only effective for persuading firms to invest in ECORD but does not motivate increased ECORD investments by firms with existing ECORD activities.

Chapter 7 by Simon Porcher addresses the relationship between regulation and investment in information and communications technology (ICT) in a sample of 11 manufacturing industries in 10 OECD countries over 26 years, from 1980 to 2005. Porcher tries to establish whether different measures of regulatory stringency on their own or in interaction with closeness to the technology frontier can explain ICT intensity (i.e., the ratio of ICT investments to value added) at the industry-country level. To do this, he assembles data for a range of regulatory measures and other control variables that are used in the literature.

Porcher utilizes four proxies for regulation, all of which are taken from OECD data. These include: (i) a regulatory environment indicator (*REGREF*) for network industries (telecoms, electricity, gas, post, rail, air passenger transport, road freight), the output of which is heavily used by manufacturing firms in the sample; (ii) an indicator that measures the extent to which industries are constrained by administrative burdens, entry regulation and other market barriers in key non-manufacturing sectors such as network services, retail distribution, financial services and professional business services (*REGIMP*); (iii) an indicator of product-market regulation (*PMR*) that provides information about barriers to entry in each country; and (iv) an indicator of public sector presence in product markets (*PMRP*).

Closeness to the frontier (*FRONT*) is calculated using productivity levels for each industry in each country from 1980 until 2005. Closeness to the productivity frontier is measured as the ratio between the productivity in industry i in country j at time t and the highest productivity level in the same industry i at the same time t. The range of control variables captures different factors that influence ICT intensity and includes: the capital/labor ratio (*KL*), externalities (*EXT*) which captures the international intensity of the ICT capital input, and import penetration (*MPEN*) as a measure of the extent to which the market is open to external competition.

Estimation results indicate that closeness to the frontier has a negative effect on ICT investment intensity across all estimations. This is to be expected because industries closer to the frontier need to invest less in ICT to remain competitive. Secondly, regulation also tends to have a negative partial effect on ICT intensity. This is in line with the received wisdom, which expects a negative relationship between regulation and innovation. However, this partial effect does not tell the whole story as regulation interacts with closeness to the frontier and the interaction term (*REG*FRONT*) has a positive and significant effect in three out of four estimations. This means that an increase in regulation mitigates the negative effect of the closeness to the frontier and drives industries close to the frontier to increase their investment in ICT technology. It also indicates that regulation reduces the innovation effort in laggard industries that are distant from the frontier.

Porcher tests if the marginal effect of regulation (i.e., the combined effects of regulation and the interaction term) is significant at different levels of closeness to the frontier. The test results indicate that the marginal effect is positive and significant when industries are at the technology frontier and negative and significant when closeness to the frontier is minimum. In between, the marginal effect is insignificant. Hence, regulation is more likely to slow down innovation when industries are far from the technology frontier, but it is not likely to slow down the innovation effort of the industries that are close to the frontier. Porcher proposes two explanations for these results. First, regulation may induce firms to remain competitive by investing in ICT as a means of improving quality standards and product variety rather than cutting costs. Secondly, regulation may encourage firms to undertake drastic rather than piecemeal innovation. Hence, the product market deregulation prescription of the Lisbon Agenda may be counterproductive. The Lisbon Agenda may be effective in securing innovation convergence between European industries by encouraging the laggards to invest in cost-cutting innovation; but it may remain ineffective in securing its declared aim of achieving convergence between EU and USA levels of innovation.

The relationship between regulation and innovation is also an issue that Eshref Trushin investigates in chapter 8. Trushin utilizes a panel dataset for more than 1,000 pharmaceutical firms in 11 countries for the period 1997–2007. The data is compiled from financial statements of the sample firms in the Orbis database. The analysis in this chapter is conducted in three steps. In step 1, Trushin conducts Pearson Chi-square and likelihood ratio independence tests to establish if R&D intensity (R&D/sale and R&D/assets ratios) is related to the stringency of price regulation and market concentration in the pharmaceutical industry. Then, he estimates average technical efficiency levels for firms within each country, using stochastic frontier modelling and a production function with three inputs: intangible assets, tangible assets, and labour. In the third step, he conducts independence tests to verify if the average technical inefficiency at the country level is related to the stringency of price regulation and market concentration.

Trushin reports that there is no evidence indicating that the stringency of drug price regulations is systematically associated with R&D intensities or technical production inefficiency. The same result is obtained with respect to the relationship between market concentration and R&D intensities or technical production inefficiency. There is partial evidence indicating that the most liberal pharmaceutical price regimes in the UK and the US have the lowest inefficiency in the truncated normal time invariant random effect panel specification, but this result is not robust across other specifications for the inefficiency term. The policy implication of this result is that price regulations do not seem to prevent firms from achieving the highest level of output given factor inputs.

A major limitation of the findings is that the small sample of only eleven countries reduces the power of the tests. Another major problem is the difficulty involved in accounting for the quality of intangible assets. Time discounting of patents and quality of patent portfolios can be major confounding factors, which must be taken into account in further research.

The last chapter in Part II is Freddy Huet and Simon Porcher, who investigate how investment in innovation affects the balance between reputational and opportunistic behaviour of private water companies in the French public-private partnership contracts (PPPs). Drawing on the relevant literature, Huet and Porcher demonstrate that water supply firms engaged in PPPs can be expected to increase their chances of winning the contract at the renewal stage by following two strategies: opportunistic behaviour aimed at reducing the probability of rivals' market entry, or building a good reputation that might increase their probability of winning the contract. Although a rich literature exists on the determinants of opportunistic behaviour or reputational concerns in a principal-agent setting, the effects of investment in innovation on corporate behaviour in regulated industries are not investigated. Huet and Porcher set out to address this issue.

The authors utilize a dataset on the French water industry, compiled by the French Environment Institute (IFEN), the French Health Ministry (DGS) and the National Statistics Institute (INSEE). The dataset contains information on more than 4,000 French municipalities with water services under private management in 2004 and 2008. They argue that network update information transmitted by private suppliers to municipalities can be considered as a measure of reputational behaviour because such information reduces information asymmetries. Then, they set out to investigate whether investment in geo-referring information systems (GIS) for leak detection is related to the probability of providing network information updates in 2008, taking into the account the effects of competition and a range of control variables.

Investment in innovative leak detection systems is expected to have two effects on the probability of disclosing information to the municipality. On the one hand, GIS investment may induce incumbents to withhold network update information in order to reinforce the 'lock-in' situation that makes the incumbent more likely to win the contract at the renewal stage. In this case, the incumbent is acting opportunistically. On the other hand, large investments made by an operator can be a signal of reputational concerns. In this case, investments in GIS leak detection systems will be associated with higher probability of transmitting information.

The authors test these hypotheses by estimating a probit model, in which they control for a range of variables that relate to the competition environment, the contractual characteristics and some control variables.

Their findings indicate that investment in specific innovation capital input (GIS) has a positive and significant effect on the probability of reputational behaviour, which is measured as the probability of disclosing network information to the municipality. They explain this result by the fact that innovative investment in itself is a signal for reputational concerns and that information disclosure follows in tandem to reinforce the reputational signals. Furthermore, operators with GIS leak detection systems are able provide more timely and detailed information at lower variable cost compared to rivals with older systems.

Huet and Porcher also report that competition from public-sector suppliers of water services and closeness to the end of the contract tends to increase the probability of opportunistic behaviour. Furthermore, when interacted with innovation, competition from public-sector providers has a substitution effect on reputational behaviour. In other words, as the number of public-sector providers increases, the probability of reputational behaviour decreases among incumbents that invest in GIS. Hence, they conclude that incumbents that invest in GIS tend to disclose less information when faced with competition from public-sector providers compared to other incumbents with the same level of investment in GIS but lower level of competition from public providers.

Huet and Porcher argue that their findings show that firms involved in PPP contracts in the water sector may strategically react to the competitive environment by concealing network information in order to raise rivals' entry costs. Therefore, some policies that aim to foster competition in this industry may fail if they don't take into account the strategic behaviours that firms could adopt to protect their rents. Hence, they suggest that regulatory policies that reinforce the obligation for incumbents to invest in innovative capital may reduce the probability of opportunistic behaviour by incumbents.

In the last chapter, Erickson revisits the theme of corporate governance and innovation, but asks a different question: does the emergence of intellectual capital as a wider concept of innovation require a re-think on corporate governance? His answer is positive and depends on growing evidence that softer knowledge assets, i.e., the class of assets that are less amenable to be defined by structured innovation mechanisms, are additional sources of competitive advantage for the firm. Hence, Erickson makes the case for: (i) adding knowledge asset development and use to the remits of national innovation systems; and (ii) devising new corporate governance mechanisms that would induce managers to manage, report and protect these assets more effectively.

According to Erickson, the national innovation system (NIS) approach has proved valuable during the past decades. It has provided a guide to the right national governance approach that would support innovation. However, the concept has remained practical and taxonomic; and does not lend itself to addressing the new type of knowledge assets that he describes as intellectual capital. Although intellectual capital is considered critical to firm performance, it is not protected by traditional intellectual property legislation. Hence, it is necessary to devise national innovation system approaches that would encourage the development and application of softer forms of knowledge by creating government programs to grow knowledge (education, infrastructure, etc.), by encouraging the establishment of common metrics and reporting standards, by creating protection mechanisms, and by forming procedures that would make government use of such assets predictable.

However, effective governance in this realm may not be easy to develop and implement, as returns on intellectual capital are often not accruing until some years in the future. Therefore, corporate governance rules should be developed to facilitate the management, reporting and protection of intellectual capital. Corporate managers should be able to show that they have procedures and rules to protect such valuable proprietary assets, both from prying competitors and from sloppy collaborators, including government. In short, effective corporate governance faces a number of new concerns that were not even on the radar two decades ago.

CONCLUDING REMARKS

As indicated above, this volume is based on papers presented to an international conference on governance and innovation held at the University of Greenwich in June 2011. At the time, the call for papers indicated that the relationship between innovation and governance is a relatively under-studied area of research. This has been the case despite extensive work on the relationship between governance quality and other performance indicators such as growth, firm value, investment, and income distribution. In addition, potential synergies that may result from combining economic governance, market structure, corporate governance and regulation remain to be explored. The conference aimed to bring together innovative research papers that explore the relationship between governance widely defined and innovation, taking into account the interactions between governance and market structure as well as between different dimensions of governance.

The contributors to the conference and to this edited volume have risen to this challenge very well by undertaking innovative and empirically rich studies. The summary above does reflect these qualities to some extent, but it is far from doing justice either to the effort of the contributors or to the richness of their analysis. Hence, I would like to conclude this introductory chapter by thanking the contributors again and inviting the reader to explore the perspectives and evidence they provide on governance and innovation outcomes at firm, industry and country levels.

REFERENCES

Acemoglu, D. (2006), 'A simple model of inefficient institutions', *Scandinavian Journal of Economics*, 108(4): 515–546.

Acemoglu, D., P. Antràs and E. Helpman (2007), 'Contracts and technology adoption', *American Economic Review*, 97(3): 916–943.

Acs, Z.J., D.B. Audretsch and M. Feldman (1994), 'R&D Spillovers and innovative activity', *Managerial and Decision Economics*, 15(2): 131–138.

Aghion, P. and P. Howitt (1992), 'A model of growth through creative destruction', *Econometrica*, 60(2): 323–351.

Aghion, P., M. Dewatripont, and P. Rey (1999), 'Competition, financial discipline and growth', *The Review of Economic Studies*, 66(4): 825–852.

Aghion, P., N. Bloom, R. Blundell, R. Griffith and P. Howitt (2002a), 'Competition and innovation: an inverted-U relationship', *National Bureau of Economic Research Working Papers*, no. w9269.

Aghion, P., W. Carlin, and M. Schaffer (2002b), 'Competition, innovation and growth in transition: exploring the interactions between policies', William Davidson Working Paper, No. 501, http://papers.ssrn.com/sol3/papers.cfm?abstract_id=311407.

Aghion, P., N. Bloom, R. Blundell, R. Griffith and P. Howitt (2005), 'Competition and innovation: an inverted-U relationship, *Quarterly Journal of Economics*, 120(2): 701–728.

Arrow, K. (1962), 'Economic welfare and the allocation of resources for invention', in H.M. Groves (ed.), *The Rate and Direction of Inventive Activity: Economic and Social Factors*, NBER, 609–626. http://papers.nber.org/books/univ62-1

Atanassov, J. (2012), 'Do hostile takeovers stifle innovation? Evidence from anti-takeover legislation and corporate patenting', Working Paper, http://papers.ssrn.com/sol3/papers.cfm?abstract_id=967421

Barbosa, N. and Faria, A.P. (2011), 'Innovation across Europe: how important are institutional differences?', *Research Policy*, 40(9), 1157–1169.

Baysinger, B. and R.E. Hoskisson (1990), 'The composition of boards of directors and strategic control', *Academy of Management Review*, 15(1): 72–88.

Baysinger, B.D., R.D. Kosnik and T.A. Turk (1991), 'Effects of board and ownership structure on corporate R&D strategy', *Academy of Management Journal*, 34(1): 205–214.

Beck, N., and J.N. Katz (1995), 'What to do (and not to do) with time-series cross-section data', *American Political Science Review*, 89: 634–647.

Belloc, F. (2012), 'Corporate governance and innovation: a survey', *Journal of Economic Surveys*, 26(5): 835–864.

Chen, X., S. Lin and W.R. Reed (2009), 'A Monte Carlo evaluation of the efficiency of the PCSE estimator', *Applied Economics Letters*, 17(1): 7–10.

Clarke, G.R.G. (2001), 'How institutional quality and economic factors impact technological deepening in developing countries', *Journal of International Development*, 13(8): 1097–1118.

Dakhli, M. and D. De Clercq (2004), 'Human capital, social capital, and innovation: a multi-country study', *Entrepreneurship & Regional Development*, 16(2): 107–128.

Dixit, A. (2009), 'Governance institutions and economic activity', *American Economic Review*, 99(1): 3–24.

Dosi, G., C. Freeman, R.R. Nelson, G. Silverberg and L. Soete (eds) (1988), *Technological Change and Economic Theory*, London: Pinter.

Egger, P. (2002), 'An econometric view on the estimation of gravity models and the calculation of trade potentials', *The World Economy*, 25(2): 297–312.

Freeman, C. (1987), *Technology Policy and Economic Performance: Lessons from Japan*, London: Pinter.

Gilbert, Richard (2006), 'Looking for Mr. Schumpeter: where are we in the competition-innovation debate?', in Adam B. Jaffe, Josh Lerner and Scott Stern (eds), *Innovation Policy and the Economy – Volume 6*, Cambridge, Mass.: MIT Press, pp. 159–215.

Giménez, G. and J. Sanaú (2007), 'Interrelationship among institutional infrastructure, technological innovation and growth: an empirical evidence', *Applied Economics*, 39(10): 1267–1282.

Graves, S.B. (1988), 'Institutional ownership and corporate R&D in the computer industry', *Academy of Management Journal*, 31(2): 417–428.

Hill, C.W.L. and S.A. Snell (1988), 'External control, corporate strategy, and firm performance in research-intensive industries', *Strategic Management Journal*, 9(6): 577–590.

Hill, C.W., M.A. Hitt and R.E. Hoskisson (1988), 'Declining US competitiveness: reflections on a crisis', *Academy of Management Executive*, 2(1): 51–60.

Honoré., F., F. Munari and B. Pottelsberge de la Potterie (2011), 'Corporate governance practices and companies' R&D orientation: evidence from European countries', Working Paper. Available at: http://aei.pitt.edu/15489/1/110124_WP_CORPORATE_GOVERNANCE_PRACTICES.pdf

Jaffe, A.B. (1986), 'Technological opportunity and spillovers of R&D: evidence from firms' patents, profits, and market value', *American Economic Review*, 76(5): 984–1001.

Jensen, M. (1988), 'Takeovers: causes and consequences', *Journal of Economic Perspectives*, 2(1): 21–48.

Jones, C.I. and J.C. Williams (1998), 'Measuring the social return to R&D', *Quarterly Journal of Economics*, 113(4): 1119–1135.

Keefer, P., and S. Knack (1997), 'Why don't poor countries catch up? A cross-national test of an institutional explanation', *Economic Inquiry*, 35(3), 590–602.

Kim J., I. Krinsky and J. Lee (1997), 'Institutional holdings and trading volume reactions to quarterly earnings announcements', *Journal of Accounting, Auditing & Finance*, 12(1): 1–14.

Lang M. and M. McNichols (1997), 'Institutional trading and corporate performance', Research Paper no. 1460, Graduate School of Business Research, Stanford University, Stanford, CA.

Lundvall, B.-Å. (1988), 'Innovation as an interactive process: from user-producer interaction to the national innovation systems', in G. Dosi, C. Freeman, R.R. Nelson, G. Silverberg and L. Soete (eds), *Technological Change and Economic Theory*, London: Pinter.

Lundvall, B.Å., B. Johnson, E.S. Andersen and B. Dalum (2002), 'National systems of production, innovation and competence building', *Research Policy*, 31(2), 213–231.

Mansfield, E. (1985), 'How rapidly does new industrial technology leak out?', *Journal of Industrial Economics*, 34(2): 217–223.

Munari, F., R. Oriani and M. Sobrero (2010), 'The effects of owner identity and external governance systems on R&D investments: a study of Western European firms', *Research Policy*, 39(8), 1093–1104.

Nelson, R.R. (ed.) (1993), *National Innovation Systems*, New York: Oxford University Press.

North, Douglass (1990), *Institutions, Institutional Change, and Economic Performance*, Cambridge and London: Cambridge University Press.

North, D.C. (1994), 'Economic performance through time', *American Economic Review*, 84 (3): 359–368.

Peneder, M. (2012), 'Competition and innovation: revisiting the inverted-U relationship', *Journal of Industry, Competition and Trade*, 12(1): 1–5.

Potter, G. (1992), 'Accounting earnings announcements, institutional investor concentration and common stock returns', *Journal of Accounting Research*, 30(1): 146–155.

Sapra, H., A. Subramanian, and K. Subramanian (2009), 'Corporate governance and innovation: theory and evidence', Discussion paper published in *Corporate Governance and Capital Markets Ideas*, edited by the Chicago Booth School of Business. http://faculty.chicagobooth.edu/haresh.sapra/docs_WP/GI_01Oct09_SSRN.pdf

Schumpeter, Joseph A. (1934), *The Theory of Economic Development*, Cambridge, MA: Harvard University Press. (First published in German, 1912.)

Schumpeter, Joseph A. (1942), *Capitalism, Socialism, and Democracy*, New York: Harper and Brothers. (Harper Colophon edition, 1976.)

Shleifer, A. and L. Summers (1988), 'Breach of trust in hostile takeovers', in Alan J. Auerbach (ed.), *Corporate Takeovers: Causes and Consequences*, Chicago: University of Chicago Press, pp. 33–56.

Stein, J.C. (1988), 'Takeover threats and managerial myopia', *The Journal of Political Economy*, 96(1): 61–80.

Tebaldi, E. and B. Elmslie (2013), 'Does institutional quality impact innovation? Evidence from cross-country patent grant data', *Applied Economics*, 45(7): 887–900.

PART I

Governance and innovation

2. Governance, market power and innovation: evidence from OECD countries

Mehmet Ugur

INTRODUCTION

Since Joseph Schumpeter's seminal contribution, the relationship between market structure and innovation has been a highly debated issue in economics. This issue, however, tends to be treated as non-problematic in policy statements. For example, the analysis in OECD (2007) does not reflect on whether or not innovation and competition go hand in hand or on whether competition and governance have complementary or offsetting effects on innovation. Instead, it makes a blanket call for regulatory and institutional reform with a view to foster innovative activities. Similar statements have been made by the Commission of the European Union (EU) in the context of the Lisbon Agenda. According to the Commission's policy documents, the EU will become 'the most dynamic and competitive knowledge-based economy in the world' by 2010 as a result of reforms that increase competition in goods and services markets (EU Commission, 2005).This view is echoed in OECD (2006, 57–80), which argues that innovation performance is driven by a wide range of factors that include competitive product markets, macroeconomic stability, availability of internal and external finance, and economic openness.

Yet, the extensive literature on the relationship between product-market competition and innovation provides conflicting findings, some of which indicate a positive relationship while some report a negative or non-linear relationship. Hence, there is an evident need to verify if product-market competition is conducive to innovation or whether innovation entails deadweight losses associated with market power as a driver of innovation. In addition, both academic and policy debate has paid little attention to how market power interacts with governance quality and with what effects on innovation.

As Dixit (2009) has indicated, governance institutions may affect economic outcomes in general and innovation in particular because good governance is necessary for securing three essential prerequisites for market economies: (i) security of property rights; (ii) enforcement of contracts; and (iii) resolution of collective action problems. Institutions that secure property rights foster innovation by enabling investors in innovative activities to appropriate post-innovation profits, the level of which depends on the market structure. Governance institutions that secure contract enforceability reduce transaction costs and foster innovation by enabling firms to choose advanced technologies that prevail in contracted-intensive sectors (Acemoglu et al., 2007). Finally, institutions that minimize or resolve collective action problems also foster innovation because they facilitate internalization of the externalities associated with innovation, hence enabling countries or firms to avoid prisoners' dilemmas in the management of common pool resources such as knowledge.

A number of empirical studies have investigated the determinants of innovation at the macro level. These include Clarke (2001), Griffith et al. (2006a, 2006b), Guan and Chen (2012), and Tebaldi and Elmslie (2013). However, none of these studies examine the interactions between market structure and governance institutions as potential determinants of innovation. For example, Clarke (2001) examines the effects of macroeconomic variables and institutional factors on innovation, but without controlling for the level of market power. Similarly, Tebaldi and Elmslie (2013) examine the effects of governance institutions on patenting activity but without controlling for market structure and only with a small number of control variables that include R&D expenditures, geographical factors and demographic characteristics. Griffith et al. (2006a, 2006b) do examine the relationship between market power and innovation, but neither the effects of macroeconomic variables nor the interactions between market structure and governance quality. Of other work, Tselios (2011), Weinhold and Nair-Reichert (2009) and Foellmi and Zweimüller (2006) investigate the relationship between income inequality and innovation; Guloglu et al. (2012) and Baldwin and Gu (2004) examine the effects of trade liberalization on innovation; and Altman (2009) and Zhou et al. (2011) examine the relationship between labour costs and innovation. However, in all of this work, governance institutions are usually absent and so is the interaction between governance and market structure.

As such, the findings reported in the existing work may be subject to model specification bias. In this chapter, we aim to contribute to existing work in three ways. First, we control for both market structure and governance institutions, taking into account the interactions between the two. Our measure of market structure consists of excess profits over and above the total costs of capital and labour. The governance measure, on the other hand, consists of a composite index composed of five governance dimensions: bureaucracy quality, control of corruption, investment profile, law and order, and government stability. Secondly, we control for a wide range of potential determinants of patenting activity, including income distribution, depth of equity markets, economic openness, labour's share in national income, the level of military expenditures, and research and development (R&D) expenditures. Third: in line with Aghion and his co-authors' work on innovation at the firm level (Aghion et al., 2002, 2005), we control for non-linear relationship between market power and innovation. As a result, we will be able to provide evidence on whether governance and market structure have *complementary* or *offsetting* effects on innovation and whether the relationship between market structure and innovation is U-shaped or whether it has an inverted-U shape.

Our sample consists of 24 OECD countries for which data is collected from various sources for the period 1981–2008. The panel dataset is unbalanced, but it allows for estimation over 24 countries and 20 years for all relevant variables (see data and methodology section below). The dataset also enables us to check whether the relationship between innovation and its potential determinants differs between the full sample and the set of countries that have higher than sample average levels of per capita GDP, economic openness and governance scores in each year. We report that the relationship between innovation and its potential determinants have the same signs across samples with the exception of profit mark-ups. We discuss the significance and policy implications of these findings below.

The chapter is organized in five sections. In the following section, we provide a brief review of the related literature. We take stock of the existing evidence and identify the scope for adopting a more comprehensive approach to modelling the relationship between innovation and its potential determinants at the national level. In the third section, we introduce the data and elaborate on estimation methodology. The data is collected from a number of sources, including the OECD's Main Science and Technology Indicators (MSTI) database, the World Bank's World Development Indicators (WDI) database, the International Country Risk Guide (ICRG) database, the Standardized World Income Inequality database (Solt, 2009), and the UNDP study on factor shares in national income (Rodriguez and Jayadev, 2010). For estimation, we use generalized least-squares (GLS) estimation with panel-corrected standard errors (PCEs). This method allows for estimation in the presence of panel heteroskedasticity, panel autocorrelation, and contemporaneous correlation (HPAC). In the fourth section, we provide evidence on the relationship between innovation and potential determinants. We use two measures of innovation: number of patents granted by the US Patent and Trademark

Office (USPTO) and the number of triadic patent families registered with USPTO, the European Patent Office (EPO) and Japan Patent Office (JPO). Finally, in the last section we summarize the main findings and elaborate on their implications for policy and further research.

RELATED LITERATURE

Studies of innovation at the national level tend to adopt a national innovation system (NIS) approach based on pioneering work by Freeman (1987), Dosi et al. (1988) and Lundvall (1992). In this approach, the NIS has two dimensions: the knowledge innovation process (KIP) and the innovation environment (IE) that consists of institutional factors, macroeconomic conditions and government policy (Faber and Hesen, 2004; Guan and Chen, 2012). This chapter focuses on the environmental factors that influence the KIP and its outcomes. Specifically, we focus on the factors that may affect the number of USPTO-granted and triadic patents.

One of the most frequently researched environmental factors has been market structure and the level of competition it depicts. The debate on the innovation-competition relationship dates back to Schumpeter (1934, 1942), who posited that firms' innovation effort is likely to be higher when markets are concentrated and/or firm size is large. This is because market power enables firms to generate excess profits that can be used to hire highly qualified personnel and respond to competition quickly by utilizing internal finance instead of relying on costly external finance. In addition, market power enables firms to enjoy the benefits of innovation by erecting new barriers against future entry.

Arrow (1962) takes issue with the Schumpeterian hypothesis and demonstrates that a monopoly shielded against competition has less incentive to innovate because it can earn positive profits with or without innovation. However, a firm in a perfectly competitive market does not earn positive profits unless it innovates and its innovation is protected through exclusive rights. However, Arrow (1962) compares a pure monopolist with a perfectly competitive firm. When the market as a whole is modelled as imperfectly competitive, Gilbert and Newbery (1982) demonstrate that an incumbent firm with significant market power can be expected to invest more in innovation compared to a newcomer with less market power.

The result obtained by Gilbert and Newbery (1982) depends on the assumption that the patent is obtained by the highest bidder – i.e., by the firm that invests more in R&D. This assumption is challenged by Reinganum (1983, 1985) who argues that innovation expenditures increase the probability of obtaining the patent but do not guarantee success.

Given this uncertainty, the incumbent monopolist will decide to invest in innovation depending on the nature of innovation (drastic versus incremental innovation) and on the probability of innovation by the newcomer. Reinganum (1983, 1985) shows that the expected profits for the monopolist that invests in drastic innovation are less than the expected profits for a competitor; and this result holds even if innovation becomes less drastic on a drastic/non-drastic scale.

As demonstrated in Gilbert's (2006) extensive review, conflicting findings tend to be the norm in both theoretical and empirical work. Peneder (2012) argues that the conflicting results may be due to assuming a linear relationship between market power and innovation. Yet, such assumption overlooks the possibility that the relationship may depend on the degree of initial market power assumed. Schumpeter (1934, 1942) assumes that the initial degree of market power is low and this is evident from his argument that endogenous innovation under perfect competition is impossible. In Arrow (1962), on the other hand, the initial level of market power is assumed to be high: the comparison is between a legally protected monopoly and duopoly. Therefore the incentives analysed by Schumpeter and Arrow unfold exactly at the opposite ends of the market-power spectrum.

The inverted-U relationship between competition and innovation is central to the theoretical and empirical work by Aghion et al. (2002, 2005). In this work, incumbent firms tend to operate with similar technologies and innovation consists of neck-and-neck rather than drastic innovation when the level of competition is low. When this is the case, an increase in competition induces incumbent firms to innovate as a means of escaping competition. Hence, at low levels of initial competition, the relationship between competition and innovation is positive. In contrast, when the initial level of competition is high, innovation is more likely to be drastic and will be undertaken by newcomers who would have lower profits. Given that further increase in competition would reduce firm profits, fewer and fewer newcomers will be able to invest in innovation. Hence, at high levels of initial competition, the relationship between competition and innovation is negative. The dynamic that drives the non-linear relationship between competition and innovation is the type of innovation (neck-and-neck versus drastic innovation), and the type of innovators (incumbents versus newcomers) is determined endogenously by the level of competition. Phrased in terms of market power, the findings by Aghion et al. (2002, 2005) imply that the relationship between market power and innovation would have a U-shape: innovation would fall when market power increases from a low initial level and would increase when market power increases from a high initial level.

Following the work by Aghion and his co-authors, we can detect a degree of convergence towards the affirmation of a non-linear relationship between competition and innovation. This tendency is confirmed in recent work published in a special issue of the *Journal of Industry, Competition and Trade*. In an introductory article to the special issue, Peneder (2012) states that the non-linear model is technically sophisticated and has intuitive appeal – not the least because it can reconcile the Schumpeterian and Arrow-like arguments. Three empirical papers in the special issue test explicitly for non-linear relationship between competition and innovation. While Berubé et al. (2012) and Polder and Veldhuizen (2012) confirm the existence of an inverted-U relationship in Canadian and Dutch micro-data respectively, Peroni and Gomes Ferreira (2012) report a U-shaped relationship in Luxembourg firm-level data.

Nevertheless, the work reviewed above examines the relationship between market power and innovation at the firm level. To our knowledge, Griffith et al. (2006a, 2006b) is the only work that investigates the relationship between market power and innovation at the national level. Using the ratio of business R&D expenditures to GDP as measure of innovation, and average profitability as measure of market power, Griffith et al. (2006a: 30–31) report a positive relationship between average market power and R&D intensity for 13 OECD countries from 1986 to 2000. However, when three Scandinavian countries (Finland, Sweden and Denmark) are excluded, the relationship is found to be negative. To address the sensitivity to sample size, the authors also use sector-level average profitability and log R&D (instead of R&D intensity). The results indicate a negative relationship between market power and log R&D for all sectors taken together and for individual sectors classified on the basis of their exposure to competition through the Single Market reforms in the EU (Griffith et al., 2006a: 32–34; Griffith et al., 2006b: 28). The measure of profitability (market power) used is the ratio of value added to total cost of capital and labour at sector or macro level.

Another factor that may affect innovation at the national level is the quality of governance institutions. According to North (1990, 1994), a country's institutional environment constrains actors' choice sets and behaviour, and as such hinders or supports economic performance in general and innovation in particular. Governance institutions can be considered as the 'rules of the game' and consist of both formal and informal institutions. Formal institutions include written rules, regulations, laws and contracts; whereas informal institutions consist of values and belief systems that a society has developed and internalized over time.

Knack and Keefer (1997: 591) is the first attempt at relating innovation to a country's institutional quality. In their approach, returns on innovation investment are spread over long time periods and are essentially uncertain. Hence, firms tend to make less investment in new technologies or continue with obsolete ones if rule of law is weak and the risk of 'expropriation' is high. Lundvall et al. (2002) take the debate further by providing a systematic analysis of how governance institutions affect a society's interactive learning and innovation capabilities. The authors demonstrate that arbitration institutions, labour market regulation, and property rights institutions affect the level of innovation by shaping actors' ability to trust, learn and share knowledge.

Acemoglu and his co-authors provide theoretical justification for examining the relationship between governance institutions and innovation. For example, Acemoglu (2006) develops a model of economic and political institutions that lead to poor economic performance, including low levels of investment in long-term innovation projects. In the model, groups with political power choose policies to increase their income by revenue extraction, factor price manipulation and political consolidation. These choices lead to inefficient economic institutions, under which equilibrium taxes and regulations are worse than the elite would like them to be from an *ex ante* point of view. *Ipso facto*, economic institutions that provide additional security of property rights to other groups can have a positive effect on long-term investment and growth. Acemoglu et al. (2007) focus on the quality of contracting institutions and demonstrate that this tends to explain productivity differences between countries as well as the choice between contract-dependent and vertically integrated firm structures.

Empirical work on the relationship between governance institutions and innovation is few and far in between. Clarke (2001) is the first attempt at investigating the relationship between rule of law and innovation in a panel of developed and developing countries. The study reports that R&D expenditures tend to be lower in countries where the risk of expropriation is higher and the rule of law is weaker. Giménez and Sanaú (2007) provide a model where rule of law has a positive effect on technological development and economic growth. Using evidence for 64 countries averaged over 1985–97, the authors report that the model's prediction is confirmed by the data. A similar result is established by Dakhli and de Clercq (2004), who report that a reliable legal system and effective patent registration are conducive to higher levels of innovation. More recently, Tebaldi and Elmslie (2013) also propose a model where institutional quality affects innovation by helping in the process of registering new patents, diffusion of ideas across researchers, enforcement of property rights and reducing the uncertainty of new projects. Using data averaged over 1970–2003 for 110 countries, the authors report a positive and significant relationship between USPTO-granted patents and individual institutional indicators, which consist of control of corruption, market-friendly policies, protection of property rights and a more effective judiciary system. The results remain robust when initial level of knowledge stock (proxied by country shares in book production) is controlled for with a sample of 76 countries.

The control variables included in our analysis are also based on the existing literature. One such factor is income distribution, which may affect innovation from the demand or supply side. Zweimüller (2000) and Foellmi and Zweimüller (2006) propose a demand-induced innovation model where income inequality and concentration has a positive effect on innovation. Their model is based on hierarchical preferences for new products and higher willingness of the rich to pay higher prices for the new products. Firms that cater for the preferences of the rich are able to extract rents whereas others catering for the mass market with standardized products are not. Hence, income inequality and the persistence of inequality may be associated with higher levels of innovation. However, high concentration of wealth may also hinder innovation by preserving a poor majority, which restricts the market size.

Income inequality may affect innovation from the supply side too. If income is related to ability, economic agents may interpret income inequality as a signal of an economic system that rewards ability, an endowment that is distributed unequally. This expectation will encourage risk taking and innovation, the benefits of which are known to have a skewed distribution (Scherer et al., 2000). Hence, income inequality can be expected to increase the supply of innovation (Galor and Tsiddon, 1997; Hassler and Mora, 2000). However, income inequality may also induce resistance to innovation due to feelings of unfairness by lower income groups and wage earners – as indicated in Akerlof and Yellen (1990). In addition, income inequality may be associated with poor institutional quality, which reduces innovation.

The relationship between income inequality and innovation has been investigated by some empirical studies. For example, Weinhold and Nair-Reichert (2009) report that the number of patents registered by residents in a sample of 53 countries is related positively to size of the middle class over the period 1994–2000. However, Tselios (2011) report a positive relationship between income inequality and innovation, using data for 102 European regions over the period 1995–2000. Their findings indicate that, given the existing levels of income inequality in the European Union (EU), an increase in a region's inequality favours innovation.

Another factor that may affect innovation is labour cost. The question here is whether higher labour costs induce firms to innovate as a means of reducing unit costs and/or increasing productivity. Altman (2009) utilizes a behavioural-institutional model of induced technical change and reports that higher labour costs induce firms to innovate to remain competitive or to maintain current profit rates. Zhou et al. (2011), however, provide mixed results. Using firm-level survey data for Dutch firms, the authors report that functional (as opposed to numerical) labour market flexibility is associated with higher levels of products that are new to the firm. The relationship, however, does not hold for numerical flexibility. This evidence suggests that human resource management practices aiming to dampen wage costs may not be conducive to firm-level innovation.

A larger volume of work exists on the relationship between union power and innovation. Menezes-Filho and Van Reenen (2005) provide an excellent review of this literature. Their overall conclusion is that the sign, size and statistical significance of the association between unions and innovation vary dramatically between studies. Nevertheless, some patterns could be identified. First, North American studies tend to report a negative relationship between unions and R&D expenditures; but the evidence from Europe (mainly the UK) is mixed. Secondly, the ability of the unions to extract rents and hinder innovation depends on whether the strategic game between unions and employers is a one-shot or repeated game. If the game is repeated, unions are less likely to hinder innovation by extracting rents. This is because employers can retaliate by setting employment at lower levels. However, the repeated game is associated with multiple equilibria and it can boil down to a single-shot game – especially if the industry is in decline. Finally, the results also differ depending on whether unions bargain for wages only or for wages and employment at the same time. If the latter is the case, stronger unions may be conducive to higher innovation.

Innovation may also depend on the level of per capita income. As Clarke (2001) has indicated, wealthier countries tend to have higher levels of human capital and this may have a positive effect on economic agents' willingness to invest in innovation. Secondly, higher levels of income may lead to demand-induced innovation as higher average incomes increase the demand for novel products. Third, Taskin and Zaim (1997) report that countries with low initial per capita GDP levels catch up at a faster rate while countries with relatively high income depend more on technological progress for their productivity increases. Hence, higher per capita income may be associated with higher levels of investment in innovation. Finally, and from an empirical perspective, per capita GDP might capture other sources of innovation and as such it can help control for omitted variables.

Access to capital might also affect firms' ability to finance innovation. The moral hazard and adverse selection problems associated with debt finance in general and debt-financing of innovation in particular are well known (Stiglitz and Weiss, 1981). In addition, debt financing may be costly for another reason: the collateral value of intangible assets such as patents is low and innovative firms may have to provide extra collateral.

Hence, equity issue emerges as an alternative method of financing innovation. Indeed, Brown et al. (2009) report that equity finance has become a significant source of financing R&D investments in the 1990s by young firms. In this chapter, we will investigate whether stock market turnover (i.e., the value of traded stocks) as a percentage of GDP is related to innovation.

Military expenditures may have a positive effect on innovation for two reasons. On the one hand, there may be spillover effects from government-financed innovation expenditures in the defence sector into R&D expenditures or patenting activity of private firms. On the other hand, there may be geographical spillover effects, whereby the level of military expenditures may be associated with local/regional or international investment in innovation (Clarke, 2001). However, military expenditure may divert resources from innovation investment into the production of non-productive goods, leading to lower levels of innovation in non-defence sectors (Kentor and Kick, 2008).

Finally, economic openness (i.e., openness to trade, foreign direct investment and portfolio investment) may also be related to innovation. For example, Baldwin and Gu (2004) report that Canadian firms that moved into export markets increased investments in R&D and in capacity building aimed at absorbing foreign technologies. A similar finding is reported by Pla-Barber and Alegre (2007), who investigate 121 French biotechnology firms. The authors find that firm size is not a determinant for innovation but export intensity is. At country level, however, the evidence is mixed. For example, Guloglu et al. (2012) examine the relationship between technological change and a series of macroeconomic variables in G7 countries. The authors find no significant relationship between technological change and trade openness. Furthermore, when other indicators of openness are taken into account, economic openness tends to be negatively related to innovation. For example, Clarke (2001) reports a negative relationship between foreign direct investment (FDI) and R&D expenditures, and the negative correlation is robust to different model specifications. One possible reason is that FDI may be a substitute for investment in R&D. This is in contrast to frequent statements made by international organizations or national policy makers, who tend to emphasize the positive effects of globalization on innovation.[1]

The review above indicates that the work on the relationship between innovation and potential determinants has a long history, with the majority of the work being focused on the relationship between market structure and innovation. A relatively smaller number of studies investigate the relationship between innovation and governance quality, income distribution, labour costs, depth of equity markets and the extent of economic openness. Even then, the existing work does not take account of how these potential predictors interact with market power and with what consequences for innovation.

The aim of this chapter is to contribute to the existing work in three ways. First, we will try to establish if the non-linear relationship between market power and innovation that is established at the firm level also holds at the national level. To our knowledge, this is the first exercise in this direction. Secondly, we aim to expand the limited evidence base by investigating whether governance quality and market power have complementary or offsetting effects on innovation. Finally, we address the risk of model specification bias by controlling for a wide range of potential determinants, which include per capita GDP, income distribution, labour costs, economic openness, military expenditures, and R&D expenditures as inputs into patenting activity. Extension of the research effort in these directions can support evidence-based policy debate by: (a) correcting for potential bias; (b) identifying the extent of complementary and offsetting effects from governance and market power; and (c) identifying the extent to which competition tends to drive or hinder innovation.[2]

METHODOLOGY AND DATA

We have collected data for 24 OECD countries from 1981 to 2008. The dataset is an unbalanced panel that allows estimation for 24 countries over 20 years from 1988 to 2007. For estimation, we use a Prais-Winsten estimator that takes into account panel heteroskedasticity, panel autocorrelation, and contemporaneous correlation (HPAC) (see Beck and Katz, 1995). Formally, the model to be estimated can be stated as follows:

$$Y_{it} = \beta_0 + \sum_{k=1}^{K} \beta_k X_{kit} + u_{it}. \tag{2.1}$$

We assume that the error terms (u_{it}) are heteroskedastic, contemporaneously correlated and autoregressive (i.e, serially correlated). These assumptions can be stated as follows:

$$E(u_{it}^2) = \sigma_{ii} \text{ (heteroskedasticity)} \tag{2.1.1}$$

$$E(u_{it} u_{jt}) = \sigma_{ij} \text{ (contemporaneous correlation)} \tag{2.1.2}$$

and

$$u_{it} = \rho_i u_{i,t-1} + \varepsilon_{it} \text{ (country-specific serial correlation)} \tag{2.1.3}$$

The model is estimated with generalized least squares (GLS), using the Prais-Winsten estimator. The estimator is suitable for cross-sectional time-series data and allows for estimating coefficients with panel-corrected standard errors (PCSE). It also allows for error structures that are heteroskedastic and contemporaneously correlated across panels (Beck and Katz, 1995; Egger, 2002). The estimator is found to be efficient when the number of time period is close to the number of cases (countries) (Chen et al., 2009). Our dataset satisfies this condition with 24 countries and 20 years. In the estimation, we correct for first-order autocorrelation (AR(1)) that is specific to each panel (2.1.3). This specification is in line with methods typically used to estimate autocorrelation in time-series analysis.

The Prais-Winsten estimator with panel-corrected standard errors (PCSEs) yields standard errors that are robust to two types of violation of the standard ordinary least-squares (OLS) assumptions. First, the standard errors are robust to each country having a different variance of disturbances. Secondly, they are robust to each country's observations being correlated with those of other countries over time. The control for within-panel serial correlation is an additional feature that allows for assuming two types of autocorrelation coefficients: a single coefficient that is common to all countries; and different autocorrelation coefficients that are specific to each country. This additional feature enables us to avoid the inefficient estimate problem that arises when the data follows an autoregressive process. Hence, the model for estimation can be stated as follows:

$$
\begin{aligned}
Innov_{it} = {} & \beta_0 + rent_{it-1} + rent\_sq_{it-1} + gov\_score_{it-1} + gov\_score\_rent_{it-1} + \\
& gini\_gross_{it-1} + lab\_share_{it-1} + pc\_gdp_{it-1} + milit\_\exp\_gdp_{it-1} + \\
& traded\_stocks\_gdp_{it-1} + ec\_global_{it-1} + TRIPS\_dummy_{it} + berd\_va_{it-1} + \\
& berd\_va_{it-2} + u_{it}
\end{aligned}
\tag{2.2}
$$

We use two measures of innovation as dependent variables: number of patents granted by USPTO (*patents_uspto*) and number of patents in triadic patent families (*triadic_patents*) registered with EPO, JPO and USPTO. We have chosen patents as measures of innovation because patents indicate the extent to which patent holders consider the innovation as 'new to the market' (OECD, 2005). Being new to the market does not provide a reliable indication of quality though. However, patent registration is a costly exercise and patent holders will be willing to incur the cost only if they expect benefits from patenting the innovation – i.e., if patents protect a process or a product that provides a competitive advantage in the market place. Because we cannot observe the extent to which this is the case, empirical studies at the firm-level tend to use citations-weighted patents as a measure of quality (see, for example, Aghion et al., 2002, 2005).

As citations data was not available to us, we have decided to use two measures of registered patents. *Patents_uspto* is the number of patents that innovators register with the USPTO. Compared to patents registered with national patent offices, *patents_uspto* provides slightly better information about patent quality. This is because of extra cost associated with multiple registrations. However, *patents-uspto* may be affected by home bias so far as the registration of US patents is concerned (on home bias, see OECD, 2006). To check whether this may affect the results and to enhance the information content of the measure with respect to quality, we also use *triadic_patents*. This measure reflects the number of patents registered within patent families at three major patenting offices – EPO, JPO and USPTO. Compared to patent filings with a single office, triadic patent families cover a homogeneous set of inventions. These are considered as the most important inventions, and the resultant indicator is less influenced by patent offices' rules, regulations, and patenting strategies. Consequently, 'counting triadic patent families provide indicators of an improved quality and international comparability for measuring innovation' (Dernis and Khan, 2004). The patent count data is obtained from OECD's MSTI database. From the same source, we have also obtained data for business R&D expenditures as percentage of value added (*BERD_VA*), which is used as input into the innovation process. *BERD_VA* is financed mainly by industry, but it also includes government subsidies.

The *rent* variable is calculated as the ratio of value-added to the total cost of capital and labour, in accordance with (2.3) below.

$$rent_{it} = VA_{it}/(CK_{it} + CL_{it}) \tag{2.3}$$

VA = gross value added at current prices, excluding the output of indirectly measured financial intermediation services. As indicated in paragraph 8.14 of ESA (1995), financial intermediation services indirectly measured (FISIM) are not allocated to user sectors. Hence the value of the output of FISIM is treated as intermediate consumption of a nominal sector with zero output and negative value added equal in size but opposite in sign to intermediate consumption.

CK = cost of capital. The cost of capital is not provided in national accounts. We have calculated it by multiplying the net capital stock by US interest rates adjusted for country risk (see below).

CL = cost of labour. This is the compensation of employees item in national accounts. Compensation of employees consists of wages and salaries and employers' social contributions.

Thus defined, the *rent* variable measures the average rate of profits retained by owners of capital (or entrepreneurs). It is used as such by Griffith et al. (2006a, 2006b). The measure is similar to the price-cost margin (or Lerner Index) calculated at the firm or industry level. As a measure of market power, it is better than country-level concentration indices such as a macro-level Herfindahl-Hirschman index (HHI). Macro-level HHI provides inadequate information about market power because the definition of the market over which the concentration index is calculated is imperfect (see Aghion et al., 2002, 2005).

However, the market power index also has some shortcomings. First, it is based on the assumption of constant returns to scale (or the unobservable marginal cost is proxied by average costs). Therefore, it will underestimate (overestimate) the level of profit mark-up if there is increasing (decreasing) returns to scale (Griffith et al., 2006a, 2006b). Secondly, the cost of capital is not directly observable and has to be calculated by making assumptions about the appropriate interest rates. Griffith et al. (2006a, 2006b) use long-term US interest rates as a proxy, assuming full capital mobility and a single world interest rate. They also conduct a sensitivity check by using national interest rates and found that the results are not sensitive to different ways of constructing the cost of capital.

In this chapter, we use long-term US interest for lending to the private sector and adjust for other countries by taking into account each country's composite risk rating (CRR) compiled by ICRG. The higher the value of the CRR, the more risky the country is. Subtracting the US CRR from each country's CRR, we have obtained relative CRR (*CRR_relative*) for each country/year. Using *CRR_relative*, we have adjusted the interest rate for each country/year upward if the country's CRR in that year is higher than the US CRR. We also carry out sensitivity checks to see if results differ when US interest rates are used as world interest rates for calculating the cost of capital. The adjustment is carried out in accordance with the following procedure:

If *CRR_relative* = 0 or MINUS, use US interest rates
If *CRR_relative* = 0.1 to 2.0, use US interest rates + 1 percentage point.
For example if US interest rates is 10%, use 11%
If *CRR_relative* = 2.1 to 4.0, use US interest rates + 2 percentage points.
If *CRR_relative* = 4.1 to 6.0, use US interest rates + 3 percentage points.

If *CRR_relative* = 6.1 to 8.0, use US interest rates + 4 percentage points.
If *CRR_relative* = 8.1 or more, use US interest rates + 5 percentage points.

We model the relationship between innovation and profit mark-ups (*rent*) as non-linear. Hence model (3) includes the square of the *rent* variable. This is in line with the firm-level work reviewed above.

The governance indicators are obtained from ICRG and they include the following: bureaucracy quality, control of corruption, investment profile, law and order, and government stability. The indicators range from 0 to 4 for bureaucratic quality; from 0 to 6 for control of corruption, democratic accountability and law and order; and from 0 to 12 for government stability and investment profile. The higher the value of the indicator the better is the governance quality.

These indicators measure perceptions of the respondents to ICRG surveys. As such, their use as a measure of governance (or institutional) quality is debated extensively in the literature (see Kurtz and Schrank, 2007; Kaufmann et al., 2007). The debate revolves around the issue of endogeneity and reverse causality. Because respondents' perceptions of governance are likely to be influenced by economic performance (e.g., growth rate or level of unemployment) of the country, governance scores may be measuring economic performance rather than governance quality *per se*. Hence, their use as predictors of economic performance creates endogeneity problems that lead to spurious results. This issue is addressed by using instrumental variable (IV) techniques or by using lagged values. In this chapter, we examine the relationship between governance and patenting activity. Unlike growth or unemployment, the effect of patenting activities on perceptions is likely to be weak and hence the reverse causality problem is less severe in our case. To address the risk of any residual endogeneity, we use one-year lagged values of the governance indicators – and indeed all other covariates in equation (2.3).

Using the ICRG indicators, we have conducted principal component analysis (PCA) and constructed an aggregate governance score (*gov_score*) from five indicators: bureaucracy quality, control of corruption, investment profile, law and order, and government stability. The *gov_score* is constructed by excluding components with eigenvalues of less than 1 – as recommended in the literature (see, for example, Jolliffe, 2002). In our estimation, we control for the partial effect of *gov_score* and for the effect of its interaction with the level of profit mark-ups through the interactive term *gov_score*rent*. The inclusion of an interaction term in models with quadratic terms (such as *rent_squared* here) is reported to provide more reliable estimates of the coefficients. Using both simulation data and a genuine dataset on parents' education and children's educational performance, Ganzach (1997) concludes as follows: if appropriate inter-action terms are not included, then the estimated quadratic model may indicate a concave relationship between the independent variables and the dependent variable, whereas the true relationship is, in fact, convex. Conversely, when quadratic terms are omitted despite being justified by theory or by the data structure, the omission causes the interaction terms to have complementary effects whereas the true effect is offsetting.

The income inequality measure (*gini_gross*) is obtained from the Standardized World Income Inequality Database (SWIID). *Gini_gross* measures income inequality before taxes and subsidies and is standard-ized using the United Nations University's World Income Inequality Database. Standardization is carried out by minimizing reliance on problematic assumptions in existing income inequality data and by using as much information as possible from proximate years within the same country (for details, see Solt, 2009). The SWIID data has been used in recent empirical research (see Bergh and Nilsson, 2010; Mahutga et al., 2011). We control for *gini_gross* because it has been demonstrated that income inequality can influence innovation, but the direction of its effect can be either negative or positive (see literature review above).

Another factor we control for is the share of labour in national income (*lab_share*). We have obtained the labour share data from Rodriguez and Jayadev (2010). The authors report that both economy-wide and manufac-turing industry labour shares have declined from the 1980s in most coun-tries. Their findings are robust to adjustments for self-employment and adjustments for unbalanced panel structure. They also report that declines in labour shares are driven by declines in intra-sector labour shares rather than movements in activity towards sectors with lower labour shares. We have used their data to establish if innovation is driven by considerations related to reducing labour costs. The aim here is to contribute to existing evidence, which tends to use union power as a proxy for labour costs.

OECD (2007) claims that globalization is a major driver of innova-tion. The logic in such arguments rests on a positive relationship between increased competition (i.e., reduced rents) and innovation. Although trade liberalization is usually found to have a positive effect on innovation, the evidence on the relationship between economic openness (including open-ness to trade, FDI and portfolio investment) is inconclusive. Hence, we use a measure of economic globalization constructed by Dreher (2006). The Economic Globalization Index is based on 'hard evidence' in the sense that it synthesizes data on actual economic flows (trade, FDI and portfolio investment flows) and data on restrictions. In our data set, the economic globalization index (*econ_global*) ranges from 34 to 98, with higher values indicating higher levels of economic openness.

Other factors we control for include per capita GDP (*pc_GDP*), military expenditures as percentage of GDP (*milit_exp_GDP*), traded stock as percentage of GDP (*traded_stocks_GDP*) and lagged values of business R&D expenditures as percentage of value added (*BERD_VA*). The rationale for including per capita GDP, value of traded stocks and military expenditures is discussed briefly in the literature review above. Further elaboration on the relevance of these predictors can be found in Clarke (2001). We will use the remainder of this section to say a few words about inclusion of the dummy variable (*TRIPS_dummy*) and the business R&D expenditures as percentage of value added (*BERD_VA*).

The *TRIPS_dummy* captures two important developments in 1994 that are likely to affect patenting activity: (a) the conclusion of the Paris Convention for Protection of Industrial Property and Patent Cooperation; and (b) the conclusion of Trade-Related Intellectual Property Rights (TRIPs) within the World Trade Organization (WTO). The inclusion of *TRIPS_dummy* is justified for two reasons. First, the conclusion of the Paris convention has led to convergence in the criteria used for granting patents. Secondly, the TRIPs agreement has strengthened intellectual property rights and may have had a positive effect on registration of patents.

Pakes and Griliches (1984) and Hall et al. (1986) are first to study the lag structure in the relationship between R&D expenditures and patenting at the firm level. They control for contemporaneous R&D and its three lags and report that the relationship between R&D expenditures and patenting has a U-shape – with closest and furthest lags having large effects and intermediate lags having small effects. The empirical work that has followed tends to control for R&D expenditures not only as an input measure of innovation but also as a predictor of innovation productivity. Therefore, we include lagged values of R&D in model (3), but we restrict the number of lags to two in order to reduce the risk of multicollinearity.

Our examination of the summary statistics by year and by country suggests that heteroskedasticity and serial correlation are likely to confound the estimation results. The patent counts for some countries (US, Japan, Germany and the UK) are much larger than the rest of the sample. To a lesser extent, this is the case for per capita GDP too. Such differences in the magnitude of the variables are likely to cause the variance of the error terms to be heteroskedastic. The data also reveals an upward trend over time. This is evident with respect to patent counts, per capita GDP, stock market turnover, and income inequality; and indicates risk of serial correlation. Therefore, the choice of Prais-Winsten estimator seems appropriate as it corrects for heteroskedasticity, serial correlation and contemporaneous correlation across countries.

Summary statistics of the variables are given in Table 2.1. The variables

Table 2.1   Summary statistics: patenting activity and country-level variables

Variable	Obs.	Mean	Std. Dev.	Min.	Max.
Patents_USPTO (Log)	610	6.23	2.52	0.69	12.39
Triadic_patents (Log)	610	4.80	2.48	0.00	9.68
Rent (Ratio)	487	1.44	0.40	0.80	3.21
Rent_squared	487	2.24	1.50	0.63	10.29
Gov_score (Index)	608	0.04	1.60	−5.57	2.02
Gov_score*rent	487	0.31	2.87	−12.89	3.17
Gini_gross (%)	636	42.88	5.64	26.09	61.69
Traded_stocks_GDP (%)	593	62.59	55.73	0.19	479.74
Lab_share (%)	580	51.82	9.29	0.00	73.64
PC_GDP (Log)	634	9.62	0.73	7.92	10.94
Milit_exp_GDP (%)	622	1.87	0.99	0.00	5.79
Econ_global (Index)	624	73.72	13.69	38.53	98.69
BERD_VA (%)	508	1.53	1.06	0.01	5.35
TRIPS_dummy	640	0.70	0.46	0.00	1.00

are measured in four different scales. Patents (*patents_uspto* and *triadic_patents*) are count variables, which are known to have a Poisson distribution with positive integer values and mean equal to variance. Hence, Poisson-distributed data is not suitable for OLS estimation. Instead, Poisson regression is recommended. However, for ease of interpretation, we have decided to take the natural logarithm of the patent data. The log of patent data is approximately normal and as such can be used for estimating model (3). The other variable in log is per capita GDP (*pc_GDP*). The *rent* variable is a ratio; whereas *gini_gross, lab_share, traded_stocks_GDP, milit_exp_GDP* and *BERD_VA* are percentages. Two variables (*gov_score* and *econ_global*) are indices. *Gov_score* is computed using principal component analysis methodology but *econ_global* is taken as given and ranges between 38.53 and 98.69 in the dataset.

RESULTS

The results in Table 2.2 are based on data for the full sample of 24 countries from 1988 to 2007. They indicate that the majority of the covariates have a significant relationship with the number of patents. Moreover, the sign and significance of the relationship are consistent across two types of patents: patents granted by USPTO and triadic patents. This is a significant finding because it suggests that the number of triadic patents that

Table 2.2   Predictors of patenting activity: full OECD sample

Dependent variable	USPTO Patents (1)	Triadic Patents (2)
Rent	−1.959***	−1.367**
	(0.536)	(0.614)
Rent_sq	0.676***	0.450**
	(0.176)	(0.185)
Gov_score	0.301**	0.243*
	(0.118)	(0.126)
Gov_score*Rent	−0.235***	−0.162*
	(0.084)	(0.083)
Gini_gross	−0.024***	−0.029***
	(0.008)	(0.010)
Lab_share	0.019	0.034***
	(0.012)	(0.011)
Ln_pcGDP	3.025***	2.381***
	(0.293)	(0.211)
Mili_texp_GDP	0.284***	0.435***
	(0.086)	(0.055)
Traded_stocks_GDP	0.003***	0.002*
	(0.001)	(0.001)
Econ_global	−0.041***	−0.044***
	(0.005)	(0.006)
TRIPS_dummy	0.313***	0.241**
	(0.099)	(0.102)
L1.BERD_VA	0.315	0.540**
	(0.192)	(0.237)
L2.BERD_VA	0.180	0.249
	(0.234)	(0.272)
Constant	−20.107***	−16.568***
	(2.821)	(1.968)
Observations	333	331
Number of countries	24	24
Number of coefficients	14	14
R-squared	0.96	0.946
Chi^2	769.243	1408.934
Model degrees of freedom	13	13
P>Chi^2	0.000	0.000

Notes: Standard errors in brackets are based on Prais-Winsten regression, with heteroskedastic panels, panel-specific AR(1) autocorrelation and contemporaneously correlated panel disturbances. ***, **, * indicates significance at 1%, 5% and 10% respectively. All independent variables are lagged by one year.

reflects higher innovation quality is proportional to the number of registered patents across countries and over time.

The results also indicate that patenting activity has a U-shaped relationship with the level of profit mark-ups (*rent*). When the profit mark-up increases by one decimal point (for example from 1.4 to 1.5 as a proportion of total cost), the number of patents registered with USPTO decreases by 19.59 per cent. The decrease in the number of triadic patents is 13.67 per cent. However, the decrease is non-monotonic. The positive and significant coefficient of *rent_squared* indicates that the number of patents decreases at lower rates until *rent* reaches the turning point of the parabolic curve. From that level, the number of patents begins to increase at a non-monotonic rate. This result is in line with findings obtained with firm-level data (Aghion et al., 2002, 2005; Berubé et al., 2012; and Polder and Veldhuizen, 2012). The U-shaped relationship we find here is based on market power rather than competition and therefore it is the mirror image of the inverted-U relationship found in the firm-level literature that investigates the relationship between competition and innovation.

The turning point for rent can be calculated easily by taking the partial derivative of the models with respect to rent and setting equal to zero. The terms with rent are as follows:

$$ln\_patents\_uspto = -1.959rent + 0.676rent^2 - 0.235rent * gov\_score \tag{2.4a}$$

$$ln\_triadic\_patents = -1.367rent + 0.45rent^2 - 0.162rent * gov\_score \tag{2.4b}$$

Differentiating with respect to rent:

$$\partial(ln\_patents\_uspto)/\partial(rent) = -1.959 + 1.352rent - 0.235gov\_score = 0 \tag{2.4a'}$$

$$\partial(ln\_triadic\_patents)/\partial(rent) = -1.367 + 0.90rent - 0.162gov\_score = 0 \tag{2.4b'}$$

The turning point for rent depends on governance score. Taking the sample average of the governance score (which is 0.04), the turning points can be calculated as follows:

$$\text{For USPTO-granted patents, } rent = 1.97/1.352 = 1.46 \tag{2.4a''}$$

$$\text{For Triadic patents, } rent = 1.373/0.9 = 1.53 \tag{2.4b''}$$

These values are close to the average level of rent in the sample (1.44) and enable us to conclude that an increase in *rent* leads to a fall in patenting activity when the initial level of rent is approximately less than the sample average; however a unit increase in rent leads to an increase in patenting activity when the initial level of rent is higher than average.

The governance coefficient is positive and significant and can be interpreted in the same way: a one-decimal-point increase in governance score is associated with an increase of 3.01 per cent in the number of patents registered with USPTO and an increase of 2.43 per cent in the number of triadic patents. This finding is in line with earlier findings on the governance-innovation relationship reported by Clarke (2001), Giménez and Sanaú (2007), Dakhli and de Clercq (2004), and Tebaldi and Elmslie (2013). The difference from earlier findings is that our result is based on an aggregate score that captures six dimensions of governance quality: bureaucracy quality, control of corruption, democratic accountability, investment profile, law and order and political stability. As such, it does not indicate which dimension is the most influential but it does provide evidence that overall governance quality matters. To our knowledge, this is the first estimate of the relationship between overall governance quality and patenting activity.

More importantly, however, we also find a negative and significant relationship between the interaction term (*gov_score*rent*) and patenting activity. Given the positive coefficient on governance, this finding indicates that rent has an offsetting effect on the relationship between governance and patenting activity. This can be seen easily by calculating the marginal effects of governance, taking into account the interaction between rent and governance. The marginal effects of the governance score and the rent are given in panels A and B of Table 2.3.

From summary statistics, rent has an average of 1.44 and ranges from 0.80 to 3.21. In other words, rent is always positive. Hence, the marginal effect indicates that rent always has an offsetting effect on the relationship between governance and innovation (Panel A of Table 2.3). To our knowledge, this is the first finding that establishes not only a positive partial effect from governance to innovation but also an offsetting (substitution) effect from rent when the latter is interacted with governance quality. This finding indicates that the partial effect of governance usually reported in the existing literature can be misleading because the true marginal effect of governance on innovation depends on market power, which has an offsetting effect on the relationship between governance and innovation.

The marginal effect of market power on innovation depends both on the level of rent and the governance score (Panel B of Table 2.3). From (2.4a″) and (2.4b″) above, the relationship between rent and innovation is positive

Table 2.3   Marginal effects of governance and market power: full sample

Panel A: marginal effect of governance	Rent: complementary or offsetting?
$\dfrac{\partial\,ln\_patents\_uspto}{\partial\,gov\_score} = 0.301 - 0.235\ rent$	Offsetting
$\dfrac{\partial\,ln\_triadic\_patents}{\partial\,gov\_score} = 0.243 - 0.162\ rent$	Offsetting
Panel B: marginal effect of rent	Governance: complementary or offsetting?
$\dfrac{\partial\,ln\_patents\_uspto}{\partial\,rent} = -1.959 + 1.352\ rent$ $-0.235\ gov\_score$	Complementary until rent = 1.46; offsetting thereafter
$\dfrac{\partial\,ln\_triadic\_patents}{\partial\,rent} = -1.367 + 0.90\ rent$ $-0.162\ gov\_score$	Complementary until rent = 1.53; offsetting thereafter

until the rent values that correspond to the turning points and negative thereafter. Hence, an increase in governance score tends to complement the negative effect of the rent on governance until the turning points; but it tends to offset it thereafter. Again, to our knowledge, this is the first finding that establishes not only a non-linear relationship between rent (i.e., market power) and innovation at the macro level, but also complementary and offsetting effects that augment or weaken the relationship between market power and innovation. This finding also indicates that the partial effect of market power on innovation reported in Griffith et al. (2006a, 2006b) can be misleading because the true marginal effect of market power on innovation is mediated via governance quality.

With respect to control variables, the results in Table 2.2 indicate that the relationship between income inequality and innovation is negative and significant: one percentage point increase in the *gini* index is associated with a decrease of 2.4 and 2.9 per cent in the number of patents registered with USPTO and the number of triadic patents, respectively. This is in contrast to empirical findings reported by Foellmi and Zweimüller (2006) and Tselios (2011); but in line with Weinhold and Nair-Reichert (2009). We think that our finding is driven by the characteristics of the sample. Recall that the sample consists of OECD countries with an average per capita GDP of 21,703 US dollars. The high level of per capita GDP indicates that firms engage in innovation to cater not only for the preferences of the high-income groups but also the average-income groups who have a substantial purchasing power. Hence, our finding lends support to

Weinhold and Nair-Reichert (2009) who report that innovation is related positively to size of the middle class in a sample of 53 countries from 1994 to 2000. Furthermore, the negative relationship between income inequality and patenting activity is compatible with the finding of a positive relationship between governance quality and patenting activity. Higher levels of income inequality may be reflecting relatively poorer governance quality.

As indicated in the literature review, the cost of labour is another factor that may affect innovation. The results in Table 2.2 indicate that labour share has a positive and significant relationship with innovation only in the case of triadic patents. This finding is in line with Altman (2009) whose behavioural-institutional model predicts that higher labour costs induce firms to innovate to remain competitive or to maintain current profit rates. However, the finding is in contrast to the US-based empirical results reviewed in Menezes-Filho and Van Reenen (2005), which tend to report a negative relationship between union power and innovation.

Due to space limitations, we are unable to elaborate on the findings concerning the effects of per capita GDP, military expenditures and stock market turnover as percentage of GDP. Suffice it to say that the results are in line with the existing literature. A similar comment can be made about the effect of lagged business R&D expenditures: the coefficient on the first lag of *BERD_VA* is always positive, but significant only with respect to triadic patents. Hence, we are unable to verify the existence or absence of the lag structure identified by Pakes and Griliches (1984) and Hall et al. (1986). However, we can report that frequent claims about globalization as a driver of innovation (e.g., OECD, 2007) are not supported by the OECD data: the index of economic globalization is related negatively to the number of patents registered with USPTO and triadic patents.

We have conducted three sensitivity checks to verify the robustness of the results in Table 2.2. First, we have estimated the model by normalizing the standard errors of the coefficients by N − k (N is number of observation and k is the number of estimated coefficients) instead of N. Secondly, we used unadjusted US interest rates instead of adjusted interest rates for calculating the cost of capital. In both cases, the results remain consistent with those reported in Table 2.2.[3]

The third sensitivity check involved splitting the sample into two: countries with higher than sample average for per capita GDP, governance score and economic globalization against those with lower than average in each year. The results from the split sample of higher-than-average countries are given in Table 2.4.

The signs of the coefficients in the split sample are largely in line with those obtained with the full sample – with the notable exception of the *rent* variable and its square. The coefficients on governance score (*gov_score*)

Table 2.4 Predictors of patenting activity: split samples

Dependent variable	USPTO patents [PC_GDP > Mean PC_GDP]	Triadic patents [PC_GDP > mean PC_GDP]	USPTO patents [GOV_SCORE > mean GOV_SCORE]	Triadic patents [GOV_SCORE > mean GOV_SCORE]	USPTO patents [EC_GLOBAL > mean EC_GLOBAL]
Regressors	(1)	(2)	(3)	(4)	(5)[++]
Rent	5.743***	2.158	7.517***	1.107	4.185***
	(1.818)	(1.715)	(1.971)	(2.040)	(1.588)
Rent_sq	-2.440***	-1.008	-2.783***	-0.397	-1.904***
	(0.706)	(0.635)	(0.784)	(0.786)	(0.525)
Gov_score	0.454***	0.107	1.312***	0.995**	0.506*
	(0.155)	(0.136)	(0.374)	(0.442)	(0.307)
Gov_score*Rent	-0.476***	-0.221**	-1.266***	-0.985***	-0.579**
	(0.119)	(0.103)	(0.293)	(0.336)	(0.248)
Gini_gross	-0.010	-0.014	-0.026**	-0.053***	-0.023*
	(0.009)	(0.010)	(0.011)	(0.011)	(0.013)
Lab_share	-0.021*	-0.022*	-0.002	0.018	-0.005
	(0.011)	(0.012)	(0.014)	(0.013)	(0.016)
Ln_pcGDP	2.485***	1.224***	2.506***	1.565***	2.251***
	(0.470)	(0.385)	(0.434)	(0.386)	(0.514)
Mili_texp_GDP	0.576***	0.562***	0.521***	0.537***	0.630***
	(0.068)	(0.057)	(0.085)	(0.076)	(0.053)
Traded_stocks_GDP	0.004***	0.002**	0.006***	0.004***	0.003***
	(0.001)	(0.001)	(0.001)	(0.001)	(0.001)
Econ_global	-0.053***	-0.052***	-0.068***	-0.058***	-0.024**
	(0.006)	(0.005)	(0.005)	(0.006)	(0.010)

TRIPS_dummy	0.225*	0.278**	0.353***	0.420***	0.308***
	(0.117)	(0.113)	(0.095)	(0.112)	(0.105)
L1.BERD_VA	0.249	0.509**	0.225	0.327	0.216
	(0.159)	(0.203)	(0.197)	(0.230)	(0.199)
L2.BERD_VA	0.346**	0.254	0.351*	0.271	0.250
	(0.174)	(0.199)	(0.207)	(0.219)	(0.190)
Constant	−17.399***	−4.050	−18.173***	−6.905	−16.493***
	(5.089)	(4.313)	(4.731)	(4.286)	(4.185)
Observations	252	252	216	216	178
Number of countries	18	18	20	20	17
Number of coeff.	14	14	14	14	14
R-squared	0.968	0.961	0.981	0.966	0.981
Chi²	372.075	464.009	1018.880	560.996	374.668
Model d.f.	13	13	13	13	8
P > Chi²	0.00	0.00	0.00	0.00	0.00

Notes: Standard errors in brackets are based on Prais-Winsten regression, with heteroskedastic panels, panel-specific AR(1) autocorrelation and contemporaneously correlated panel disturbances. ***, **, * indicates significance at 1%, 5% and 10% respectively. All independent variables are lagged by one year.

++: The sixth model with triadic patents and countries with economic globalization index higher than average could not be estimated as the variance matrix turned out to be non-symmetric.

and the interaction term (*gov_score*rent*) have the same sign as the full sample, but the magnitudes in the split sample are larger. Hence, it can be concluded that governance tends to have stronger effects on innovation when countries are wealthier, more open and have higher-than-average governance scores. This finding indicates governance quality is not subject to diminishing returns with respect to its effects on innovation: better governance is good for innovation and it matters even more when countries have higher-than-average governance scores.

The coefficients on the interaction term (*gov_score*rent*) also have the same sign as the full sample: they range from −0.22 to −1.27 and are significant in all models. Yet, their magnitudes are larger when compared to −0.16 and −0.24 in the full sample. Hence, it can be concluded that rent tends to have a stronger offsetting effect on innovation when interacted with governance in wealthier, more open and better-governance countries.

The coefficients on rent are significant only when we estimate the model with USPTO-granted patents, even though there is sign consistency between USPTO-registered and triadic patents. Moreover, the signs of the coefficients are opposite to the signs obtained with full sample. Focusing on USPTO-registered patents only, the results indicate that the relationship between market power and patenting activity has an inverted-U shape rather than U-shape when countries are characterized by higher-than-average per capita GDP, governance scores and economic openness. Hence, higher market power is associated with higher (lower) levels of innovation when the initial level of market power is low (high). This is just the opposite of the finding with respect to full sample.

The turning points of the concave parabola take place at rent = 1.19 when the sample is split on the basis per capita GDP; 1.36 when the split is based on governance scores; and 1.11 when it is based on economic openness. These values are lower than the average rent value in the full sample, which is 1.44. They are also lower than the average values of the rent for the split samples, which are 1.36, 1.38 and 1.33 respectively. Hence, we can conclude that market power drives innovation initially but begins to be detrimental for innovation relatively sooner when countries are characterized by higher-than-average per capita GDP, governance scores and economic openness.

The inverted-U shape of the relationship between market power and innovation in the split samples contradicts the findings of Aghion et al. (2002, 2005) at firm level and those reported by Griffith et al. (2006a, 2006b) at sector level across EU countries. We explain the difference as follows: the potential threat of entry is higher when countries have higher-than-average per capita GDP, governance scores and economic openness. This is because higher-than-average per capita GDP indicates deep markets and encourages newcomers with low initial profits to contest the market through drastic innovation. Similarly, higher-than-average governance quality provides better protection of property rights and induces new entrants with drastic or neck-and-neck innovations. Finally, higher levels of economic openness erode profits and induce drastic innovation as a means of escaping competition. However, the average levels of rent in relatively richer and more open countries with higher-than-average governance scores (1.36, 1.38 and 1.33, respectively) are lower than the average for the full sample (1.44). Stated differently, the level of competition in these countries is higher than the sample average and therefore an increase in market power is necessary to convert the potential threat of entry into actual entry based on investment in innovation. Hence, we can conclude that the Schumpeterian hypothesis that innovation is driven by market power is more likely to hold when countries are relatively richer, more open to international competition and have better governance institutions.

The relationship between income inequality and innovation has the same sign as the full sample, but the relationship is significant only in countries with higher-than-average governance and economic openness scores. The relationship between labour share and innovation, however, has the opposite sign compared to full sample; but the negative relationship is significant only in countries with higher-than-average per capita GDP. Economic openness is related negatively to innovation across models and in both full and split samples.

The TRIPS dummy is positive in both full and split samples and across estimations. However, it is also important to note that the coefficient on the dummy variable is larger when estimation is in the split sample and especially when the dependent variable is triadic patents. This finding indicates that countries tend to register relatively larger numbers of triadic patents after the conclusion of the Paris Convention and of the TRIPS agreement within the World Trade Organization (WTO). It appears that better protection of intellectual property rights has induced countries to increase the number of better-value patents. This can be explained by better scope for making claims against infringement after the conclusion of the Paris Convention and the TRIPs agreement.

Two interesting findings relate to effects of stock market turnover and military expenditures as percentage of GDP. The size of the stock market is positively related to patenting activity in full and split sample, but the relationship is stronger in the split samples. This finding indicates that the stock market could be a more important source of finance for innovation in wealthier, more open and better-governance countries. Similarly, military expenditures also tend to have a stronger positive effect on patenting activity in countries with higher-than-average per capita GDP, economic openness and governance scores.

Finally, we have found positive but partial evidence between lagged R&D expenditures and patenting activity. However neither the lag structure nor its significance is stable across samples and between USPTO-granted and triadic patents.

CONCLUSIONS

The analysis above indicates that patenting activity in OECD countries from 1988 to 2007 is related to a range of macro-level variables, which include governance quality, profit mark-ups, income distribution, labour share in national income, per capita GDP, size of the stock market, and economic openness. With the exception of market power, the sign of the relationship between the explanatory variables and patenting activity is consistent between the full sample and the split samples based on higher-than-average levels of per capita GDP, openness and governance quality. Hence, we can conclude that the number of USPTO-registered and triadic patents is positively related to governance quality, per capita GDP, size of the stock market relative to GDP, military expenditures as percentage of GDP, and TRIPs dummy. The positive relationship between these explanatory variables and patenting activity is stronger in countries with higher-than-average per capita GDP, economic openness and governance scores.

The relationship between economic openness and innovation is consistently negative across samples and patent types. Similarly, the relationship between income inequality and patenting activity is also negative; but it is significant for both patent types only in the full sample and in some of the split samples.

We have also found that the relationship between market power and patenting activity is non-linear. The relationship has a U-shape in the full sample but an inverted-U shape in countries with higher-than-average per capita GDP, economic openness and governance scores. This finding strengthens the case for non-linear modelling of the competition-innovation relationship. However, it also indicates that it is necessary to check whether the relationship is convex or concave to the origin. In this study, we have found that the relationship is convex to the origin in the full sample but it is concave in countries with higher-than-average per capita GDP, economic openness and governance scores. The difference is due to higher levels of entry threat in these countries, which have average rent levels that are lower than the full-sample average.

In full and split samples market power has an offsetting effect on patenting activity when it is interacted with governance; and the offsetting effect is stronger in countries with higher-than-average per capita GDP, economic openness and governance scores. The stronger offsetting effect, coupled with stronger and positive partial effects, suggest that rents are the main driver of patenting activity in countries with higher-than-average per capita GDP, economic openness and governance scores.

Our findings suggest that the existing estimates of the relationship between governance and innovation and/or between competition and innovation may be biased due to model misspecification. Model misspecification can be due to exclusion of competition or governance variables; or the interactions between the two. In addition, they suggest that the innovation rhetoric in national and international policy debate tends to rely on short cuts and as such may be misleading. The OECD sample does not provide evidence to support the assertion that competition and openness are drivers of innovation under all conditions. In the full sample, the relationship between competition and innovation is positive only when the initial levels of market power are low. In split samples, the competition-innovation relationship is positive only when the initial level of market power is high. Furthermore, governance may complement or offset the effects of competition (market power) on innovation depending on the initial level of competition (market power); and openness is negatively related to innovation in both full and split samples.

Our findings also suggest that better governance is associated with higher patenting activity in full and split samples; and the positive relationship is stronger in countries with higher-than-average per capita GDP, economic openness and governance scores. However, when interacted with market power, the latter tends to offset the positive effect of governance on innovation; and the offsetting effect is stronger in split samples. This finding suggests that governance is a significant driver of innovation in its own right, but its positive effect on innovation is dampened by market power.

NOTES

1. For example, OECD (2007: 3) makes the following observation: 'In addition to the rapid advances in scientific discovery and in general-purpose technologies such as ICTs and biotechnology, the accelerating pace of innovation is being driven by globalisation.'
2. The policy statements suggest that innovation is both a necessary condition for and an outcome of competitiveness at the same time. The concept of competitiveness is also quite fuzzy, implying either an ability to maintain market shares (i.e., absence of competition) or the existence of product-market competition. In addition, the policy statements suggest a linear relationship between competition (or competitiveness) and innovation – as can be seen in OECD and EU policy documents.
3. The results are not reported here, but they can be provided on request.

REFERENCES

Acemoglu, D. (2006), 'A simple model of inefficient institutions', *Scandinavian Journal of Economics*, 108(4): 515–546.

Acemoglu, D., P. Antràs and E. Helpman (2007), 'Contracts and technology adoption', *American Economic Review*, 97(3): 916–943.

Aghion, P., W. Carlin and M. Schaffer (2002), 'Competition, innovation and growth in transition: exploring the interactions between policies', *William Davidson Working Paper* Number 501 (March).

Aghion, P., N. Bloom, R. Blundell, R. Griffith and P. Howitt (2005), 'Competition and innovation: an inverted-U relationship', *The Quarterly Journal of Economics*, 120(2): 701–728.

Akerlof, G.A., and J.L. Yellen (1990), 'The fair wage-effort hypothesis and unemployment', *Quarterly Journal of Economics*, 55: 255–283.

Altman, M. (2009), 'A behavioural-institutional model of endogenous growth and induced technical change', *Journal of Economic Issues*, 43(3): 685–713.

Arrow, K. (1962), 'Economic welfare and the allocation of resources for invention', in H.M. Groves (ed.), *The Rate and Direction of Inventive Activity: Economic and Social Factors*, NBER, 609–626.

Baldwin, J.R. and W. Gu (2004), 'Trade liberalization: export-market participation, productivity growth, and innovation', *Oxford Review of Economic Policy*, 20(3): 372–392.

Beck, N., and J. N. Katz (1995), 'What to do (and not to do) with time-series cross-section data', *American Political Science Review*, 89: 634–647.

Bergh, A. and T. Nilsson (2010), 'Do liberalization and globalization increase income inequality?', *European Journal of Political Economy*, 26(4): 488–505.

Berubé, C., M. Duhamel and D. Ershov (2012), 'Market incentives for business innovation: results from Canada', *Journal of Industry, Competition and Trade*, 12(1), 47–65.

Brown, J.R., S.M. Fazzari and B.C. Petersen (2009), 'Financing innovation and growth: cash flow, external equity, and the 1990s R&D boom', *Journal of Finance*, 64(1): 151–183.

Chen, X., S. Lin and W.R. Reed (2009), 'A Monte Carlo evaluation of the efficiency of the PCSE estimator', *Applied Economics Letters*, 17(1): 7–10.

Clarke, G.R.G. (2001), 'How institutional quality and economic factors impact technological deepening in developing countries', *Journal of International Development*, 13(8): 1097–1118.

Dakhli, M., and D. De Clercq (2004), 'Human capital, social capital, and innovation: a multi-country study', *Entrepreneurship & Regional Development*, 16(2): 107–128.

Dernis, H. and M. Khan (2004), 'Triadic patent families methodology', OECD Science, Technology and Industry Working Papers, 2004/02, OECD.

Dixit, A. (2009), 'Governance institutions and economic activity', *The American Economic Review*, 99(1), 3–24.

Dosi, Giovanni, Christopher Freeman, Richard Nelson and Luc Soete (1988), *Technical Change and Economic Theory: Global Process of Development*, London: Pinter.

Dreher, A. (2006), 'Does globalization affect growth? Evidence from a new Index of Globalization', *Applied Economics*, 38(10): 1091–1110.

Egger, P. (2002), 'An econometric view on the estimation of gravity models and the calculation of trade potentials', *The World Economy*, 25(2): 297–312.

ESA (1995), *European System of Accounts*, European Commission, http://circa. europa.eu/irc/dsis/nfaccount/info/data/esa95/en/een00348.htm

EU Commission (2005), *Common Actions for Growth and Employment: The Community Lisbon Programme*, COM(2005) 330 final, 20.7.2005, Brussels.

Faber, J. and A.B. Hesen (2004), 'Innovation capabilities of European nations: cross-national analyses of patents and sales of product innovations', *Research Policy*, 33 (3), 193–207.

Foellmi, R. and J. Zweimüller (2006), 'Income distribution and demand-induced innovations', *Review of Economic Studies*, 73(4), 941–960.

Freeman, Christopher (1987), *Technology Policy and Economic Performance: Lessons from Japan*, London: Pinter.

Galor, O., and D. Tsiddon (1997), 'Technological progress, mobility and economic growth', *American Economic Review*, 87: 363–382.

Ganzach, Y. (1997), 'Misleading interaction and curvilinear terms', *Psychological Methods*, 2(3): 235–247.

Gilbert, Richard (2006), 'Looking for Mr. Schumpeter: where are we in the competition-innovation debate?', in Adam B. Jaffe, Josh Lerner and Scott Stern (eds), *Innovation Policy and the Economy – Volume 6*, Cambridge, Mass.: MIT Press, pp. 159–215.

Gilbert, R. and D. Newbery (1982), 'Pre-emptive patenting and the persistence of monopoly', *American Economic Review*, 72(2): 514–526.

Giménez, G. and J. Sanaú (2007), 'Interrelationship among institutional infrastructure, technological innovation and growth: an empirical evidence', *Applied Economics*, 39(10): 1267–1282.

Griffith, R., R. Harrison and H. Simpson (2006a), 'The link between product market reform, innovation and EU macroeconomic performance', *European Economy*, no. 243 (February): 1–123.

Griffith, R., R. Harrison and H. Simpson (2006b), 'Product market reforms and innovation in the EU', *Institute of Fiscal Studies Working Papers*, No. WP06/17.

Guan, J. and K. Chen (2012), 'Modeling the relative efficiency of national innovation systems', *Research Policy*, 41(1): 102–115.

Guloglu, B., R.T.R. Baris and E. Saridogan (2012), 'Economic determinants of technological progress in G7 countries: a re-examination', *Economics Letters*, 116(3): 604–608.

Hall, B.H., Z. Griliches and J.A. Hausman (1986), 'Patents and R&D: is there a lag?', *International Economic Review*, 27(2): 265–283.

Hassler, J., and J.V. Rodriguez Mora (2000), 'Intelligence, social mobility and growth', *American Economic Review*, 90: 888–908.

ICRG – International Country Risk Guide database, PRS Group. http://www. prsgroup.com/ICRG_Methodology.aspx

Jolliffe, I.T. (2002), *Principal Component Analysis* (2nd ed.), Heidelberg: Springer.

Kaufmann, D., Kraay, A. and Mastruzzi, M. (2007), 'The Worldwide Governance Indicators project: answering the critics', *World Bank Policy Research Working Paper* 4149.

Keefer, P., and S. Knack (1997), 'Why don't poor countries catch up? A cross-national test of an institutional explanation', *Economic Inquiry*, 35 (3), 590–602.

Kentor, J. and E. Kick (2008), 'Bringing the military back in: military expenditures and economic growth 1990 to 2003', *Journal of World-Systems Research*, 14(2): 142–172.

Knack, S. and P. Keefer (1997), 'Does social capital have an economic payoff? A cross-country investigation', *Quarterly Journal of Economics*, 112(4): 1251–88.

Kurtz, M.J. and Schrank, A. (2007), 'Growth and governance: models, measures, and mechanisms', *Journal of Politics*, 69 (2): 538–554.

Lundvall, Bengt-Åke (1992), *National Systems of Innovation: Towards a Theory of Innovation and Interactive Learning*, London: Pinter.

Lundvall, B.Å., B. Johnson, E.S. Andersen and B. Dalum (2002), 'National systems of production, innovation and competence building', *Research Policy*, 31(2), 213–231.

Mahutga, M.C., R. Kwon and G. Grainger (2011), 'Within-country inequality and the modern world-system: a theoretical reprise and empirical first step', *Journal of World-Systems Research*, 27(2): 279–307.

Menezes-Filho, Naercio and John Van Reenen (2005), 'Unions and innovation: a survey of the theory and empirical evidence', Chapter 9 in John T. Addison and Claus Schnabel (eds), *The International Handbook of Trade Unions*, Cheltenham, UK and Northampton, MA, USA: Edward Elgar Publishing.

MSTI – *Main Science and Technology Indicators (MSTI) Database*, OECD. http://www.oecd.org/sti/scienceandtechnologypolicy/mainscienceandtechnology indicatorsmsti20122edition.htm

North, Douglass (1990), *Institutions, Institutional Change, and Economic Performance*, Cambridge and London: Cambridge University Press.

North, D.C. (1994), 'Economic performance through time', *American Economic Review*, 84 (3), 359–368.

OECD (2005), *Oslo Manual: Guidelines for Collecting and Interpreting Innovation Data*, 3rd edition, Paris: OECD.

OECD (2006), *Economic Policy Reforms: Going for Growth*, Paris: OECD. http://www.keepeek.com/Digital-Asset-Management/oecd/economics/economic-policy-reforms-2006_growth-2006-en

OECD (2007), *Innovation and Growth: Rationale for an Innovation Strategy*, Paris: OECD. http://www.oecd.org/edu/ceri/40908171.pdf

Pakes, A. and Z. Griliches (1984), 'Patents and R&D at the firm level: a first look', in Z. Griliches (ed.), *R and D, Patents and Productivity*, Chicago: Chicago University Press, pp. 55–72.

Peneder, M. (2012), 'Competition and innovation: revisiting the inverted-U relationship', *Journal of Industry, Competition and Trade*, 12(1): 1–5.

Peroni, C. and I.S. Gomes Ferreira (2012), 'Competition and innovation in Luxembourg', *Journal of Industry, Competition and Trade*, 12(1): 93–117.

Pla-Barber, J. and J. Alegre (2007), 'Analysing the link between export intensity, innovation and firm size in a science-based industry', *International Business Review*, 16(3): 275–293.

Polder, M. and E. Veldhuizen (2012), 'Innovation and competition in the Netherlands: testing the inverted U for industries and firms', *Journal of Industry, Competition and Trade*, 12(1): 67–91.

Reinganum, J.F. (1983), 'Uncertain innovation and the persistence of monopoly', *American Economic Review*, 73: 741–748.

Reinganum, J.F. (1985), 'A two-stage model of research and development with endogenous second-mover advantages', *International Journal of Industrial Organization*, 3 (3), 275–292.

Rodriguez, F. and A. Jayadev (2010), 'The declining labour share of income', *UNDP Human Development Research Paper*, no. 2010/36. http://hdr.undp.org/en/reports/global/hdr2010/papers/HDRP_2010_36.pdf

Scherer, F.M., D. Harhoff and J. Kukies (2000), 'Uncertainty and the size distribution of rewards from innovation', *Journal of Evolutionary Economics*, 10(1–2): 175–200.

Schumpeter, Joseph A. (1934), *The Theory of Economic Development*, Cambridge, MA: Harvard University Press. (First published in German, 1912).

Schumpeter, Joseph A. (1942), *Capitalism, Socialism, and Democracy*, New York: Harper and Brothers. (Harper Colophon edition, 1976.)

Solt, F. (2009), 'Standardizing the World Income Inequality Database', *Social Science Quarterly*, 90(2): 231–242. See also: http://dvn.iq.harvard.edu/dvn/dv/fsolt/faces/study/StudyPage.xhtml?studyId=36908

Stiglitz, J.E. and A. Weiss (1981), 'Credit rationing in markets with imperfect information', *American Economic Review*, 71: 393–410.

Taskin, F. and O. Zaim (1997), 'Catching-up and innovation in high- and low-income countries', *Economics Letters*, 54(1): 93–100.

Tebaldi, E. and B. Elmslie (2013), 'Does institutional quality impact innovation? Evidence from cross-country patent grant data', *Applied Economics*, 45(7): 887–900.

Tselios, V. (2011), 'Is inequality good for innovation?', *International Regional Science Review*, 34(1): 75–101.

WDI – *World Development Indicators Database*, the World Bank. http://data.worldbank.org/data-catalog/world-development-indicators

Weinhold, D. and U. Nair-Reichert (2009), 'Innovation, inequality and intellectual property rights', *World Development*, 37 (5): 889–901.

Zhou, H., R. Dekker and A. Kleinknecht (2011), 'Flexible labour and innovation performance: evidence from longitudinal firm-level data', *Industrial and Corporate Change*, 20(3), 941–968.

Zweimüller, J. (2000), 'Schumpeterian entrepreneurs meet Engel's Law: the impact of inequality on innovation-driven growth', *Journal of Economic Growth*, 5(2): 185–206.

3. Effects of firm-level corporate governance and country-level economic governance institutions on R&D curtailment during crisis times

Peter-Jan Engelen and Marc van Essen

INTRODUCTION

The 2007–09 financial crisis has been the world's deepest since the Great Depression of the last century. This particular financial crisis can be characterized as the burst of the US real estate bubble in 2007 which caused sharp decreases in asset values and overall uncertainty in financial markets and resulted in the collapse of a number of major financial institutions in the US and Europe. This had far-reaching spillover effects on non-financial firms as well. In times of economic distress companies are particularly exposed to environmental threats that could hamper the firm's performance and potentially even the firm's existence. Such circumstances typically push companies to save on costs and scrutinize research and development (R&D) budgets: 'In fact, R&D is a perennially attractive target for corporate belt-tightening rituals, since it doesn't produce cash directly. Now more than ever, many companies are trying to generate quick savings [. . .] by asking their development groups to cut costs across the board' (Barrett et al., 2009: 1).

The credit crisis is a particularly interesting time frame to examine R&D cuts as a recent survey among more than 1000 Chief Financial Officers indeed reveals that, during the credit crisis, firms were planning major cuts in almost all corporate policy parameters such as technology expenditures, capital expenditures, and marketing expenditures, among others (Campello et al., 2010). For instance European firms were planning to cut back technology expenditures by 10.8 per cent, marketing expenditures by 10.6 per cent and capital expenditures by 4 per cent (see Figure 3.1). This survey shows that firms seem to postpone or cancel expenditures and particularly technology investment plans when financing constraints are severe.

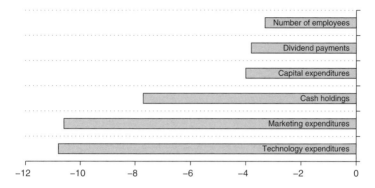

Source: Campello et al. (2010).

Figure 3.1 European firms' planned changes (% per year; as of 2008Q4)

While the early classic economic theory of innovation assumes all firms to be alike when taking R&D decisions, the recent literature on corporate governance demonstrates that companies are not monolithic entities. Differences in internal corporate governance mechanisms and in the institutional framework in which companies operate do matter for a firm's innovation performance (Belloc, 2012). In this chapter, we therefore investigate the effects of the quality of country-level economic governance institutions (EGI) and firm-level corporate governance mechanisms (CG) on innovation effort of listed companies in the European context during the financial crisis from 2007 until 2009. Our measure of innovation effort is investment in R&D, which is a key determinant of a firm's innovation capacity.

Our contribution to the existing literature is threefold. First, to our knowledge, this is the first study that combines firm-level corporate governance and country-level institutions variables with respect to R&D decisions (and controls for industry differences). Earlier studies focused solely on firm-level data (Munari et al., 2010), or combined industry-level data with country-level data (Barbosa and Faria, 2011). Second, our study focuses on R&D decisions during the recent financial crisis. Therefore we contribute to the limited amount of studies that investigate the relationship between corporate governance and R&D investments in Europe during normal times (Honoré et al., 2011; Munari et al., 2010). Third, we examine the question whether firm-level corporate governance and country-level institutions interact with each other with respect to R&D investment decisions. We test whether both levels are complementary, substitutes or independent of each other. This is an important research question as it provides evidence on whether firm-level corporate governance dimensions reinforce or offset the effects of country-level institutions on innovation. This gives policy makers further insight into fine-tuning corporate governance rules.

THEORY AND HYPOTHESES

R&D investments are generally regarded as inherently risky (Baysinger et al., 1991) due to their long-term horizon (Laverty, 1996) and high failure rates (Cassimon et al., 2011). Although investments in long-term R&D projects do not guarantee high returns ex-post (Chan et al., 2001; Kothari et al., 2002), continuous innovation is essential to realize growth and to sustain competitive advantages and firm rents (Schumpeter, 1934; Romer, 1994). Empirical research has largely confirmed the view that firms with higher R&D investments outperform those that invest less (Hill and Snell, 1988; Jaruzelski and Dehoff, 2010). In this section we examine the potential impact of firm-level corporate governance mechanisms and country-level economic governance institutions on R&D investments, and we subsequently develop our hypotheses. A corporate governance system or regime can be seen as a configuration of different mechanisms that condition the generation and the distribution of residual earnings in publicly owned firms (Zingales, 1998). These mechanisms exist both internally and externally to public firms, and they function at both firm- and country-level of analysis (Shleifer and Vishny, 1997).

Firm-level Corporate Governance and R&D Expenditure

Investments in R&D are usually found to be subject to financing constraints (Bhagat and Welch, 1995; Bougheas et al., 2003; Hall, 2002). When internal cash flow is high or external funding is easily available, investments in R&D will be set at their first best level. If the company is faced with financial constraints, such as during crisis times, there will be underinvestment in R&D (Bougheas et al., 2003). Agency theory suggests that managers are less inclined to make R&D investments when confronted with financing constraints because they are assumed to be more risk-averse than diversified shareholders. In crisis times managers prefer short-term efficiency gains over R&D investments because the costs of R&D investments are incurred in the present, and will only pay off after a longer period of time when the same managers may not occupy the same position any more (the so-called horizon problem) (Cazier, 2011) or because they are close to retirement (Barker and Mueller, 2002).

For instance, in the pharmaceutical industry R&D investments tend to pay off ten to fifteen years after the start of the R&D phase (Cassimon et al., 2004). The currently incurred costs, however, reduce the corporate bottom-line immediately and can have a negative influence on the reputation and careers of managers (David and Hitt, 2001). The high failure risk of R&D investments makes managers risk-averse because risk is an immediate threat for their job security as their entire non-diversifiable human capital is invested in a single firm (Alchian and Demsetz, 1972). Therefore, managers are expected to have a shorter investment horizon (Laverty, 1996; Munari et al., 2010). R&D curtailment by managers is even more aggravated when their remuneration is correlated with short-term firm performance. In that case managers' decisions and actions are very likely to be even more biased towards a short-term investment horizon. This is supported by empirical evidence, which indicates a particularly strong negative relationship between performance-related remuneration and R&D expenses (Honoré et al., 2011).

Especially during the credit crisis, when firms are confronted with huge losses, managers will be more inclined to cut on costs, despite the fact that it might hurt the long-term returns. From a shareholder perspective, investments in R&D are crucial as they contribute to the long-term performance of the firm, creating competitive advantages and firm rents. As shareholders can diversify their investment portfolio, they are also able to spread the associated risk from R&D investments (Baysinger et al., 1991). Firm-level corporate governance can therefore play a key role in inducing managers to keep up R&D investment levels during crisis times.

Board of directors
The potential problem of R&D cutbacks will first arise within the board of directors. This is not only the primary decision making organ within a public firm, but is also the most direct agent of the shareholders that, at least in theory, serves to mitigate the agency costs that result from the separation of ownership and control in public firms (Jensen and Meckling, 1976; Fama and Jensen, 1983). In this view, the board's first and foremost responsibility is to monitor the management (Zahra and Pearce, 1989). A widely shared view is that a board performs its monitoring function well when there is a separation between the roles of the chief executive officer (CEO) and Board Chair, which puts more constraints on CEO authority (in our case, CEO power to cut back on R&D investments) (Coles et al., 2001), when the board is smaller (Yermack, 1996) and when the board consists of a majority of independent directors (Johnson et al., 1996).

Our chapter is related to studies examining the effects of board characteristics on firm critical decisions. A meta-analysis by Deutsch (2005) finds little empirical support for theoretical predictions on the impact of board composition on critical decisions that involve a potential conflict of interest between managers and shareholders, such as executive turnover, takeover defenses and diversification. Our study examines whether board characteristics influence R&D decisions in crisis times.

The downside of having a board with a higher level of independence might be that it is less informed, as independent directors may not have important firm specific know-how of the capabilities, processes and environment in which the firm operates (Honoré et al., 2011). This is specifically true for firms with a high level of R&D investments because in these boards the information asymmetry between board members is more severe (Boone et al., 2007). As a consequence of this lack of information, independent board members are more likely to make their decisions on the basis of available financial information. This financial information is usually showing information with a short time horizon, which makes R&D investments look less attractive (Hoskisson et al., 2002; Lorsch and MacIver, 1989). The current economic crisis makes it presumably even more difficult to evaluate long-term investments because there are more fluctuations in the environmental conditions. High quality information is especially important for strategies with considerable levels of uncertainty, such as R&D (Honoré et al., 2011). We therefore formulate the following hypothesis:

Hypothesis 1:   Stronger board monitoring (as characterized by the absence of CEO duality, a smaller board size and a higher fraction of independent directors) will reduce R&D curtailment during the crisis.

Ownership structure
Ownership concentration is presumably an important external corporate governance mechanism because blockholders typically have both the means and the motive to monitor managers effectively (Coffee, 1991; Shleifer and Vishny, 1986). However, extant literature does not provide a clear cut direction concerning the effect of ownership concentration on R&D spending. Some researchers have found a positive relation (Hosono et al., 2004; Wahal and McConnell, 2000) while others support a negative relation (Yafeh and Yosha, 2003; Jones and Danbolt, 2003) or even no relationship at all (Francis and Smith, 1995). Tribo et al. (2007) take this view one step further and investigate, for Spanish firms, the influence of ownership concentration on R&D spending for different blockholders. Their findings show that this relation becomes negative when blockholders are banks, positive when blockholders are non-financial institutions and null for individual investors. Recent studies, such as Munari et al.

(2010), therefore stress the role of different large owners on innovation activities. We therefore distinguish between institutional, relational, and governmental largest blockholders (Van Essen et al., 2012b).

The institutional investor is the quintessential transactional block-holder. On the one hand, firms having an institutional owner as largest shareholder are expected to be more vulnerable to short-term market discipline. First, institutional shareholders act like traders instead of owners. The rewards of institutional money managers depend on short-term assessments, such as quarterly or annual results. This creates incentives to go for short-term returns and relatively risk free investments (Graves and Waddock, 1990). Second, institutional money managers focus too much on easily retrievable information and therefore do not possess the right information to value long-term investment opportunities appropriately. This makes these managers excessively focused on short-term gains (Kochhar and David, 1996). Furthermore, the assessment of long-term opportunities is even more difficult in crisis times because stock markets are less stable and thus more uncertain. Hill and Snell (1988) and Graves (1988) indeed find that institutional investors negatively affect innovation because of their short-term interests. On the other side, institutional investors are thought to positively affect innovation, first, because they 'cannot exit the ownership in the short run without depressing the price of their other stocks' (Hansen and Hill, 1991; Kochhar and David, 1996) and, second, because they (especially banks – Lee, 2005), generally, increase monitoring (Aghion et al., 2009).

Relational blockholders, such as family owners, are typically tied strongly to their firm and consequently have longer investment horizons (Van Essen et al., 2012a). As a consequence, large family owners are expected to have a positive impact on the level of R&D investments. Moreover, family owners often want to pass on the firm to their progeny (Anderson and Reeb, 2003). For these family owners, it is more important to stay in business than to gain from short-term profits. As investors with longer investment horizons they are more likely to pressure management to invest in long-term R&D projects. Family executives can also bring innovative and value-increasing specific skills to the firm that non-family executives usually do not have (Morck et al., 1988). At the downside, family-controlled firms are more prone to risk aversion since a significant amount of the family's wealth is locked-up in the company. This might negatively influence R&D investment decisions.

The impact of state-ownership on the level of R&D spending is less clear from the literature. Using seven French and Italian privatization case studies, Munari (2002) finds that the share of ownership controlled by the state positively affects the level of firms' R&D investments. Munari et al.

(2002) argue that state-controlled firms have longer investment horizons, making them less prone to the discipline of the market. This is a surprising finding as most studies show that state-owned firms make less capital investments, are run less efficiently and perform worse than private firms (Boardman and Vining, 1989; Megginson et al., 1994; Megginson and Netter, 2001). Munari et al. (2010) do not find any relationship between state-ownership and R&D investment, while Gupta (2005) finds a negative relationship. In crisis times we expect governmental blockholders to have a negative influence on R&D investments of listed firms as governments often have more stringent national/social financial priorities which might put their involvement in R&D investments on a second plan. Government sensitivity to concerns of stakeholders such as employees and suppliers will put the company under pressure to save on R&D expenses to benefit the interest of those stakeholders. Accordingly, we formulate the following hypotheses regarding ownership identity:

Hypothesis 2a   Firms with family and corporate ownership will not exhibit R&D curtailment during the crisis.

Hypothesis 2b   Firms with institutional and government ownership will exhibit R&D curtailment during the crisis.

Economic Governance Institutions and R&D Expenditure

The economic governance institutions of a country can be summarized as 'the structure and functioning of the legal and social institutions that support economic activity and economic transactions by protecting property rights, enforcing contracts, and taking collective action to provide physical and organizational infrastructure' (Dixit, 2009). From this perspective, it is clear that well-developed economic governance is of crucial importance to the good functioning of the country's economic activity – that is, the main source of growth. An emerging but fast-growing paradigm in comparative corporate governance and international business therefore emphasizes the importance of the institutional context in understanding firm strategies as well as their outcomes (Judge et al., 2010).

In countries with better legal protection, the set of legal rights and enforcement mechanisms makes financial contracts more effective and provides investors with more certainty about realizing the appropriate return on their investment. Recent studies in the comparative corporate governance literature extend this view and have been focusing on the relationship between country-level institutions and corporate behavior and governance of companies. Researchers have shown that cross-country differences in the legal framework affect, among others, availability of external finance (La Porta et al., 1997), asset structure (Claessens and Laeven, 2003), IPO underpricing (Engelen and Van Essen, 2010), dividend policy (La Porta et al., 2000), portfolio choices (Leuz et al., 2009), equity risk premiums (Chiou et al., 2010), business group effectiveness (Carney et al., 2011), and female board representation (Grosvold and Brammer, 2011).

Before anything else, the confidence in a country's institutions is very important as firms might be unwilling to commit necessary funds for R&D if they are skeptical about the institutional environment (Clarke, 2001). Keefer and Knack (1997: 591) find that 'more secure property rights and credible policy regimes increase the incentives of entrepreneurs to adopt those techniques that maximize long-run profits. Firms make less efficient adjustments and continue to use obsolescent technology if those policies are not credible, or if optimal firm adjustments leave them more vulnerable to expropriation.' R&D expenditures indeed tend to be lower in countries where the risk of expropriation is higher and the rule of law is weaker (Clarke, 2001). Claessens and Laeven (2003) demonstrate as well that firms operating in a jurisdiction with weak (intellectual) property rights protection underinvest in intangible assets compared to similar firms in a strong environment. Related studies focused on the impact of labor market regulations (Samaniego, 2006), of product regulations (Griffith et al., 2007), of educational institutions (Varsakelis, 2006) and of intellectual property rights protection (Kanwar, 2007) on innovation processes. Barbosa and Faria (2011) examine institutional differences in the European context and find that stricter labor market regulations and heavier product market regulations negatively impact innovation in Europe. They also find that the level of intellectual property rights protection has a negative impact on innovation. This suggests that too strict intellectual property rights do not lead to further increases in innovation.

As far as R&D curtailment becomes problematic during crisis times, we expect that firms operating in a country with stronger shareholder protection will cut back less on R&D investments as investors in those jurisdictions are better equipped to put constraints on management. As R&D is constrained by financing, we expect that stronger creditor rights lead to increased availability of credit, which might be more valuable during crisis times as it keeps the external funding available to finance the R&D investments (Djankov et al., 2007; Djankov et al., 2008a). Barbosa and Faria (2011) find that better credit information and credit access has a positive impact on R&D investments, which confirms earlier findings of Carpenter and Petersen (2002). Considering the above, we expect that good economic governance institutions have a positive influence on R&D investments:

Hypothesis 3:   Companies operating in a more developed country-level legal framework (as measured by the rule of law, shareholder protection, creditor right protection and market-based financial system) are prone to less R&D curtailment during the crisis.

Interactions

We also examine how firm-level corporate governance and country-level economic governance institutions interact with each other during the financial crisis to jointly influence R&D investments. Some scholars suggest that country- and firm-level governance mechanisms may be substitutes for one another (Durnev and Kim, 2005; Klapper and Love, 2004), while others suggest that firm-level governance mechanisms develop strong complementarities with country-level financial systems (Aggarwal et al., 2010). Alternatively, they may have no impact on one another (Chhaochharia and Laeven, 2009). We therefore formulate the following hypotheses with respect to R&D investments:

Hypothesis 4a: During the financial crisis, firm-level governance and country-level legal protection are substitutes with respect to R&D curtailment.

Hypothesis 4b: During the financial crisis, firm-level governance and country-level legal protection are complements with respect to R&D curtailment.

DATA AND METHOD

Our sample consists of 411 firms from 16 European countries. We manually collected the data for the period from 2006 until mid-2009. In addition, digital information sources such as *Datastream*, *Mint GlobalWorldscope*, *BoardEx*, and the EU Industrial R&D Investment Scoreboard for 2010 were used to obtain firm-specific control variables and board characteristics. Country-specific data such as overall quality of legal background institutions, shareholder minority protection, credit right index, and market- versus bank-based system were obtained from Kaufmann et al. (2009), Djankov et al. (2007, 2008b), Doing Business (World Bank), La Porta et al. (1998), and Demirguc-Kunt and Levine (2001). The countries with German civil law included in our sample are Austria, Germany, and Switzerland. The countries with French civil law tradition are Belgium, France, Italy, Netherlands, Portugal, Spain, and Turkey. The countries with Scandinavian civil law are Denmark, Finland, Norway, and Sweden.

Finally, the countries with English common law are Ireland and United Kingdom.

Dependent Variable

In the regression models, the percentage change in annual R&D expenditure during the financial crisis is used as the dependent variable to capture R&D curtailment (Butler and Newman, 1989; Dechow and Sloan, 1991; Murphy and Zimmerman, 1993). Following Beltratti and Stulz (2009) and Fahlenbrach and Stulz (2010), we measure the crisis period from 2007 until 2009. As a robustness check we used the percentage change in annual R&D expenditure at the firm level for the periods 2008–09 and 2007–08.

Firm-level Variables

The first set of firm-level variables captures the impact of ownership structure on R&D expenditure. We constructed five dummy variables to distinguish the influence of concentrated and dispersed ownership on the one hand and that of the identities of the concentrated owner on the other hand. *Dispersed ownership* is defined as a firm with no shareholder with more than 10 per cent of the voting rights of the shares (Maury, 2006). The largest shareholders who reach this threshold level are divided into the following four identity categories: corporation, family, government, and institutional owner (Faccio and Lang, 2002).

We also included several other conventional firm-level corporate governance variables from the corporate governance literature. *Board size* measured as the total number of directors who serve on the board is a traditional firm-level corporate governance variable that captures the strength of monitoring (Yermack, 1996). *Board independence* measured as the percentage of non-executive directors captures board composition (Hermalin and Weisbach, 2003). We measured *CEO duality* with a dummy variable which is set to one if the chair of the board is taken up by the CEO and zero otherwise (Coles et al., 2001).

In order to assess the impact of general firm characteristics on R&D expenditures, we collected the following control variables: *firm age* (Brown et al., 2009), *firm size* (Francis and Smith, 1995), *firm leverage* (Czarnitzki and Kraft, 2009), *market-to-book ratio* (DiVito et al., 2010), the firm's *R&D intensity* (Becker-Blease, 2011), *firm diversification* (Baysinger and Hoskisson, 1989), and *industry dummies* to control for industry effects (Barbosa and Faria, 2011). Table 3.1 gives an overview of the precise definition of each control variable.

Table 3.1 Description and summary of the firm-specific variables

Variable	Description	Source	Statistics		
			Obs.	Mean	SD
Percentage change in annual R&D expenditure 2007–09	The percentage change in annual R&D expenditure during the financial crisis in the period 2007–09	DataStream, Mint Global and 2010 EU Industrial R&D Investment Scoreboard	411	0.11	0.99
Corporate largest blockholder	The largest shareholder is a corporate owner with more than 10% of the (voting rights of the) shares	Annual reports, company website, and other websites	411	0.15	0.36
Family largest blockholder	The largest shareholder is a family owner with more than 10% of the (voting rights of the) shares	Annual reports, company website, and other websites	411	0.21	0.41
Government largest blockholder	The largest shareholder is the government with more than 10% of the (voting rights of the) shares	Annual reports, company website, and other websites	411	0.09	0.28
Institution largest blockholder	The largest shareholder is an institutional owner with more than 10% of the (voting rights of the) shares	Annual reports, company website, and other websites	411	0.24	0.43
Widely held firm	There is no shareholder with more than 10% of the (voting rights of the) shares	Annual reports, company website, and other websites	411	0.31	0.46
Board size	Total numbers of directors who serve on the board	Annual reports, company website, and BoardEx	411	12.63	5.25

Variable	Description	Source	N	Mean	SD
CEO duality	Situation where the positions of board chairman and CEO are held by one individual	Annual reports, company website, and BoardEx	411	0.13	0.33
Board independence	A variable which reflects the degree to which the board of directors operates independently from corporate insiders	Annual reports, company website, and BoardEx	411	0.75	0.15
Firm size	An indicator of the size of the firm, measured as a firm's logarithm of total assets	Worldscope	411	8.56	2.00
Firm age	A variable measuring the logarithm of number of years since the company was established	Worldscope	411	3.91	1.01
Firm leverage	A variable reflecting the degree of leverage of the firm, measured as total debt divided by total assets	Worldscope	411	0.24	0.16
R&D intensity	The annual R&D expenditure of previous year divided by total assets	DataStream, Mint Global and 2010 EU Industrial R&D Investment Scoreboard	411	0.28	0.61
Firm diversification	Herfindahl-Hirschman index of the difference business segment sales	Worldscope	411	0.55	0.25
Industry	Dummy variable for two-digit SIC codes	Worldscope			

Country-level Variables

To investigate cross-country differences in governance quality, the literature on EGI typically uses several proxies to measure the quality of institutions: (1) a proxy measuring the general quality of the legal system (Heugens et al., 2009), (2) a proxy measuring investor protection (Liu and Magnan, 2011) and creditor protection (Barbosa and Faria, 2011), and (3) a proxy measuring the quality of the financial system (Engelen and Van Essen, 2010).

To measure the impact of the overall quality of legal background institutions in various European jurisdictions, we used Kaufmann et al. (2009) 'rule of law' measure. This variable measures the extent to which agents have confidence in and abide by the rules of society (Kaufmann et al., 2009). A higher score for the rule of law implies more confidence in the legal system. To measure the impact of the jurisdictional level of shareholder protection against misuse of corporate assets by directors or large shareholders for their personal gain, we used the Doing Business 'Protecting investors' indicator provided by the World Bank (see Table 3.2). To assess the impact of creditor right protection in each country we used Djankov et al.'s (2007) 'creditor right protection index'. Djankov et al. (2007, 2008a) show that stronger creditor rights lead to increased availability of credit.

Finally, we also distinguished between market- and bank-based financial systems. We followed the methodology of Demirguc-Kunt and Levine (2001) to classify a country as having a 'market- versus bank-based financial system' in order to test whether the distinction between both financial architectures is an important determinant of R&D decisions in times of crisis.

Models

To test for the impact of firm-level corporate governance and country-level institutions variables on R&D curtailment during the crisis, we use three different models. Our first model estimates the following regression equation:

$$\Delta R\&D_{i,t} = \alpha_i + \sum_j \beta_{i,j} \cdot CG_{i,j,t-1} + \sum_k \gamma_{i,k} \cdot F_{i,k,t-1} + \varepsilon_i \qquad (3.1)$$

with $\Delta R\&D_{i,t}$ the percentage change in annual $R\&D$ expenditure for firm i during the crisis period t, $CG_{i,j,t-1}$ the vector of j firm-level corporate governance variables for firm i during the pre-crisis period $t-1$, and $F_{i,k,t-1}$ the vector of k firm-level control variables for firm i during the pre-crisis

Table 3.2   Description and summary of the country-specific variables

Variable	Description	Source	Statistics		
			Obs.	Mean	SD
Rule of law	A variable which measures the extent to which agents have confidence in and abide by the rules of society in year 2007. These include perceptions of the incidence of violent and non-violent crime, the effectiveness and predictability of the judiciary, and the enforceability of contracts. A higher value means a better rule of law	Kaufmann et al., 2009	411	1.54	0.50
Shareholder protection	The strength of minority shareholder protections against misuse of corporate assets by insiders and large owners in year 2007. A higher value means more protection of minority shareholders	Doing Business, World Bank, 2010	411	6.02	1.39
Creditor right protection	Creditor right protection, an index aggregating different creditor rights. A higher value means better creditor protection	Djankov et al., 2007	411	2.34	1.34
Market financial system	A dummy variable that equals 1 if the country's financial system is market-based and 0 if it is bank-based.	Demirguc-Kunt and Levine, 2001	411	0.45	0.50

period $t-1$ (see above). We add country-level institutional variables to obtain Model 2 by including l country-specific variables for each firm i:

$$\Delta R\&D_{i,t} = \alpha_i + \sum_j \beta_{i,j} \cdot CG_{i,j,t-1} + \sum_k \gamma_{i,k} \cdot F_{i,k,t-1} + \sum_l \delta_{i,l} \cdot C_{i,l} + \varepsilon_i \quad (3.2)$$

Finally, we include in Model 3 interactions terms between firm-level and country-level variables:

$$\Delta RD_{i,t} = \alpha_i + \sum_j \beta_{i,j} \cdot CG_{i,j,t-1} + \sum_k \gamma_{i,k} F_{i,k,t-1} + \sum_l \gamma_{i,l} \cdot C_{i,l}$$

$$+ \sum \theta_{i,j,l} \cdot (CG_{i,j,t-1} \cdot C_{i,l}) + \varepsilon_i \qquad (3.3)$$

ANALYSIS AND RESULTS

The data were analysed using ordinary least square regression (OLS). All of our firm and country-level independent variables lag the dependent variable, and are measured before the financial crisis to avoid possible confounding affects that are associated with the crisis (Durnev and Kim, 2005; Peng and Jiang, 2010). More specifically, we measure firm-level corporate governance and other characteristics at the end of 2006 and relate them to the percentage change in annual R&D expenditure over the period from 2007 until 2009. To test interaction effects, we included product terms linking country-level institutions to firm-level corporate governance. Prior to multiplication, we grand-mean centered the institutional variables to facilitate subsequent interpretation of their product terms and avoid multicollinearity. We use the White's (1980) modified standard error estimates to correct for possible heteroskedasticity. Finally, we also check for the presence of any problematic correlations for the dependent and main independent firm-level variables in our regressions.[1]

Firm-level Corporate Governance

We start by examining the impact of firm-level corporate governance while controlling for other firm characteristics in Model 1 of Table 3.3. First, we examine the impact of the ownership structure on R&D investments in crisis times. The empirical results show that having an institutional largest blockholder significantly reduced the R&D spending of the firm during the credit crisis ($p<0.10$). This finding confirms our expectation that the short-termism of institutional investors will put companies under pressure to curtail R&D expenditures (acceptance of Hypothesis 2b). During the credit crisis every penny counts, inducing institutional investors to have a preference for short-term gains over long-term R&D plans. We also find that having the state as the largest owner is detrimental for R&D spending during the credit crisis ($p<0.05$), again confirming Hypothesis 2b. State-controlled firms probably use a wider set of objectives such as job security for their employees. Such companies might temporarily save on R&D spending in favor of sponsoring jobs in crisis times.

Having a corporation or a family as the largest owner does not lead to

Table 3.3   Effect of firm-level CG and country-level EGI on R&D during the credit crisis

Variables	Model (1)	Model (2)	Model (3)
Firm-level CG variables			
Corporate largest blockholder	−11.44 (14.23)	−16.32 (15.73)	−19.31 (16.41)
Family largest blockholder	−16.40 (12.57)	−26.03 (16.45)	**−28.11 (17.03)***
Government largest blockholder (GB)	**−39.49 (15.47)*****	**−45.21 (15.68)*****	**−60.83 (26.60)****
Institution largest blockholder (IB)	**−30.09 (15.40)***	**−25.76 (13.79)****	**−52.53 (23.49)****
Board size	0.38 (1.36)	−2.52 (2.80)	−2.22 (2.76)
CEO power	−4.11 (9.34)	−5.10 (13.82)	−8.17 (14.09)
Board independence	0.17 (0.36)	−0.05 (0.36)	0.02 (0.36)
Country-level variables			
Rule of law		−15.12 (16.51)	−17.16 (16.85)
Shareholder protection		−8.72 (7.09)	−9.11 (7.20)
Creditor right protection (CRP)		**16.31 (7.48)****	**18.76 (9.09)****
Market-based financial system (MBFS)		**−48.31 (27.83)***	**−60.80 (33.08)***
Interaction terms			
GB * CRP			**−15.98 (9.51)***
GB * MBFS			−4.07 (27.64)
IB * CRP			−7.11 (7.79)
IB * MBFS			**−55.36 (25.81)****
Firm-level control variables			
Firm size	**5.91 (3.03)***	3.26 (2.24)	**5.21 (3.11)***
Firm age	1.87 (5.45)	0.71 (5.58)	0.79 (4.33)
Firm leverage	−2.36 (45.97)	−8.20 (44.02)	−14.10 (45.31)
Firm diversification	−14.22 (26.93)	−10.62 (23.44)	−7.60 (23.05)

Table 3.3　(continued)

Variables	Model (1)	Model (2)	Model (3)
Firm-level control variables			
Firm's market to book ratio	−1.03 (4.14)	0.40 (4.64)	0.29 (4.78)
Firm's R&D intensity	**2.11 (1.32)****	**2.09 (1.08)****	**2.19 (1.26)***
Industry controls	Yes	Yes	Yes
N	411	411	411
R^2	0.06	0.14	0.15

Notes:
Dependent variable: percentage change in R&D expenditures during the crisis years of 2007–09.
Significant figures in bold.
Significance levels: *p<0.10; **p<0.05; ***p<0.01 (two-tailed test).
Model 1 corresponds to regression equation (3.1), Model 2 corresponds to regression equation (3.2) and Model 3 corresponds to regression equation (3.3).
Please see Tables 3.1 and 3.2 for the definitions of the variables.

R&D curtailment in crisis times, confirming Hypothesis 2a. Our finding that family ownership is not connected to R&D curtailment supports the idea that families are typically tied strongly to their firm and consequently are less subject to shareholder pressure for short-term returns.

Board-level corporate governance characteristics (board size and board independence) seem not to have any impact on R&D spending during crisis times (rejection of Hypothesis 1); nor are the variables board size, CEO duality, and board independence significantly related to R&D curtailment in crisis times at the conventional levels of significance. There seems to be no relation between those conventional measures of monitoring and the size of R&D curtailment in crisis times. These results corroborate with Deutsch (2005) who finds little impact of boards on critical decisions that involve a potential conflict of interest between managers and shareholders.

Country-level Institutional Factors

Besides the firm-level corporate governance and firm-level control variables, we now add country-level EGI variables in model 2 of Table 3.3. We do not find any impact of shareholder protection and the rule of law on R&D spending during crisis times. Using a sample of 48 countries over

1993–2006, Belloc (2009) even finds that countries with stronger share-holder protection tend to have lower innovation activity. For our sample of 16 European countries shareholder protection and the rule of law do not seem to drive R&D curtailment decisions of the firms in our sample. The non-significant variable of investor protection at the country-level in Model 2 mirrors the non-significant results of our measures of better CG monitoring at the firm-level in Model 1.

However, we find that better credit rights have a positive impact on R&D spending during crisis times. This result is consistent with Djankov et al. (2007, 2008a) who show that strong creditor protection is associated with greater availability of credit. Creditor protection laws ensure that creditors are protected from default (Claessens and Laeven, 2003). As default becomes more probable during a financial crisis, stronger creditor rights will be more valuable during times of crisis as they keep the credit line open (Van Essen et al., 2013). This suggests that credit rights are an important EGI in crisis times because creditor protection secures debt financing to support the funding of R&D programs. The availability of external financing therefore puts less pressure on curtailing R&D invest-ments. Barbosa and Faria (2011) report similar findings for a sample of 10 European countries using industry-level data, showing that creditor rights are important in supporting innovation.

Finally, we find a negative impact of market-based financial systems on R&D spending during crisis times. Our results are in line with Lazonick and O'Sullivan (1996) and Munari et al. (2010) who suggest the existence of a greater pressure towards the reduction of R&D in market-based gov-ernance systems. Our results show that, during crisis times, bank-based financial systems outperform market-based financial systems with respect to R&D spending. Due to the provisions for greater bank-firm coordina-tion in bank-based systems, bankers are better placed to take a leadership role in assisting cash-flow restrained firms (Van Essen et al., 2013). Our regression results therefore suggest that a bank-based financial system with strong creditor rights is the best guarantee for not having to cut on R&D expenses. Our results also corroborate with Hall and Soskice (2001) who argue that market forms of coordination (e.g. US, UK) are better at sup-porting radical innovation (e.g. biotech), while non-market forms of coor-dination (e.g. continental Europe – the majority of firms in our sample) are better at supporting incremental innovation (e.g. mechanical engineering).

Adding the country-level variables does not alter the conclusions from Model 1; all other firm-level variables in Model 2 remain similar to the findings of Model 1.

To sum up, we can conclude that Hypothesis 3 is only partly accepted as better creditor rights have a positive impact on R&D spending in crisis times, while the rule of law and shareholder protection have no impact and a market-based financial system has a negative impact.

Interaction Effects

In this section we also add interaction effects in our model. Model 3 of Table 3.3 combines the firm-level CG variables, the firm-level control variables, the country-level EGI variables and interaction terms. We only present interaction terms between the significant CG and EGI variables from Models 1 and 2.[2] The results of Model 3 indicate that the presence of institutional investors curtailing R&D spending is the most problematic in market-based financial systems. The interaction term between institutional investors (IB) and market-based financial system (MBFS) shows that MBFS reinforces the effect of IB on R&D curtailment.[3] This result is no surprise as our earlier findings show that institutional investors save more on R&D expenditures (Model 1) and that market-based financial systems have a negative impact on R&D spending during crisis times (Model 2). Institutional investors are the quintessential transactional investors in a market-based financial system. They have therefore little incentive to prop up or bail out an underperforming firm during crisis times (Van Essen et al., 2013). Instead, our results show that institutional investors push firms towards short-term stock price gains by saving on R&D expenses. Our results therefore point in the direction of better bank-firm coordination in bank-based systems during crisis times as they cut back less on R&D than market-based financial systems. Banks often have better information than arms-length investors (such as institutional investors), which gives them a longer investment horizon to support R&D investment decisions (Van Essen et al., 2013).

The interaction term between government largest blockholders (GB) and creditor rights protection (CRP) indicates that the effect of GB on R&D curtailment is stronger as CRP increases.[4] State-controlled firms seem to cut more on R&D expenditures when credit rights are better protected. This result seems a bit counter-intuitive. A possible explanation is the disciplinary role of debt. Better credit rights reduce the amount of free cash flows as debt holders are better placed to secure their debt payments. Lower free cash flows leave state-controlled firms with less leeway to service other objectives such as job security for their employees. This, in turn, puts more pressure to save costs elsewhere, in this case on R&D programs.

Summarizing, we can conclude that there is a complementary effect between two types of blockholders (government and institutional investors) and two country-level EGI (creditor rights protection and market-based financial system) with respect to R&D spending during crisis times. The negative impact of having an institutional blockholder is more severe in a market-based financial system, while the negative impact of a government blockholder is stronger as creditor rights improve. Both interaction effects confirm Hypothesis 4b. As we do not find any other significant interaction effects between firm-level CG variables and country-level EGI, we reject both Hypothesis 4a and 4b and conclude that overall firm-level CG and country-level EGI function independently with respect to R&D investments in crisis times.

Firm-level Control Variables

Surprisingly, with the exception of firm size and R&D intensity, none of the other firm-level control variables turned out to be significantly related to R&D curtailment during the credit crisis. First, we do find a scale effect in R&D spending as the variable firm size is significantly positive. This is in line with earlier studies that show a positive relationship between firm size and R&D investments (Baysinger et al., 1991), but contradicts the results of Barker and Mueller (2002). Hao and Jaffe (1993) provide corroborating evidence that large firms do not experience any liquidity constraint. Second, we do not find any impact of firm age on R&D spending during crisis times. This result contrasts the finding of Huergo and Jaumandreu (2004) who find a negative relationship between firm age and innovative output during normal times, but confirms recent results of DiVito et al. (2010). Third, despite the credit crisis, we do not find any impact of firm leverage on R&D investments. Earlier studies found mixed results: positive (DiVito et al., 2010), negative (Baysinger and Hoskisson, 1989) or no impact (Munari et al., 2010) effects. Fourth, the insignificant results of the variable market to book ratio can be interpreted that firms with more growth options do not reduce R&D investments during crisis times. These results are in line with DiVito et al. (2010). Fifth, firm diversification had no effect on R&D investments during the credit crisis. Finally, the firm's R&D intensity had a significant effect on R&D investments during the credit crisis. It seems that firms with a high level of R&D spending before the crisis continue to spend at higher levels in the subsequent years. This might indicate that firms crucially depending on innovation will not temporarily save on R&D costs to maintain a certain profit level, on the contrary they might use it as an opportunity to make themselves more competitive (Barrett et al., 2009). Bond et al. (2003) indeed find for a sample of UK firms that cash flow predicts whether a firm engages in R&D, but not how much it invests in R&D. Firms that engage in R&D keep investing in R&D.

78   *Governance, regulation and innovation*

CONCLUSIONS

In this chapter, we have examined the combined effects of firm-level corporate governance and country-level institutions on R&D investments at the firm level during the recent financial crisis for a large sample of 411 firms across 16 European countries. The credit crisis is a particularly interesting time frame as firms would be inclined to cut costs and reduce spending such as R&D, capital expenditures, or marketing expenditures under strict financial constraints. We have therefore analysed whether more developed country-level economic governance institutions (EGI) and better firm-level corporate governance indicators (CG) have an impact on the R&D investment decisions of listed firms in Europe during the financial crisis from 2007 until 2009. Our study has enabled us to identify the CG and EGI characteristics that are most crucial in explaining differences in R&D curtailment patterns between firms.

First, we find that the firm-level CG characteristic with the strongest effects on R&D expenditures in crisis times is the identity of the largest shareholder. Our results show that having an institutional largest blockholder significantly reduced the R&D spending of the firm during the credit crisis. This finding points towards short-termism of institutional investors to push firms to curtail R&D expenditures to realize short-term gains over long-term R&D plans. We also find that state-controlled firms have a negative impact on R&D spending. Probably governments have more urgent policy items to be realized in crisis times than long-term R&D spending. We do not find any impact of having a family as largest shareholder on R&D curtailment. In contrast to ownership, board-level CG characteristics seem not to have a significant effect on R&D spending during crisis times. Neither board size nor CEO duality or board independence has any impact on R&D curtailment during crisis times.

Secondly, of the EGI, we find that market-based financial systems have a negative impact on R&D spending during crisis, whereas the effect of credit rights is positive. During crisis times, bank-based financial systems outperform market-based financial systems with respect to R&D spending. This is because banks are better placed to coordinate cash-flow restraints with the firms, leading to less short-term pressure to cut R&D expenses at the expense of long-term returns.

Finally, the short-termism of market-based financial systems that leads to curtailment of R&D spending during crisis times is the most problematic when institutional investors hold a large block in the firm. We furthermore find that strong creditor rights are an important EGI in crisis times because it secures the availability of external financing to fund R&D programs and therefore puts less pressure on curtailing R&D investments.

Our results suggest that a bank-based financial system with strong creditor rights is the best guarantee for not having to save on R&D expenses.

NOTES

1. Table not reported here, but available upon request.
2. We have also included other interaction terms between CG and EGI variables in Model 3 which might interact from a theoretical viewpoint. We included, for instance, interaction terms between credit right protection and leverage, between market-based financial system and R&D intensity, between shareholder right protection and board independence, between rule of law and R&D intensity. None of the other interaction terms showed up significantly in our model, therefore we do not present these results in Table 3.3. An extended table is available from the authors upon request.
3. The marginal effect of IB on R&D curtailment is $-52.53 - 55.23 \times$ MBFS.
4. The marginal effect of GB on R&D curtailment is $-60.83 - 15.98 \times$ CRP.

REFERENCES

Aggarwal, R., I. Erel, R. Stulz and R. Williamson (2010), 'Differences in governance practices between US and foreign firms: measurement, causes and consequences', *Review of Financial Studies*, 23(3): 3131–3169.

Aghion, P., J. van Reenen and L. Zingales (2009), 'Innovation and institutional ownership', Centre for Economic Performance, Discussion Paper No 911 (February), accessed on 11 January 2012, at http://cep.lse.ac.uk/pubs/download/dp0911.pdf

Alchian, A.A. and H. Demsetz (1972), 'Production, information costs, and economic organization', *American Economic Review*, 62(5): 777–95.

Anderson, R. and D. Reeb (2003), 'Founding-family ownership and firm performance: evidence from the S&P 500', *Journal of Finance*, 58(3): 1301–1328.

Barbosa, N. and A.P. Faria (2011), 'Innovation across Europe: how important are institutional differences?', *Research Policy*, 40(9): 1157–1169.

Barker, V. and G. Mueller (2002), 'CEO characteristics and firm R&D spending', *Management Science*, 48(6): 782–801.

Barrett, C.W., C.S. Musso and A. Padhi (2009), 'Upgrading R&D in a downturn', *McKinsey Quarterly*, February, 1–3.

Baysinger, B.D. and R.E. Hoskisson (1989), 'Diversification strategy and R&D intensity in large multiproduct firms', *Academy of Management Journal*, 32(2): 310–332.

Baysinger, B.D., R.D. Kosnik and T.A. Turk (1991), 'Effects of board and ownership structure on corporate R&D strategy', *Academy of Management Journal*, 34(1): 205–214.

Becker-Blease, J.R. (2011), 'Governance and innovation', *Journal of Corporate Finance*, 17(4): 947–958.

Belloc, F. (2009), 'Law, finance and innovation: the dark side of shareholder protection', *Working Paper*, Quaderni del Dipartimento di Economia Politica No. 583/2010, University of Siena. Available at SSRN: http://ssrn.com/abstract=1452743.

Belloc, F. (2012), 'Corporate governance and innovation: a survey', *Journal of Economic Surveys*, 26(5): 835–864.

Beltratti, A. and R. Stulz (2009), 'Why did some banks perform better during the credit crisis? A cross-country study of the impact of governance and regulation', *NBER Working Papers*, no.15180.

Bhagat, S. and I. Welch (1995), 'Corporate research and development investments: international comparisons,' *Journal of Accounting and Economics*, 19(2–3): 443–470.

Boardman, A. and A. Vining (1989), 'Ownership and performance in competitive environments: a comparison of the performance of private, mixed, and state-owned enterprises', *Journal of Law and Economics*, 32(1): 1–33.

Bond, S., H. Dietmar and J. Van Reenen (2003), 'Investment, R&D and financial constraints in Britain and Germany' Working Paper no. 595, Centre for Economic Performance, London School of Economics and Political Science, London, UK.

Boone, A., L. Field, J. Karpoff and C. Raheja (2007), 'The determinants of corporate board size and composition: an empirical analysis', *Journal of Financial Economics*, 85(1): 66–101.

Bougheas, S., H. Görg and E. Strobl (2003), 'Is R&D financially constrained? Theory and evidence from Irish manufacturing,' *Review of Industrial Organization*, 22(2): 159–174.

Brown, J., S. Fazzari and B. Petersen (2009), 'Financing innovation and growth: cash flow, external equity and the 1990s R&D boom', *Journal of Finance*, 64(1): 151–185.

Butler, S. and H. Newman (1989), 'Agency control mechanisms, effectiveness and decision making in an executive's final year with a firm', *Journal of Institutional and Theoretical Economics*, 145(3): 451–464.

Campello, M., J.R. Graham and C. Harvey (2010), 'The real effects of financial constraints: evidence from a financial crisis', *Journal of Financial Economics*, 97(3): 470–487.

Carney, M., E.R. Gedajlovic, P.P.M.A.R. Heugens, M. Van Essen and J. Van Oosterhout (2011), 'Business group affiliation, performance, context, and strategy: a meta-analysis', *Academy of Management Journal*, 54(3): 437–460.

Carpenter, R. and B. Petersen (2002), 'Capital market imperfections, high-tech investment, and new equity financing', *The Economic Journal*, 112(477): 54–72.

Cassimon, D., P.J. Engelen, L. Thomassen and M. Van Wouwe (2004), 'Valuing new drug applications using n-fold compound options', *Research Policy*, 33(1): 41–51.

Cassimon, D., M. De Backer, P.J. Engelen, M. Van Wouwe and V. Yordanov (2011), 'Incorporating technical risk into a compound option model to value a pharma R&D licensing opportunity', *Research Policy*, 40(9): 1200–1216.

Cazier, R. (2011), 'Measuring R&D curtailment among short-horizon CEOs', *Journal of Corporate Finance*,17(3): 584–594.

Chan, L. K.C., J. Lakonishok and T. Sougiannis (2001), 'The stock market valuation of research and development expenditures', *Journal of Finance*, 56(6): 2431–2456.

Chhaochharia, V. and L. Laeven (2009), 'Corporate governance norms and practices', *Journal of Financial Intermediation*, 18(3): 405–431.

Chiou, W.J.P., A.C. Lee and C.F. Lee (2010), 'Stock return, risk, and legal environment around the world', *International Review of Economics and Finance*, 19(1): 95–105.

Claessens, S. and L. Laeven (2003), 'Law, property rights and growth', *Journal of Finance*, 58(6): 2401–2436.

Clarke, G.R.G. (2001), 'How the quality of institutions affects technological deepening in developing countries', *Journal of International Development*,13(8): 1097–1118.

Coffee, J. (1991), 'Liquidity versus control: the institutional investor as corporate monitor', *Columbia Law Review*, 91(6): 1277–1368.

Coles, J.W., V.B. McWilliams and N. Sen (2001), 'An examination of the relationship of governance mechanisms to performance', *Journal of Management*, 27(1): 23–50.

Czarnitzki, D. and K. Kraft (2009), 'Capital control, debt financing and innovative activity', *Journal of Economic Behavior and Organization*, 71(2): 372–383.

David, P., M.A. Hitt and J. Gimeno (2001), 'The influence of activism by institutional investors on R&D', *The Academy of Management Journal*, 44(1): 144–157.

Dechow, P. and R. Sloan (1991), 'Executive incentives and the horizon problem: An empirical investigation', *Journal of Accounting and Economics*, 14(1): 51–89.

Demirguc-Kunt, A.R. and R. Levine (2001), 'Bank-based and market-based financial systems: cross-country comparisons', in A. Demirguc-Kunt and R. Levine (eds.), *Financial Structure and Economic Growth: A Cross-Country Comparison of Banks, Markets, and Development*, Cambridge, MA: MIT Press, pp. 81–140.

Deutsch, Y. (2005), 'The impact of board composition on a firm's critical decisions: a meta-analytic review', *Journal of Management*, 31(3): 424–444.

DiVito, J., C. Laurin and Y. Bozec (2010), 'R&D activity in Canada: does corporate ownership structure matter?', *Canadian Journal of Administrative Sciences*, 27(2): 107–121.

Dixit, A. (2009), 'Governance institutions and economic activity', *American Economic Review*, 99(1): 5–24.

Djankov, S., C. McLiesh and A. Shleifer (2007), 'Private credit in 129 countries', *Journal of Financial Economics*, 84(2): 299–329.

Djankov, S., C. McLiesh, O.D. Hart and A. Shleifer (2008a), 'Debt enforcement around the world', *Journal of Political Economy*, 116(6): 1105–1149.

Djankov, S., R. La Porta, F. Lopez-De-Silanes, and A. Shleifer (2008b), 'The law and economics of self-dealing', *Journal of Financial Economics*, 88(3): 430–465.

Durnev, A. and H. Kim (2005), 'To steal or not to steal: firm attributes, legal environment, and valuation', *Journal of Finance*, 60(3): 1461–1493.

Engelen, P.J. and M. Van Essen (2010), 'Underpricing of IPOs: firm-, issue- and country-specific characteristics', *Journal of Banking and Finance*, 34(8): 1958–1969.

Faccio, M. and L.H.P. Lang (2002), 'The ultimate ownership of western European corporations', *Journal of Financial Economics*, 65(3): 365–395.

Fahlenbrach, R. and R.M. Stulz (2010), 'Bank CEO incentives and the credit crisis', *Journal of Financial Economics*, 99(1): 11–26.

Fama, E.F. and M.C. Jensen (1983), 'Agency problems and residual claims', *Journal of Law and Economics*, 26(1): 327–349.

Francis, J. and A. Smith (1995), 'Agency costs and innovation: some empirical evidence', *Journal of Accounting and Economics*, 19(2–3): 383–409.

Graves, S. (1988), 'Institutional ownership and corporate R&D in the computer industry', *Academy of Management Journal*, 31(2): 417–428.

Graves, S.B. and S.A. Waddock (1990), 'Institutional ownership and control: implications for long-term corporate strategy', *The Executive*, 4(1): 75–83.

Griffith, R., R. Harrison and G. Macartney (2007), 'Product market reforms, labour market institutions and unemployment', *Economic Journal*, 117(519): 142–166.

Grosvold, J. and S. Brammer (2011), 'National institutional systems as antecedents of female board representation: an empirical study', *Corporate Governance: International Review*, 19(2):116–135.

Gupta, N. (2005), 'Partial privatization and firm performance', *Journal of Finance*, 60(2): 987–1015.

Hall, B. (2002), 'The financing of research and development', *Oxford Review of Economic Policy*, 18(1): 35–51.

Hall, P. and D. Soskice (2001), 'An introduction to varieties of capitalism', in P. Hall and D. Soskice (eds.), *Varieties of Capitalism*, Cambridge, MA: Harvard University Press.

Hansen, G.S. and C.W. Hill (1991), 'Are institutional investors myopic? A time-series study of four technology-driven industries', *Strategic Management Journal*, 12(1): 1–16.

Hao, K. and A. Jaffe (1993), 'Effect of liquidity on firms' R&D spending', *Economics of Innovation and New Technology*, 2(4): 275–282.

Hermalin, B.E. and M.S. Weisbach (2003), 'Boards of directors as an endogenously determined institution: a survey of the economic literature', *Federal Reserve Bank of New York Economic Policy Review*, 9, 7–26.

Heugens, P., M. Van Essen and J. Van Oosterhout (2009), 'Meta-analyzing ownership concentration and firm performance in Asia: towards a more fine-grained understanding', *Asia Pacific Journal of Management*, 26(3): 481–512.

Hill, C.W.L. and S.A. Snell (1988), 'External control, corporate strategy, and firm performance in research-intensive industries', *Strategic Management Journal*, 9(6): 577–590.

Honoré, F., F. Munari and B. Pottelsberge de la Potterie (2011), 'Corporate governance practices and companies' R&D orientation: evidence from European countries', Working Paper. Available at: http://aei.pitt.edu/15489/1/110124_WP_CORPORATE_GOVERNANCE_PRACTICES.pdf

Hoskisson, R.E., M.A. Hitt, R.A. Johnson, and W. Grossman (2002), 'Conflicting voices: the effects of institutional ownership heterogeneity and internal governance on corporate innovation strategies', *Academy of Management Journal*, 45(4): 697–716.

Hosono, K., M. Tomiyama and T. Miyagawa (2004), 'Corporate governance and research and development: evidence from Japan', *Economics of Innovation and New Technologies*, 13(2): 141–164.

Huergo, E. and J. Jaumandreu (2004), 'How does probability of innovation change with firm age?', *Small Business Economics*, 22 (3): 193–207.

Jaruzelski, B. and K. Dehoff (2010), 'The global innovation 1000: how the top innovators keep winning', *Strategy and Business*, 61(Winter): 1–14.

Jensen, M.C., and W.H. Meckling (1976), 'Theory of the firm: managerial behavior, agency costs and ownership structure', *Journal of Financial Economics*, 3(4): 305–360.

Johnson, J.L., C.M. Daily and A.E. Ellstrand (1996), 'Boards of directors: a review and research agenda', *Journal of Management*, 22(3): 409–438.

Jones, E. and J. Danbolt (2003), 'R&D project announcements and the impact of ownership structure', *Applied Economics Letters*, 10(14): 933– 936.

Judge, W., A. Gaur and I. Muller-Kahle (2010), 'Antecedents of shareholder activism in target firms: evidence from a multi-country study', *Corporate Governance: An International Review*, 18(4): 258–273.

Kanwar, S. (2007), 'Business enterprise R&D, technological change and intellectual property protection', *Economics Letters*, 96(1): 120–126.

Kaufmann, D., A. Kraay and M. Mastruzzi (2009), 'Governance matters VIII: Governance indicators for 1996–2008', World Bank Policy Research.

Keefer, P. and S. Knack (1997), 'Why don't poor countries catch up? A crossnational test of an institutional explanation', *Economic Inquiry*, 35(3): 590–602.

Klapper, L. and I. Love (2004), 'Corporate governance, investor protection, and performance in emerging markets', *Journal of Corporate Finance*, 10(5): 703–728.

Kochhar, R. and P. David (1996), 'Institutional investors and firm innovation: a test of competing hypothesis', *Strategic Management Journal*, 17(1): 73–84.

Kothari, S., T. Laguerre and A. Leone (2002), 'Capitalization versus expensing: evidence on the uncertainty of future earnings from capital expenditures versus R&D outlays', *Review of Accounting Studies*, 7(4): 355–382.

La Porta, R., F. Lopez-De-Silanes, A. Shleifer and R. Vishny (1997), 'Legal determinants of external finance', *Journal of Finance*, 52(3): 1131–1150.

La Porta, R., F. Lopez-De-Silanes, A. Shleifer and R. Vishny (1998), 'Law and finance', *Journal of Political Economy*, 106(6): 1113–1155.

La Porta, R., F. Lopez-De-Silanes, A. Shleifer and R. Vishny (2000), 'Agency problems and dividend policies around the world', *Journal of Finance*, 55(1): 1–33.

Laverty, K.J. (1996), 'Economic "short-termism": the debate, the unresolved issues, and the implications for management practice and research', *Academy of Management Review*, 21(3): 825–860.

Lazonick, W. and M. O'Sullivan (1996), 'Organization, finance and international competition', *Industrial and Corporate Change*, 5(1): 1–49.

Lee, P.M. (2005), 'A comparison of ownership structures and innovation of US and Japanese firms', *Managerial and Decision Economics*, 26(1): 39–50.

Leuz, C., K.V. Lins and F.E. Warnock (2009), 'Do foreigners invest less in poorly governed firms?' *Review of Financial Studies*, 22(8): 3245–3285.

Liu, M. and M. Magnan (2011), 'Self-dealing regulations, ownership wedge, and corporate valuation: international evidence', *Corporate Governance: An International Review*, 19(2): 99–115.

Lorsch, J.W. and E. Maciver (1989), *Pawns or Potentates: The Reality of America's Corporate Boards*, Boston, Mass: Harvard Business School Press.

Maury, B. (2006), 'Family ownership and firm performance: empirical evidence from Western European corporations', *Journal of Corporate Finance*, 12(2): 321–341.

Megginson, W. and J. Netter (2001), 'From state to market: a survey of empirical studies on privatization', *Journal of Economic Literature*, 39(2): 321–389.

Megginson, W., R. Nash and M. van Randenborgh (1994), 'The financial and operating performance of newly privatized firms: an international empirical analysis', *Journal of Finance*, 49(2): 403–452.

Morck, R., A. Shleifer and R.W. Vishny (1988), 'Management ownership and market valuation: an empirical analysis', *Journal of Financial Economics*, 20, 293–315.

Munari, F. (2002), 'The effects of privatization processes on corporate R&D units: evidence from Italy and France', *R&D Management*, 32(3): 223–232.

Munari, F., E. Roberts and M. Sobrero (2002), 'Privatization processes and the redefinition of corporate R&D boundaries', *Research Policy*, 31(1): 33–55.

Munari, F., R. Oriani and M. Sobrero (2010), 'The effects of owner identity and external governance systems on R&D investments: a study of Western European firms', *Research Policy*, 39(8): 1093–1104.

Murphy, K.J. and J. Zimmerman (1993), 'Financial performance surrounding CEO turnover', *Journal of Accounting and Economics*, 16(1–3): 273–315.

Peng, M.W. and Y. Jiang (2010), 'Institutions behind family ownership and control in large firms', *Journal of Management Studies*, 47(2): 253–273.

Romer, P.M. (1994), 'The origins of endogenous growth', *The Journal of Economic Perspectives*, 8(1): 3–22.

Samaniego, R. (2006), 'Employment protection and high-tech aversion', *Review of Economic Dynamics*, 9(2): 224–241.

Schumpeter, J.A. (1934), *The Theory of Economic Development*, Cambridge, MA: Harvard University Press.

Shleifer, A. and R.W. Vishny (1986), 'Large shareholders and corporate control', *Journal of Political Economy*, 94(3): 461–488.

Shleifer, A. and R. Vishny (1997), 'A survey of corporate governance', *Journal of Finance*, 52(2): 737–783.

Tribo, J.A., P. Berrone and J. Surroca (2007), 'Do the type and number of block-holders influence R&D investments? New evidence from Spain', *Corporate Governance*, 15(5): 828–842.

Van Essen, M., M. Carney, E. Gedajlovic and P.P.M.A.R. Heugens (2012a), 'How does family control influence firm strategy and performance? A meta-analysis of US publicly-listed firms', Working Paper.

Van Essen, M., H. van Oosterhout and P. Heugens (2012b), 'Competition and cooperation in corporate governance: the effects of labor institutions on blockholder effectiveness in 23 European countries', *Organizational Science*, forthcoming.

Van Essen, M., P.J. Engelen and M. Carney (2013), 'Does "good" corporate governance help in a crisis? The impact of country- and firm-level governance mechanisms in the European financial crisis', *Corporate Governance: An International Review*, forthcoming.

Varsakelis, N. (2006), 'Education, political institutions and innovative activity: a cross-country empirical investigation', *Research Policy*, 35(7): 1083–1090.

Wahal, S. and J. J. McConnell (2000), 'Do institutional investors exacerbate managerial myopia?', *Journal of Corporate Finance*, 6(3): 307–329.

White, H. (1980), 'A heteroskedasticity-consistent covariance matrix estimator and a direct test for heteroskedasticity', *Econometrica*, 48(4): 817–838.

Yafeh, Y. and O. Yosha (2003), 'Large shareholders and banks: who monitors and how?' *The Economic Journal*, 113(484): 128–146.

Yermack, D. (1996), 'Higher market valuation of companies with a small board of directors', *Journal of Financial Economics*, 40(2): 185–211.

Zahra, S.A. and J.A. Pearce (1989), 'Boards of directors and corporate financial performance: a review and integrative model', *Journal of Management*, 15(2): 291–334.
Zingales, L. (1998), 'Corporate governance', in P. Newman (ed.), *The New Palgrave Dictionary of Economics and the Law*, London: Macmillan.

4. Corporate governance and innovation in US-listed firms: the mediating effects of market concentration

Nawar Hashem and Mehmet Ugur

INTRODUCTION

With the exception of a few studies, the literature on the relationship between corporate governance (CG) and innovation tends to investigate only the partial effects of CG dimensions on innovation. The aim of this chapter is to contribute to the debate by analysing not only the relationship between CG and innovation, but also how market concentration and CG interact in their effects on innovation. The case for examining both partial and interactive effects can be summarized as follows: investment in research and development (R&D) is costly and associated with uncertain returns for shareholders and uncertain private benefits for managers. At a given level of market concentration within an industry, CG rules affect managers' innovation effort by ameliorating or exacerbating the agency problem. However, the level of market concentration also affects the managers' innovation effort by affecting the rates of pre-innovation and post-innovation profits. Given these dynamics, it is necessary to investigate not only the partial effects of CG and market concentration on R&D expenditures; but also the way in which CG rules and market structure interact and affect the level of R&D effort.

To address this issue, we estimate partial and interactive effects in a sample of over 1,500 non-financial US-listed firms, using indicators for four CG dimensions: board independence and diversity; ownership structure; anti-merger defences; and shareholders' rights. We measure market concentration with the Herfindahl-Hirschman Index (HHI) calculated on the basis of four-digit standard industrial classification code (SIC) used by the Securities & Exchange Commission (SEC) to classify a company's industry.

We report that board independence is related positively to R&D intensity and that market concentration acts as a complement that strengthens the positive relationship. All other CG indicators (number of women directors on the board, percentage of shares owned by insiders and institutional investors, and percentage of vote required to approve mergers or amend company charters) are related negatively to R&D intensity. In addition, market concentration tends to have a substitution effect when it is interacted with these CG indicators. We also report that the relationship between market concentration and innovation has a U-shape, implying that an increase in market concentration is associated with lower R&D intensity when the initial level of concentration is low; but the change is positive when the initial level of concentration is high. These results are obtained with a two-way cluster-robust estimation methodology that takes account of serial and cross-sectional dependence in the error terms; and are robust to different measures of innovation, including R&D expenditures, the ratio of R&D expenditures to sales, and R&D expenditures per employee. The results are also robust to inclusion of firm-characteristics (such as firm size, age, returns on assets, Tobin's Q, and the ratio of long-term debt to capital) as control variables.

The rest of this chapter is organized as follows. In the next section, we provide a review of the related literature and develop the case for investigating the relationship between CG and innovation by taking into account the interactions between CG dimensions and market concentration. In the following section, we first describe the data and explain the method of estimation. In the penultimate section, we report the empirical findings and relate them to the existing evidence. Finally, in the conclusions section, we summarize the main findings and distil some policy- and research-relevant conclusions.

RELATED LITERATURE

Firm's innovation effort is related to two sources of costs and incentives that affect manager decisions: the extent of product-market competition that determines the pre- and post-innovation profits and the nature of the CG rules that determine the extent to which the agency problem is ameliorated. Yet, so far and with the exception of Aghion et al. (1999 and 2002b), Sapra et al. (2009) and Atanassov (2012), the effects of CG rules and market structures on innovation have been investigated in isolation. Indeed, only Aghion et al. (1999, 2002b) have investigated the ways in which CG rules and market structure may interact to determine the innovation effort. In order to set the stage for joint analysis, we first summarize the main findings on the relationship between CG and innovation. This will be followed by a similar exercise on the relationship between market concentration and innovation. At the end, we will draw on Aghion et al. (1999 and 2002b) to develop the case for joint analysis, whereby the relationship between R&D expenditures and CG dimensions is estimated by controlling for market concentration and the interaction between the latter and CG dimensions.

Corporate Governance and Innovation

Empirical work on the relationship between CG and innovation is small in number. Nonetheless, there is an evident increase in the volume of work in this area, and the theories it draws upon (the principal-agent theory and the theory of contracting) are well established in corporate finance. Some recent studies (Belloc, 2012; Honoré et al. 2011 and Sapra et al., 2009) provide excellent reviews of this emergent literature. In what follows, we will first provide a brief overview of the related literature and discuss the case for investigating not only the partial effects of CG on innovation effort but also the way in which CG and market structure interact in their effects on innovation.

The agency theory predicts that board independence would have a negative effect on innovation. This is because independent boards can implement strict monitoring and have stronger power to determine the executive pay structure. As such, they shift the risk of innovation to risk-averse managers, who would be motivated to minimize the risk of poor performance in the short term by reducing the R&D effort. In addition, outside directors may have insufficient knowledge about the firm's capabilities and processes, and may underestimate the strategic desirability of innovation projects for future growth (see Baysinger and Hoskisson, 1990; Baysinger et al., 1991; Hill and Snell, 1988; Zahra, 1996).

However, there is also evidence indicating a positive relationship between board independence and innovation effort. This is due to independent directors' preference for long-term investment as a means of maximizing firm value for shareholders. For example, Dong and Gou 2010) report that the number of independent directors is related positively to the level R&D in Chinese firms. In addition, the interaction of family ownership and independent director ratio is found to be positively related to R&D investment in Taiwanese firms, suggesting that firms with high family ownership have higher levels of R&D investment when independent outsiders are included in the board (Chen and Hsu, 2009).

Conflicting findings have been reported with respect to board diversity too – particularly in relation to gender composition of the board. Some studies suggest that board diversity delivers a broad range of perspectives, increases the search for information, enhances the quality of brainstormed ideas, and facilitates creativity (Erhardt et al., 2003; Watson et al., 1993). These dynamics are reported to have positive effects on innovation by firms with women directors on the board (Miller and del Carmen Triana, 2009). However, Torchia et al. (2011) indicate that the positive relationship between the number of woman directors and organizational innovation requires the existence of a critical mass of at least three women rather than token representation.

Another CG dimension that is found to be related to firm innovation is the strength of anti-merger and anti-takeover defences. Drawing on agency theory, the literature has provided conflicting results. For example, Shleifer and Summers (1988) demonstrate that takeover pressure reduces investment in firm-specific innovation as managers anticipate a higher probability of *ex-post* take-over by 'raiders'. Maher and Andersson (2002) and Stein (1988) confirm this finding by drawing on managers' myopia. Concerned that low short-term profits may result in unwanted takeover attempts, managers may choose to focus on projects with short-term payoffs and on visible activities, often at the expense of long-term investment and performance. Pugh et al. (1999) use a sample of 183 US firms that adopted anti-takeover defences in 1990 and report a significant increase in the ratio of R&D expenditures to sales or assets in the following four years.

However, these findings are contradicted by Jensen (1988), who reports that anti-takeover defences shield managers against external threats and encourage managerial slack, leading to less investment in innovation projects. Furthermore, Johnston and Rao (1997) examine 649 anti-takeover amendments adopted by US firms from 1979 to 1985, and show that the ratio of R&D expenditures to sales remains unchanged in each of the five-year periods after adopting an antitakeover defence amendment compared to its value before the adoption. Finally, Atanassov (2012) uses a large panel of US firms over the 1976–2000 period and reports that the number of patents and patent citations has declined after the adoption of anti-takeover laws by US states. The negative effect tends to occur two or more years after anti-takeover laws were enacted and is mitigated by alternative governance mechanisms such as large shareholders, pension fund ownership or by leverage and product-market competition.

Taking these different findings into account, Sapra et al. (2009) propose a model where the relationship between takeover pressure and innovation is non-monotonic. In this model, firms are more likely to invest in innovative projects either when takeover pressure is high or when anti-takeover provisions are strict enough to deter takeovers. The non-monotonic relationship is a result of the trade-off faced by managers, who trade off the benefits of high takeover premiums that innovative firms may attract against the loss of control benefits that occurs when innovative firms are taken over. Hence, the relationship between anti-takeover defences and innovation can be either positive as reported in earlier work or negative/ non-linear as reported in more recent work.

A third CG dimension that is found to be related to innovation is ownership structure – particularly the share of equity held by institutional investors and insiders. According to the agency theory, a high percentage of the shares held by insiders is an indicator of better alignment between shareholder and manager interests. Hence, a positive relationship can be expected between insider ownership and innovation. The existing work tends to examine the relationship between a particular type of insiders (i.e., family owners and managers) and innovation. In their review of the literature, De Massis et al. (2012) conclude that the empirical studies tend to report a negative relationship between family ownership and innovation inputs (i.e., R&D expenditures), whilst the relationship between family ownership and innovation outcomes (i.e., product/process innovation or patents) is uncertain.

In contrast, the relationship between institutional ownership and innovation is studied widely. For example, Aghion et al. (2009) report that institutional owners encourage investment in innovation by reducing the managers' career risks that risky innovation projects may entail. However, this is by no means a common finding. In fact, the weight of the evidence suggests that the relationship between institutional ownership and innovation depends on institutional investors' investment horizons.

Several studies have reported that institutional investors are more sensitive to short-term returns and therefore they engage in high trading volumes around the announcements of quarterly earnings (Kim et al., 1997; Lang and McNichols, 1997; and Potter, 1992). Other studies such as Bushee (1998), Kochhar and David (1996) and Zahra (1996) have demonstrated different time horizons tend to influence the innovation efforts of the firms with high levels of institutional ownership. Hence, the disciplining and reassurance effect reported by Aghion et al. (2009) may not always hold. Munari et al. (2010) utilize a dataset of 1,000 publicly traded European companies and report a negative relationship between the intensity of institutional ownership within national financial markets and R&D intensity of the firms. This is in line with earlier findings. For example, Hill and Snell (1989) demonstrate that large institutional shareholders tend to wield pressure on the management to secure high short-term profits at the expense of long-term projects such as investment in innovation. Similarly, Graves (1988) found that institutional ownership has a negative effect on

R&D intensity among 22 computer-manufacturing companies; and the negative effect is related to institutional investors' short-term horizons and limited knowledge of the firms or industries in which they invest.

The fourth CG dimension we investigate in this chapter is shareholders' rights. Some studies have reported that stronger shareholder rights may lead to better company performance (Gompers et al., 2003; Klapper and Love, 2004). However, more recent work tends to indicate that shareholder rights may discourage risk taking and lead to a reduction in R&D expenditures (Bargeron et al., 2010; Cohen et al., 2009). Such findings have also been reported by Shadab (2008), who argues that the Sarbanes-Oxley Act (SOA) has been followed by falling R&D investment as US firm managers have been deterred from investing in risky innovation projects by increased shareholder activism and stronger outside monitoring. Two empirical studies lend support to this argument: Bargeron et al. (2010) and Cohen et al. (2009), who report that US firms have significantly reduced their investments in R&D after the SOA went into effect.

The brief overview above indicates that the volume of work on the relationship between CG and innovation has increased significantly since the early contributions in the late 1980s and early 1990s. In addition, the existing work has been drawing on increasingly larger datasets. However, five issues remain and call for attention. First, there is evident tension between the predictions of the agency theory and empirical findings; and an evident lack of consensus in the empirical literature. Hence, further research is required to identify the drivers of the heterogeneity in reported findings. Secondly, the assumption of linear relationship between CG dimensions and innovation needs reconsideration. As Sapra et al. (2009) have demonstrated with respect to anti-takeover defences, the relationship between CG and innovation may be non-linear. Third, the interaction between different CG dimensions may be as important as the partial effects of individual CG dimensions – as demonstrated by Chen and Hsu (2009) with respect to the interaction between board independence and ownership type. Fourth, the existing literature – with the exception of Aghion et al. (2002b), Sapra et al. (2009) and Atanassov (2012) – tends to investigate the relationship between CG and innovation without controlling for the non-linear effects of market structure. Finally, even when the non-linear effects of market structure are controlled for, the effect of interactions between corporate governance and market structure is either not estimated (e.g., Sapra et al., 2009; Atanassov, 2012) or it is estimated only with a small number of control variables for firm characteristics (e.g., Aghion et al., 2002b). This chapter aims to contribute to the literature by addressing the fourth and fifth issues: namely controlling for non-linear effects of the market structure and for interaction between the latter and corporate governance. We also contribute to the breadth of the existing evidence by providing partial and marginal effect-estimates for six measures of corporate governance while controlling for a wide range of firm characteristics. Given these aims, in the next subsection we provide a review of the literature on the relationship between market structure and innovation. Then, we justify why innovation effort should be investigated by taking into account both CG rules and the market structure and the interactions between the two.

Market Structure and Innovation

The relationship between market structure and innovation has been a subject of intense debate since Schumpeter (1934, 1942) advanced the hypothesis that 'large firms and concentrated market structures promote innovation' (Gilbert, 2006: 159). Schumpeter's argument implies that the deadweight loss associated with imperfect competition is a cost that must be borne in order to induce innovation and long-term growth. Arrow (1962) takes issue with the Schumpeterian hypothesis and demonstrates that a monopoly shielded against competition has less incentive to innovate because it can earn positive profits with or without innovation. In contrast, a firm in a perfectly competitive market does not earn positive profits unless it innovates and its innovation is protected by exclusive intellectual property rights.

The results differ when a duopoly case is analysed instead of a scenario that involves a pure monopolist and a perfectly competitive firm. For example, Gilbert and Newbery (1982) analyse innovation as a 'bid for patents' by duopoly firms, where the successful bidder (i.e., the innovator) earns higher post-innovation profits. In this scenario, market concentration is conducive to higher innovation because the incumbent monopolist will earn monopoly profits before innovation plus duopoly profits after innovation if its bid for a patent is unsuccessful. The same incumbent will earn monopoly profits in both periods if its own bid for patent is successful. Compared to the incumbent, the newcomer faces zero monopoly profits if its bid for a patent is unsuccessful and can earn only duopoly profits if it is successful. Therefore, firms with higher market power can be expected to invest more in innovation compared to newcomers with lower market power.

The neat result obtained by Gilbert and Newbery (1982) depends on the assumption that the patent is obtained by the highest bidder – i.e., by the firm that invests more in R&D. This assumption is challenged by Reinganum (1983, 1985), who demonstrates that the outcome of innovation is uncertain. R&D expenditures increase the probability of obtaining the patent but do not guarantee success. Given this uncertainty, the incumbent monopolist will decide to invest in innovation depending on the nature of innovation (drastic versus incremental innovation) and on the probability of innovation by the newcomer. The expected profits for the monopolist that invests in drastic innovation are less than the expected profits for a competitor; and this result holds even if innovation becomes less drastic on a drastic/non-drastic scale.

The large volume of the empirical literature reviewed by Gilbert (2006) yields similar conflicting results. It is evident that the debate has been dominated by antagonism between a positive 'Schumpeter effect' and a negative 'Arrow effect' from market concentration on to innovation. As Peneder (2012) observes, however, it is simplistic to assume that the effects postulated by either Schumpeter or Arrow are linear or independent of the initial level of competition assumed. In Schumpeter, the positive relationship between market concentration and innovation is due to low initial level of concentration assumed, which is evident in his argument that endogenous innovation under perfect competition is impossible. In Arrow, on the other hand, the negative effect of market concentration on innovation is derived from analysing the case of monopoly. This scenario clearly implies high levels of market concentration.

The existence of a non-linear relationship between competition and innovation is central to the theoretical and empirical work by Philippe Aghion and his co-authors. This work deserves special mention here because not only does it provide a framework that captures the diverse findings in the empirical literature, but also because it addresses the inter-action between competition and CG explicitly.

Aghion et al. (2002a, 2005) explain the non-linear relationship between product-market competition and innovation through a formal model where the incumbents and their followers can innovate; and all innova-tions occur step-by-step. Their model predicts that higher levels of com-petition lead to increased innovation when incumbent firms operate with similar technologies – i.e., when technological competition is neck-and-neck. In addition, neck-and-neck competition in technology is more likely to occur when product-market competition is low. Hence, at low levels of product-market competition, innovation increases as product-market competition increases. In contrast, when product-market competition is already high, innovation is more likely to be undertaken by newcomers with low-profits. The latter engage in innovation as a means of improv-ing their post-innovation profits. In this case, increase in competition will reduce innovation due to the squeeze on already low initial profits. The main mechanism that drives the inverted-U relationship between compe-tition and innovation is that the fraction of sectors with neck-and-neck or newcomer competitors is an endogenous outcome of the equilibrium innovation intensities in each sector.

The brief review above suggests that the relationship between market concentration and innovation can be positive or negative – depending on the initial level of competition and the kind of innovation strategies involved (neck-and-neck versus step-by-step innovation). Despite differences in modelling and findings, it is possible to detect a degree of convergence towards the affirmation of a non-linear relationship between competition and innovation. This tendency is confirmed in recent work published in a special issue of the *Journal of Industry, Competition and Trade*. In an introductory article to the special issue, Peneder (2012) states that the nonlinear model is technically sophisticated and has intuitive appeal – not the least because it can reconcile the Schumpeterian and Arrow-like arguments. Three empirical papers in the special issue test explicitly for non-linear relationship between competition and innovation. While Berubé et al. (2012) and Polder and Veldhuizen (2012) confirm the existence of an inverted-U relationship in Canadian and Dutch micro-data, Peroni and Gomes Ferreira (2012) report a U-shaped relationship in Luxembourg firm-level data.

Corporate Governance, Market Structure and Innovation: Towards a Synthesis

The convergence towards non-linear modelling of the relationship between competition and innovation has led recent studies on CG and innovation to include a measure of market concentration and its square as control variables (see for example Atanassov, 2012 and Sapra et al., 2009). According to Aghion et al. (1999) the dynamic that drives the non-linear relationship between competition and innovation is the extent to which CG rules exert discipline on managers and align manager and shareholder interests. On the one hand, risk-averse managers would be inclined to minimize the direct cost of innovation and the adjustment cost associated with implementing the new technology. On the other hand, they would be motivated to innovate as a means of reducing the risk of bankruptcy. Given these conflicting incentives, increased product-market competition reduces managerial slack and increases the risk of bankruptcy – inducing managers to increase their innovation effort. However, if CG rules are already strict enough to reduce managerial slack, increased product-market competition becomes a less significant driver of innovation. Hence, CG rules and competition tend to act as substitutes in their effects on innovation.

Nevertheless, CG may also act as a complement to competition when managerial slack is minimal or the interests of managers and shareholders are aligned. This is what Aghion et al. (2002b) propose in the light of the evidence reported by Grosfeld and Tressel (2002), who find that higher levels of product-market competition increase total factor productivity (TFP) growth in firms with concentrated ownership – i.e., when managerial and shareholder interests are more likely to be aligned. To address this conundrum, Aghion et al. (2002b) draw on earlier models where innovation occurs step-by-step. In this setting, innovation is a means of escaping the harmful effects of competition on excess profits. Introducing CG into the analysis, Aghion et al. (2002b) demonstrate that the positive effect of competition on innovation will be stronger in firms where CG provides better alignment between the interests of managers and shareholders – i.e., under concentrated ownership. This is just the opposite of the finding in Aghion et al. (1999) and implies that CG and product-market competition can also act as complements in their effects on innovation.

These findings indicate that the non-linear relationship between competition and innovation may be driven not only by different innovation intensities in different sectors – as indicated in Aghion et al. (2002a, 2005); but also by different levels of disciplining effects and/or interest alignment effects that CG rules exert on managers (Aghion et al., 1999, 2002b). Given the second source of non-linearity, there is a theoretical case for estimating the effect of CG on innovation by controlling not only for the non-linear relationship between market concentration and innovation, but also for the interaction effects of both market concentration and corporate governance.

There is also an empirical case for controlling the interactive effects because failure to do this may lead to model misspecification and cause the estimated coefficients on CG as well as market concentration to be biased. Using genuine data and simulation exercises, Ganzach (1997) has demonstrated that failure to include appropriate interaction terms in models with quadratic terms may lead to estimation results that indicate a concave (inverted-U) relationship between independent and dependent variables, whereas the true relationship is, in fact, convex (U-shaped). Furthermore, when quadratic terms are omitted despite being justified by theory or by the data structure, the omission causes the interaction terms to have complementary effects whereas the true effect is offsetting. Therefore, in what follows, we will estimate both the partial effects of corporate governance and market structure on R&D effort and the interaction effects between the two.

METHODOLOGY AND DATA

Empirical work on determinants of firm innovation tends to use panel data sets, which may contain variables that are correlated serially and cross-sectionally. Such correlations violate the assumption that regression residuals are distributed independently and identically. When this assumption is not satisfied, standard OLS estimation leads to underestimated standard errors and higher probability of rejecting the null hypothesis when the latter is false (Type I error). One method for addressing this problem has been proposed by Newey and West (1987), which yields standard errors that are robust to heteroskedasticity and autocorrelation. Another method is that of Fama and MacBeth (1973), which yields standard errors that are robust to cross-sectional dependence.

The Newey-West and Fama-Macbeth standard errors may be less biased downwards, but the former assumes cross-sectional independence while the latter assumes time-series independence. Recently, a number of studies (Cameron et al., 2006; Thompson, 2006; Petersen, 2007; and Gow et al., 2010) have proposed a new method that allows for two-way clustering to obtain standard errors that are robust to both serial and cross-sectional dependence. In a panel-data setting, the model and the assumptions about intra-cluster dependence can be stated as follows:

$$Y_{it} = X_{it}\beta + \varepsilon_{it} \tag{4.1}$$

$$X_{it} = \mu_i + \theta_t + \varepsilon_{it} \tag{4.1a}$$

$$\varepsilon_{it} = \gamma_i + \delta_t + v_{it} \tag{4.1b}$$

Specifications (4.1a and 4.1b) relax the assumption of independence in both the independent variables and the error terms due to firm-specific shocks (μ_i and γ_i) and time shocks (θ_t and δ_t), which may not be constant. These shocks are in addition to the idiosyncratic shock component that is unique to each observation ($\in_{it}$ and v_{it}). Given this data structure, the standard errors of the coefficients are calculated in accordance with equation (4.2).

$$\hat{V}(\hat{\beta}) = (X'X)^{-1} \hat{\beta}(X'X)^{-1}, \text{ where } \hat{\beta} = \sum_{h=1}^{H} X'_h u_h u'_h X_h \tag{4.2}$$

Here X_h is the $N_h \times K$ matrix of regressors; u_h is the N_h-vector of residuals for cluster h; and H is the number of clusters. The two-way cluster-robust method evaluates the expression in (4.2) three times. First, it calculates one-way cluster-robust standard errors for the firm cluster (V_{firm}). Secondly, it carries out the same procedure for the time cluster (V_{year}). Finally, it deducts the White variance-covariance matrix from the sum of (V_{firm}) and (V_{year}) to avoid double counting, which is due to the fact that both the firm- and time-clustered variance-covariance matrix include the diagonal of the White variance-covariance matrix (Petersen, 2007: 24–25). Hence, the two-way cluster-robust standard errors are obtained in accordance with equation (4.3).

$$V = V_{firm} + V_{year} - V_{White} \qquad (4.3)$$

The standard errors clustered by firm (V_{firm}) captures the unspecified correlation between observations on the same firm in different years (e.g. correlations between v_{it} and v_{it+1}). The standard errors clustered by time (V_{year}) captures the unspecified correlation between observations on different firms in the same year (e.g. correlations between v_{it} and v_{kt}). The cluster-robust standard errors obtained from (4.3) are robust to any form of within cluster correlation, which can be fixed or temporary. This is an important feature that differentiates the two-way cluster-robust estimation from fixed-effect estimations (Thompson, 2006; Cameron et al., 2006).

Petersen (2007) and Gow et al. (2010) provide simulation results that compare the two-way cluster-robust estimations with results obtained from fixed- and random-effect effect panel-data estimators and the estimator proposed by Fama and Macbeth (1973). Their findings can be summarized as follows:

- *Fixed-effect estimations with firm dummies* Standard errors are unbiased only if the firm effect is fixed. If the firm-effect changes over time, firm dummies do not capture fully the within-cluster dependence and OLS standard errors remain biased.
- *Random-effect estimations, using GLS* Estimates are efficient – both with or without firm dummies. However, GLS standard errors are unbiased only when the firm effect is permanent. If the firm effect is temporary, GLS estimates are still more efficient than OLS estimates but the standard errors remain biased downwards.
- *Fama-MacBeth procedure* The standard errors are unbiased when there is only time effect. With time effect only, the slope coefficients across years are zero. However, if there were both time and firm effects, Fama-MacBeth standard errors would be biased downwards.
- *Two-way clustering* Clustering along two dimensions (say year and firm) produces less biased standard errors compared to any method of one-way clustering. However, two-way clustering does not eliminate the risk of biased estimates altogether. When the number of the clusters along one dimension (e.g., number of firms) is large but the number of clusters along the second dimension (e.g., number of

years) is small, the method of two-way clustering produces similar results to one-way clustering based on the large number of clusters (i.e., firms). However, this is not true for results obtained from clustering along the less frequent cluster (e.g., time). In other words, two-way clustering produces at least similar or less-biased standard errors compared to one-way clustering under all conditions.

Given these findings, we estimate a two-way cluster-robust model of innovation using the procedure provided by Petersen.[1] In the model, the firm's innovation effort is a function of corporate governance (*CG*) characteristics, the level of market concentration measured by Herfindahl-Hirschman Index (*HHI*), the interaction between corporate governance and market concentration (*CG*HHI*), and a range of firm characteristics used as control variables (*CV*) in the literature.

Stated formally: $INV = f(CG, HHI, Cg * HHI, CV)$. Then, the empirical model to be estimated can be stated as follows:

$$\ln RD_{it} = \beta_0 + \beta_1 CG_{it-1} + \beta_2 CG_{it-1} * HHI_{it-1} + \beta_3 HHI_{it-1} + \beta_4 HHISQ_{it-1} + \beta_5 Age_{it-1} + \beta_6 M_{cap_{it-1}} + \beta_7 RoA_{it-1} + \beta_8 Tob\_Q_{it-1} + \beta_9 Leverage_{it-1} + \varepsilon_{it};$$

where

$$\varepsilon_{it} = \gamma_i + \delta_t + v_{it} \qquad (4.4)$$

We estimate model (4.4) with pooled cross-section and time-series data for a maximum number of 1,533 US-listed non-financial firms over the period 2004–10. The explanatory variables are lagged one year to minimize the risk of simultaneity and reverse causality.[2] The choice of firms and years is determined by availability of corporate governance (CG) data, obtained from The Corporate Library of Governance Metrics International. We have complemented the CG data with annual accounting and financial data from Thomson Reuters' Datastream.[3] In line with prior studies, we exclude financial firms (banks, investment trusts, insurance companies, and properties companies). To calculate the measure of concentration, we use four-digit industry classification code utilized by the Securities and Exchange Commission (SEC) to identify the firm's industry.

We have estimated model (4.4) with three different measures of R&D effort, all in natural logarithms: log(R&D Expenditures); log(R&D Expenditures/Employees); log(R&D Expenditures/Sales Revenue). Data for R&D effort is from Datastream and has the following codes: 01201 for R&D expenditures; 08341 for R&D expenditures/sales; and 07011 for number of employees. In the results section below, we present the results for R&D intensity of sales (R&D/Sales ratio) only. However, estimation results with other measures of R&D effort (R&D level and R&D expenditure per employee) are presented in the appendix for comparison. The comparison indicates a high degree of consistency between the results obtained for all three measures of R&D effort.

We use six corporate governance (*CG*) indicators for: (i) board independence; (ii) number of women directors; (iii) institutional majority; (iv) percentage of shares owned by insiders; (v) percentage of votes required to approve a merger or sale; and (vi) percentage of votes required to amend company charter. *Board independence* is a dummy variable that takes the value of 1 if outside directors constitute a majority over inside directors and zero otherwise. *Women directors* is the number of women directors on the board and is used as a measure of board diversity. *Merger vote percentage* is the percentage of votes required to approve a merger or sale and is used to measure the strength of anti-merger/anti-takeover defences. *Insider percentage* is the percentage of outstanding shares held by top management and directors, as reported in the company's most recent proxy statement. It is used as a measure of alignment between the interests of managers and shareholders. *Institutional majority* is a dummy variable that takes the value of 1 if institutional investors own the majority of the outstanding shares and zero otherwise. *Charter vote percentage* is the percentage of outstanding shares required to amend company charter and is used as a measure of reduced shareholders rights. CG indicators are included in model (4) one at a time, leading to six estimations for each measure of R&D effort.

The term $CG_{it-1} * HHI_{it-1}$ is the interaction between a given CG indicator and the level of market concentration measured as the Herfindahl-Hirschman Index (HHI). The interaction term captures the cross effects of corporate governance and market concentration on innovation, in line with the theoretical and empirical findings reported in Aghion et al. (1999, 2002b). The HHI is calculated for each industry and year as follows:

$$HHI_{jt} = \sum S_{ijt}^2 * 100 \qquad (4.5)$$

Here, S_{ijt} represents the share of firm i in the total sales of industry j for a given year t. The industry is defined on the basis of four-digit standard industry classification (SIC) code used by the Securities and Exchange Commission (SEC). The HHI ranges between 0 and 100, and indicates higher levels of concentration (hence lower levels of competition) as it increases. Sales revenue is obtained from Datastream (code 07240).

Finally, model (4) includes five control variables for firm characteristics: (i) company age (*Age*) for establishing whether older companies invest more or less in R&D; (ii) value of market capitalization (*M_Cap*) as an alternative measure of size beyond sales revenue and number of employees that are used to scale R&D expenditures; (iii) returns on assets (*RoA*) which is used to measure a company's operating efficiency regardless of its degree of leverage, and is calculated by dividing a company's net operating income by total assets before deducting financing costs; (iv) Tobin's Q (*Tob_Q*), which is the ratio of the company's market value to its book value and as such it indicates the profit opportunities for investors as well as the scope for financing R&D investment via equity finance; and the ratio of long-term debt to capital (*Leverage*), which represents all interest bearing financial obligations with a repayment date beyond one year. Data for two of the control variables is obtained from Datastream: return on assets (code 08326) and long-term debt as percentage of total capital (code 08216). Data for three control variables is obtained from The Corporate Library: company age in years, market capitalization in US dollars, and Tobin's Q as an index. Inclusion of these control variables is in line with current practice in the literature (see Atanassov, 2012; Sapra et al., 2009; and Munari et al., 2010).

The approach adopted here has two novelties. First, it complements the earlier work by Aghion et al. (2002b), who control only for firm size when estimating the interaction effects of corporate governance and market structure. In this chapter, we control for five firm characteristics, including size, returns on assets, Tobin's Q, long-term debt and market value of capitalization. Secondly, it complements the recent work that controls for non-linear relationship between market structure and innovation (Atanassov, 2012 and Sapra et al., 2009) but not for interactions between market structure and CG.

RESULTS

Summary statistics for the variables are presented in Table 4.1. The summary statistics indicate that the average R&D expenditures is approximately US$ 37,798 (which is the exponential of 10.54 for log R&D), and ranges from a minimum of US$18 to a maximum of US$9,435,597 (exponentials of 2.89 and 16.06, respectively). The average R&D expenditure per employee is 66 cents and ranges from a minimum of practically zero to a maximum of US$4,915. Finally, R&D expenditure as a percentage of sales is 0.22 per cent on average and ranges from a minimum of practically zero to a maximum of 119,900 per cent. The large R&D/sales ratio at the upper end of the distribution is due to large investment by start-ups that have generated very little or no sales within the estimation period.

The average level of market concentration is 34.52. This average indi-

Table 4.1   *Summary statistics: corporate governance, market concentration and R&D expenditures*

Variable	Observation	Mean	Std. Dev.	Min.	Max.
Log (R&D/Sales)	5724	−6.12	5.35	−19.86	7.09
Log(R&D/Employees)	5724	−0.41	5.30	−14.56	8.50
Log (R&D Exp.)	5724	10.54	1.80	2.89	16.06
Herfindahl-Hirschman Index (HHI) (0–100)	5724	34.52	23.80	5.80	100.00
HHI_Squared	5724	1758.12	2367.64	33.59	10000.00
Board Indep. (Dummy)	5724	0.91	0.28	0.00	1.00
Board_Indep.*HHI	5724	31.61	24.84	0.00	100.00
Women Directors (#)	5724	0.92	0.97	0.00	6.00
Women_Dir*HHI	5724	34.34	49.27	0.00	342.22
Merger Vote (%)	5724	53.53	6.41	0.00	95.00
Merger_Vote*HHI	5724	1854.94	1304.34	0.00	7992.84
Insider Share (%)	5724	14.13	18.83	0.00	97.43
Insider_Share*HHI	5724	477.00	839.70	0.00	8771.00
Inst. Maj. (Dummy)	5724	0.67	0.47	0.00	1.00
Inst_Maj*HHI	5724	23.33	25.69	0.00	100.00
Charter Vote (%)	5724	51.96	4.50	0.00	80.00
Charter_Vote*HHI	5724	1794.73	1243.80	0.00	6606.17
Company Age (Years)	5724	37.63	36.52	0.00	207.00
Log (Market Cap.)	5724	20.86	1.70	15.16	26.88
Returns on Assets (%)	5724	2.07	18.04	−187.01	157.88
Tobin's_Q (Ratio)	5724	1.52	1.33	0.02	28.25
L-T Debt / Capital (Log)	5724	2.32	1.71	−0.19	7.43

cates low level of market concentration but it is associated with a large standard deviation of 23.8 and hence a wide range from 5.8 to 100. As can be seen in Figure 4.1, market concentration tends to have a long tail to the right, with the majority of the firm-year observations below the average of 34.52.

With respect to CG characteristics, the following observations can be made. First, 91 per cent of the companies have independent boards whilst institutional owners own the majority of the shares in 67 per cent of the companies over the estimation period. The number of women directors is less than one (0.92) on average, with a range from zero to six. This indicates low level of female representation on the board as the average board size is 8.7 directors, with a range from zero to 19. The percentage of votes required to approve a merger and amend company charter is 53.53 and 51.96 per cent on average, respectively. A detailed analysis of these

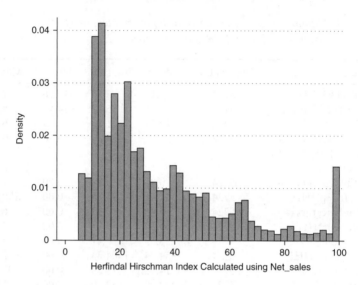

Figure 4.1   Distribution of the Herfindahl-Hirschman index

percentages indicates that the percentage of votes required to approve a merger is 51 per cent minimum and increases up to 95 per cent in the full sample. The percentage of votes required to amend company charter, on the other hand, is 51 per cent minimum and increases up to 80 per cent. These summary statistics indicate that merger approval or company charter amendments require the consent of the majority of the shareholders at a minimum. Finally, the minimum share of insiders is 14.13 per cent on average, with the share increasing to 45 per cent or higher in the top 10 per cent of the distribution.

Table 4.2 presents the estimation results based on the ratio of R&D expenditures to sales. The results are derived from two-way cluster-robust estimation, with clusters consisting of firms and years.

The results indicate that five CG dimensions (percentage of votes required to approve a merger, number of female directors on the board, percentage of insider and institutional ownership and percentage of votes required to amend company charter) are related negatively to the R&D/Sales ratio. Only board independence is positively related to the R&D/Sales ratio. The coefficients are statistically significant and robust to inclusion of market concentration and firm characteristics. The F-statistics are large and associated with p-values of less than 0.01, indicating overall significance at less than 1 per cent. The R-squared varies between 12 and 14 per cent. These values are relatively low, but the R-squared is known to

Table 4.2 Corporate governance, market structure and innovation: estimation results

Dependent variable: **R&D/sales ratio**

	(1)	(2)	(3)	(4)	(5)	(6)
Board Ind	1.4974**					
	(0.5968)					
Board Ind * HHI	0.0195**					
	(0.0098)					
Merger Vote		−0.1446***				
		(0.0423)				
Merger Vote*HHI		0.0029***				
		(0.0008)				
Women Director			−0.8434***			
			(0.2564)			
Women Dir*HHI			0.0124**			
			(0.0055)			
Insider Share				−0.0366***		
				(0.0128)		
Insider Share*HHI				−0.0004		
				(0.0003)		
Institution Maj.					−0.6871**	
					(0.3486)	
Institution Maj*HHI					0.0357***	
					(0.0090)	
Charter Vote						−0.1168***
						(0.0361)
Charter Vote*HHI						0.0019**
						(0.0008)

Table 4.2 (continued)

	(1)	(2)	(3)	(4)	(5)	(6)
HHI*100	-0.0754***	-0.2151***	-0.0604***	-0.0457**	-0.0784***	-0.1562***
	(0.0222)	(0.0488)	(0.0207)	(0.0206)	(0.0208)	(0.0444)
HHI*100_Sqd.	0.0006***	0.0006***	0.0005***	0.0005***	0.0006***	0.0006***
	(0.0002)	(0.0002)	(0.0002)	(0.0002)	(0.0002)	(0.0002)
Turning point at HHI=	**66.50**	**161.83**	**60.50**	**44.30**	**65.92**	**118.83**
Comp. Age	-0.0048	-0.0024	-0.0025	-0.0044	-0.0051	-0.0034
	(0.0038)	(0.0041)	(0.0040)	(0.0040)	(0.0041)	(0.0042)
Log(Market Cap)	0.0356	0.0508	0.1438	-0.0770	0.0336	0.0650
	(0.0967)	(0.0940)	(0.0997)	(0.1001)	(0.0992)	(0.0955)
Return on Assets	-0.0558***	-0.0571***	-0.0586***	-0.0542***	-0.0580***	-0.0582***
	(0.0050)	(0.0051)	(0.0048)	(0.0047)	(0.0046)	(0.0051)
Tobin's Q	0.4241**	0.4367***	0.4418***	0.4799***	0.4612***	0.4381***
	(0.1664)	(0.1646)	(0.1616)	(0.1768)	(0.1734)	(0.1678)
LT Debt / Capital	-0.6013***	-0.5683***	-0.5383***	-0.5687***	-0.5659***	-0.5820***
	(0.0799)	(0.0859)	(0.0913)	(0.0872)	(0.0925)	(0.0864)
Constant	-6.2551***	2.3462	-6.8335***	-2.3267	-4.5789**	0.4318
	(1.7784)	(3.0314)	(1.9012)	(1.9442)	(1.8565)	(2.6713)
Observations	4606	5328	5629	5611	5629	5332
R−squared	0.14	0.12	0.12	0.14	0.12	0.12
Model d.f.	9	9	9	9	9.0000	9.0000
F-statistic	82.65	84.57	82.95	97.06	83.68	80.82
Firm clusters	1498	1482	1503	1495	1503	1482
Year clusters	7	7	7	7	7	7

Notes: Two-way cluster-robust standard errors in brackets. ***, **, * indicates significance at 1%, 5% and 10% respectively. All independent variables are lagged by one year.

be an inefficient measure of model performance when the models are non-linear (Spiess and Neumeyer, 2010) – which is the case here.

However, these partial effects must be combined with interactive effects, which are captured by the multiplicative terms that include CG indicators and the concentration ratio (HHI). The marginal effects can be calculated easily by taking partial derivatives of the R&D/sales ratio with respect to each CG indicator. The results are presented in Table 4.3.

The partial effect of board independence is positive (1.4974), indicating that the R&D/sales ratio in firms with independent boards is approximately 1.5 times the ratio for the firms without. This finding contradicts the prediction of the agency theory that independent boards deter innovation as a result of strict monitoring and shifting the risk of innovation on to risk-averse managers (Baysinger and Hoskisson, 1990; Baysinger et al., 1991; Hill and Snell, 1988; Zahra, 1996). However, our finding lends support to empirical studies that report that independent boards encourage long-term investment as a means of maximizing firm value for shareholders (Dong and Gou, 2010; Chen and Hsu, 2009).

Yet, in the presence of interaction effects, the partial effect provides inadequate information about the relationship between board independence and R&D intensity. The marginal effect, which takes into account the interaction between board independence and market concentration, is 2.17 at the sample average for market concentration. Stated differently, firms with independent boards and in markets with higher concentration ratios have higher levels of R&D intensity compared to their peers within less concentrated markets. This finding implies that independent boards are more likely to encourage innovation when markets are more concentrated and hence managerial slack is more likely.

Two dynamics could be driving this complementarity between market power and board independence. On the one hand, independent boards may be effective in exerting discipline that may be necessary to reduce managerial slack in highly concentrated markets. On the other hand, they may be more effective in aligning managerial and shareholder interests as the level of concentration (and hence the scope for securing post-innovation profits) increases. In the former case, independent boards perform as a disciplining device. In the latter case, they perform as honest brokers that distribute the post-innovation profits between managers and shareholders in concentrated markets. In this latter case, independent boards act as anchors that encourage managers to commit to long term goals in return for better pay. This role is facilitated by the probability of higher post-innovation profits in more concentrated firms.

With respect to board diversity, our results indicate that the presence of women directors on the board is related negatively to firms' R&D inten-

Table 4.3   Marginal effects of corporate governance (CG) dimensions on R&D/sales ratio

Marginal effect	Marginal effect at sample mean HHI = 34.52	Market concentration (HHI): complementary or offsetting?
$\dfrac{\partial\,lnrd\_sales}{\partial\,Board\_indeep} = 1.4974 + 0.0195 * HHI$	$1.497+0.0195(34.52) = 2.17$	Complementary
$\dfrac{\partial\,lnrd\_sales}{\partial\,Merger\_vote} = -0.1446 + 0.0029 * HHI$	$-0.1446+0.0029(34.52) = -0.0445$	Offsetting
$\dfrac{\partial\,lnrd\_sales}{\partial\,Women\_dir} = -0.8434 + 0.0124 * HHI$	$-0.8434+0.0124(34.52) = -0.4154$	Offsetting
$\dfrac{\partial\,lnrd\_sales}{\partial\,Insid\_share} = -0.0366 + Insignificant$	Interaction term insignificant	Neither
$\dfrac{\partial\,lnrd\_sales}{\partial\,Inst\_Maj} = -0.6871 + 0.0357 * HHI$	$-0.6871+0.0357(34.52) = 0.5453$	Offsetting
$\dfrac{\partial\,lnrd\_sales}{\partial\,Charter\_vote} = -0.1168 + 0.0019 * HHI$	$-0.1168+0.0019(34.52) = -0.0512$	Offsetting

sity; but the negative relationship is attenuated as the level of market concentration increases. At the sample average for market concentration, the magnitude of the marginal effect of female representation (-0.4154) is less than half of the partial effect (-0.8434). Hence, the level of market concentration acts as a substitute that offsets the negative effect of female directors on R&D intensity. The negative marginal effect at the sample average contradicts the findings that report a positive relationship between women directors and innovation (Miller and del Carmen Triana, 2009). Instead, it indicates that concerns about token representation of women may be the cause for the negative relationship between the number of female directors and innovation effort (Torchia et al., 2011). Recall that, the average number of female directors in the sample is less than one, whereas the average board size is approximately nine directors. However, at high levels of concentration (at HHI levels over 68), the marginal effect of female representation is positive. This sign reversal strengthens the argument that female representation on the boards is below the critical threshold required for genuine diversity. This is because the positive marginal effect of female representation in highly concentrated industry firms is likely to be subsumed under the positive effect of market concentration on R&D intensity at the high end of the market concentration spectrum. The non-linear (U-shaped) relationship between R&D intensity and market concentration is discussed below.

The strength of anti-merger defences is negatively related to R&D intensity in our sample; but the adverse effect tends to diminish as the level of market concentration increases. The partial effect is –0.1446 and the marginal effect at the sample average of market concentration is –0.0445. This finding contradicts those reported by Shleifer and Summers (1988), Stein (1988), Pugh et al. (1999) and Maher and Andersson (2002). The evidence in our sample indicates that stronger anti-merger defences do not induce managers to innovate. On the contrary, it indicates that stronger anti-merger defences encourage managerial slack (Jensen, 1988; Johnson and Rao, 1997). Our finding is compatible with Atanassov (2012), who reports that the relationship between anti-takeover defences and innovation is negative across US states and that the negative effect is mediated through product-market competition. In our sample, the offsetting effect of market concentration is the driver of the non-monotonic relationship between anti-merger defences and innovation. Indeed at HHI values greater than 50, the marginal effect of anti-merger defences on R&D intensity becomes positive. This is because at high levels of market concentration the scope for securing positive post-innovation profits increases and this dominates the relationship between anti-merger defences and innovation effort.

The percentage of shares owned by insiders is negatively related to R&D

intensity, but the interaction term is insignificant. The negative partial effect is in line with Choi et al. (2011) who report that insider ownership leads to lower innovation performance by Chinese firms; and Herrmann et al. (2010) who also report that insider ownership is negatively related to R&D intensity of US-listed firms. The insignificant coefficient on the interaction term is informative because it indicates that the negative effect of insider ownership is not mediated through market concentration and is driven mainly by risk aversion of over-involved insiders (Herrmann et al., 2010).

The relationship between institutional ownership and R&D intensity is negative (−0.6871) and the interactive effect is offsetting, leading to a marginal effect of +0.5453 at the sample average of concentration. This finding contradicts Aghion et al. (2009), who report that institutional owners reduce the career risk faced by managers and induce the latter to innovate. However, the finding is compatible with Bushee (1998), Kochhar and David (1996) and Zahra (1996) who demonstrate that the effect of institutional ownership on innovation depends on the time horizons of the institutional shareholders. It also lends support to Hill and Snell (1988) and Graves (1988) who report that institutional shareholders tend to induce managers to secure high short-term profits at the expense of long-term projects such as investment in innovation. However, the evidence in our sample also indicates that the negative relationship between institutional ownership and innovation holds only at low levels of market concentration (i.e, at high levels of competition). Indeed, the sign of the marginal effect is reversed at HHI values greater than 19. The sign reversal indicates that institutional shareholders are more likely to support innovation when the firm is in a position to extract rent – i.e., when market concentration increases beyond a minimum threshold. Therefore, the positive relationship between institutional investors and innovation reported by Aghion et al. (2009) may be dominated by the level of market concentration in their sample.

Finally, the partial effect of reduced shareholders' rights on the R&D/ sales ratio is negative (−0.1163) and market concentration has an offsetting effect, leading to a marginal effect of −0.0512 at the average level of concentration in the sample. This finding contradicts those reported by Bargeron et al. (2010) and Cohen et al. (2009), who argue that *increased* shareholder rights tend to discourage risk taking and reduce innovation effort. It also contradicts the findings of studies that report that the Sarbanes-Oxley Act has had a negative effect on innovation as a result of increased shareholders' rights and external monitoring (Shadab, 2008; Bargeron et al., 2010; Cohen et al., 2009). However, the effect is mediated through market concentration. The evidence in the sample indicates that

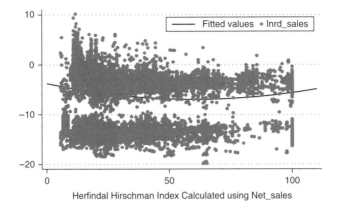

Figure 4.2   Market concentration and R&D/sales ratio for US listed firms: a U-shaped relationship

the marginal effect of reduced shareholders' rights becomes positive at HHI values of 62 and over.

Other results in Table 4.2 also indicate that the relationship between market concentration and R&D intensity is non-linear (U-shaped). This is in line with Aghion et al. (2002a, 2005) who establish an inverted-U relationship between competition and innovation. The U-shaped relationship in our sample (see Figure 4.2) suggests that an increase in market concentration is conducive to a fall in the R&D/sales ratio when the initial level of innovation is lower than the turning point of the parabolic curve. When the initial level of concentration is higher than the turning points indicated in Table 4.2, an increase in market concentration leads to an increase in the R&D/sales ratio.

The non-linear relationship implies that the marginal effects of market concentration on the R&D/sales ratio depends on the levels of market concentration and CG indicators – as indicated in Table 4.4. Given the positive coefficient on the interaction terms, CG indicators have an offsetting effect on the relationship between concentration and innovation when market concentration is below the turning point of the parabolic curve but a complementary effect thereafter.

The non-linear relationship between market concentration and the R&D/sales ratio can be explained as follows: when market concentration increases from a low initial level, the disciplining effect of product-market competition on managers is reduced and this leads to managerial slack. At the same time, the increase in market concentration from a low initial level does not guarantee positive post-innovation profits as market power is still low. The combination of both dynamics leads to lower innovation

Table 4.4   Marginal effects of market concentration on R&D/sales ratio

Marginal effect		CG dimensions: complementary or offsetting?
$\dfrac{\partial lnrd\_sales}{\partial HHI}$	$= -0.0754 + 0.0012 * HHI + 0.0195 * Board\_indep.$	Offsetting until the turning point, complementary thereafter
$\dfrac{\partial lnrd\_sales}{\partial HHI}$	$= -0.2151 + 0.0012 * HHI + 0.0029 * Merger\_vote$	Offsetting throughout HHI range of $0 - 100^{+}$
$\dfrac{\partial lnrd\_sales}{\partial HHI}$	$= -0.0604 + 0.001 * HHI + 0.0124 * Woman\_dir$	Offsetting until the turning point, complementary thereafter
$\dfrac{\partial lnrd\_sales}{\partial HHI}$	$= -0.0457 + 0.001 * HHI + $ Insignificant	Neither
$\dfrac{\partial lnrd\_sales}{\partial IHHI}$	$= -0.0784 + 0.0012 * HHI + 0.0357 * Inst\_Majority$	Offsetting until the turning point, complementary thereafter
$\dfrac{\partial lnrd\_sales}{\partial HHI}$	$= -0.1562 + 0.0012 * HHI + 0.0019 * Charter\_vote$	Offsetting throughout HHI range of $0–100^{+}$

Note: [+] The turning points are above the maximum level of $HHI = 100$ when the model is estimated with the percentage of votes required to approve mergers or to amend company charter (see Table 4.2).

110

effort. However, when the initial level of market concentration is high managerial slack is already high and an increase in market concentration does not necessarily imply further deterioration in market discipline. In addition, the scope for extracting post-innovation rents is higher when the initial level of market concentration is already high. Hence, at higher levels of market concentration an increase in the latter is more likely to be conducive to higher innovation effort by managers.

Given this setting, CG rules tend to offset the negative effect of market concentration on the R&D/sales when market concentration increases from a low initial level. At low initial levels of market concentration, CG rules offset the negative effects of increased concentration either by imposing discipline on managers (as it may be the case when the board is independent or a small number of institutional investors own the majority of the shares) or by aligning the interests of the managers with shareholders (as it may be the case when boards are independent) or by reducing the career concerns of the risk-averse managers (as it may be the case when anti-merger defences are strong and or shareholder rights are weak). When the initial levels of market concentration are higher than the values implied by the turning points, CG rules tend to have a complementary effect on the R&D/sales ratio. This is because, at high initial levels of market concentration, an increase in the latter induces managers to increase their innovation efforts and this is reinforced by the disciplining or interest-aligning effects of the CG rules.

The offsetting effect of three CG dimensions continues until the Herfindahl-Hirschman Index reaches the following values: 66.5 for board independence; 60.5 for the number of female directors and 65.9 for institutional majority of share ownership (Table 4.2, turning points). At concentration levels above these turning points, the effect of market concentration on R&D intensity is positive. Therefore, above these turning points, the positive coefficient on the interaction terms imply that an increase in board independence, female representation and institutional ownership has a complementary effect on the R&D/sales ratio.

The final set of results in Table 4.2 relate to the effects of firm characteristics, which include company age, market capitalization, returns on assets, the Tobin's Q and the log of the long-term-debt/capital ratio. The effects of company age and market capitalization on the R&D/sales ratio are insignificant. The relationship between Tobin's Q and R&D intensity is positive and in line with findings reported by O'Connor and Rafferty (2012). The positive relationship indicates that an increase in Tobin's Q (i.e., an increase in the firm's market value relative to book value) increases the investment opportunities of the firm, including investment in R&D projects. The negative relationship between long-term debt and the R&D/sales ratio is in line with findings reported by Atanassov (2012) and Graham and Harvey (2001); and indicates that creditors are less likely to finance risky innovation projects or leverage reduces managerial flexibility or a combination of both. Finally, the negative relationship between returns on assets and the R&D/sales ratio is in line with findings reported by Atanassov (2012) and indicates that firms with higher returns on assets are under less pressure to innovate as a means of enhancing profitability.

CONCLUSIONS

The analysis above demonstrates that both corporate governance rules and market structure affect the firms' innovation effort. The effect of corporate governance rules depends on the extent to which the latter exert discipline on managers and/or mitigate the agency problem and align managerial and shareholder interests. On the other hand, the effect of market concentration depends on the extent to which the latter induce managerial slack and/or affect the scope for post-innovation profits. Therefore, the relationship between corporate governance and innovation should be investigated by taking full account of the partial and interactive effects of market structure on innovation. Otherwise, the estimates would be inaccurate due to model misspecification bias.

In this chapter, we have addressed this source of bias and calculated the marginal effects of both corporate governance dimensions and market concentration on R&D/sales ratio. Our findings indicate that the partial effects on innovation effort are negative when CG rules relate to anti-takeover defences, insider and institutional ownership, number of women directors within boards, and reduction in shareholder rights; but these partial effects are subject to interaction effects caused by market concentration. With the exception of insider ownership concentration where the coefficient of the interaction term is insignificant, the marginal effects of four CG dimensions (institutional ownership, anti-takeover defences, female representation within boards, and reduced shareholder rights) on the R&D/sales ratio become weaker as the level of market concentration increases. These results are driven by the scope for higher post-innovation rents as the level of market concentration increases. We have also established that higher levels of market concentration complement the positive partial effect of board independence on the R&D effort.

Our findings confirm the existence of a non-linear relationship between market structure and innovation; but they also indicate that the effects of market structure on the R&D effort are mediated through corporate governance regimes adopted by the firms. Hence, five CG dimensions (board independence, institutional ownership, anti-takeover defences, female representation within boards, and reduced shareholder rights) offset the negative effects of market concentration on the innovation effort before the turning points of the U-shaped innovation curve; but they complement the positive effects thereafter. With respect to three CG dimensions (board independence, institutional ownership and number of female directors on the board) the turning point is within the range of market concentration index; but it is beyond the range in the case of two CG dimensions (percentage of votes required to approve a merger and amend company charter). The offsetting effects of CG rules are due to their disciplining effects and/or interest alignment effects on managers.

These findings indicate that the effects of CG rules and those of the market structure on innovation effort are non-monotonic: whilst the effects of CG rules are mediated through market concentration, the effects of the latter are mediated through CG rules. The policy and research implications of these findings can be summarized as follows: (i) the agency theory does not provide adequate guidance about the relationship between various CG dimensions and innovation because it does not have an explicit assumption about the level of market concentration (or product-market competition), nor does it analyse how CG rules and different levels of market concentration may interact in their effects on innovation; (ii) hence the predictions of agency theory are often contradicted by empirical findings and such contradictions are likely to be driven by different levels of competition that characterize the markets of the firms within different samples; (iii) the effects of CG rules tend to contradict the predictions of agency theory when market concentration is low and this is because at low levels of market concentration (i.e., at high levels of product-market competition) CG rules act as substitutes for market discipline; and (iv) hence CG rules ameliorate the deadweight losses associated with market concentration and innovation only when the levels of concentration are already low, but exacerbates the deadweight losses when the initial levels of market concentration are high. Given these findings, it can be argued that firms adopt CG rules endogenously, either to ameliorate the negative effects of market concentration on innovation or to bolster the latter's positive effects on innovation.

NOTES

1. We have used the *Stata* procedure produced by Mitchell Petersen to run two-way cluster-robust regressions with panel data. See:http://www.kellogg.northwestern.edu/faculty/petersen/htm/papers/se/se_programming.htm.

2. We have estimated model (4.4) with contemporaneous explanatory variables as well. The results are not presented here due to space limitation, but they are similar to the results with lagged estimation and can be provided on request.
3. The Corporate Library has merged with Governance Metrics International in 2010. Information on CG indicators provided by GMI can be obtained from http://www3. gmiratings.com/solutions/methodology/. For information on Datastream, see http:// online.thomsonreuters.com/datastream/.

REFERENCES

Aghion, P., M. Dewatripont, and P. Rey (1999), 'Competition, financial discipline and growth', *The Review of Economic Studies*, 66(4): 825–852.

Aghion, P., N. Bloom, R. Blundell, R. Griffith and P. Howitt (2002a), 'Competition and innovation: an inverted-U relationship', *National Bureau of Economic Research Working Papers*, no. w9269.

Aghion, P., W. Carlin, and M. Schaffer (2002b), 'Competition, innovation and growth in transition: exploring the interactions between policies', William Davidson Working Paper, No. 501, http://papers.ssrn.com/sol3/papers. cfm?abstract_id=311407, accessed on 12 March 2012.

Aghion, P., N. Bloom, R. Blundell, R. Griffith, P. Howitt (2005), 'Competition and innovation: an inverted-U relationship, *Quarterly Journal of Economics*, 120(2): 701–728.

Aghion, P., J. van Reenen, and L. Zingales (2009), 'Innovation and institutional ownership', Centre for Economic Performance, Discussion Paper No 911 (February), accessed on 11 January 2012, at http://cep.lse.ac.uk/pubs/download/ dp0911.pdf

Arrow, K.J. (1962), 'Economic welfare and the allocation of resources to invention', in Universities National Bureau (ed.), *The Rate and Direction of Inventive Activity: Economic and Social Factors*, UMI, pp. 609–626.

Atanassov, J. (2012), 'Do hostile takeovers stifle innovation? Evidence from anti-takeover legislation and corporate patenting', *Journal of Finance*, forthcoming. Also available at http://papers.ssrn.com/sol3/papers.cfm?abstract_id=967421

Bargeron, L., K. Lehn and C.J. Zutter (2010), 'Sarbanes-Oxley and corporate risk-taking', *Journal of Accounting and Economics*, 49(1): 34–52.

Baysinger, B. and R.E. Hoskisson (1990), 'The composition of boards of directors and strategic control', *Academy of Management Review*, 15(1): 72–88.

Baysinger, B.D., R.D. Kosnik and T.A. Turk (1991), 'Effects of board and ownership structure on corporate R&D strategy', *Academy of Management Journal*, 34(1): 205–214.

Belloc, F. (2011), 'Corporate governance and innovation: a survey', *Journal of Economic Surveys*, doi: 10.1111/j.1467-6419.2011.00681.x

Belloc, F. (2012), 'Corporate governance and innovation: a survey', *Journal of Economic Surveys*, 26(5), 835–864.

Berubé, C., M. Duhamel and D. Ershov (2012), 'Market incentives for business innovation: results from Canada', *Journal of Industry, Competition and Trade*, 12(1), 47–65.

Bushee, B.J. (1998), 'The influence of institutional investors on myopic R&D investment behaviour', *Accounting Review*, 73(3): 305–333.

Cameron, A.C., J.B. Gelbach and D.L. Miller (2006), 'Bootstrap-based improvements for inference with clustered errors', University of California, Davis working paper, no. 06–21.

Chen, H.L. and W.T. Hsu (2009), 'Family ownership, board independence, and R&D investment', *Family Business Review*, 22(4): 347–362.

Choi, S.B., S.H. Lee and C. Williams (2011), 'Ownership and firm innovation in a transition economy: evidence from China', *Research Policy*, 40(3): 441–452.

Cohen, D., A. Deys and T. Lys (2009), 'The Sarbanes-Oxley Act of 2002: implications for compensation contracts and managerial risk-taking', unpublished working paper, New York University Stern School of Business.

De Massis, A., F. Frattini and U. Lichtenthaler (2012), 'Research on technological innovation in family firms: present debates and future directions', *Family Business Review* (forthcoming), ISSN: 0894-4865. DOI: 10.1177/0894486512466258.

Dong, J. and Y. Gou (2010), 'Corporate governance structure, managerial discretion, and the R&D investment in China', *International Review of Economics and Finance*, 19(2): 180–188.

Erhardt, N.L., J.D. Werbel and C.B. Schrader (2003), 'Board of director diversity and firm financial performance', *Corporate Governance: An International Review*, 11(2): 102–111.

Fama, E.F. and J.D. MacBeth (1973), 'Risk, return, and equilibrium: empirical tests', *Journal of Political Economy*, 81(3): 607–636.

Ganzach, Y. (1997), 'Misleading interaction and curvilinear terms', *Psychological Methods*, 2(3): 235–247.

Gilbert, R. (2006), 'Looking for Mr. Schumpeter: where are we in the competition-innovation debate?', in Adam B. Jaffe, Josh Lerner and Scott Stern (eds), *Innovation Policy and the Economy – Volume 6*, Cambridge, Mass.: MIT Press, pp. 159–215.

Gilbert, R. and D. Newbery (1982), 'Preemptive patenting and the persistence of monopoly', *American Economic Review*, 72(2): 514–526.

Gompers, P., J. Ishii and A. Metrick (2003), 'Corporate governance and equity prices', *The Quarterly Journal of Economics*, 118(1): 107–156.

Gow, I.D., G. Ormazabal and D. Taylor (2010), 'Correcting for cross-sectional and time-series dependence in accounting research', *The Accounting Review*, 85(2): 483–512.

Graham, J., and C. Harvey (2001), 'The theory and practice of corporate finance: evidence from the field', *Journal of Financial Economics*, 60(2): 187–243

Graves, S.B. (1988), 'Institutional ownership and corporate R&D in the computer industry', *Academy of Management Journal*, 31(2): 417–428.

Grosfeld, I. and T. Tressel (2002), 'Competition and ownership structure: substitutes or complements? Evidence from the Warsaw Stock Exchange', *The Economics of Transition*, 10(3): 525–551.

Herrmann, P., J. Kaufmann and H. van Auken (2010), 'The role of corporate governance in R&D intensity of US-based international firms', *International Journal of Commerce and Management*, 20(2): 91–108.

Hill, C.W.L. and S.A. Snell (1988), 'External control, corporate strategy, and firm performance in research-intensive industries', *Strategic Management Journal*, 9(6): 577–590.

Hill, C.W., and S.A. Snell (1989), 'Effects of ownership structure and control on corporate productivity', *Academy of Management Journal*, 32(1): 25–46.

Honoré, F., F. Munari and B. van Pottelsberghe de la Potterie (2011), 'Corporate governance practices and companies' R&D orientation: evidence from European countries', Bruegel Working Paper 2011/01, 24 January 2011. http://aei.pitt.edu/15489/1/110124_WP_CORPORATE_GOVERNANCE_PRACTICES.pdf

Jensen, M. (1988), 'Takeovers: causes and consequences', *Journal of Economic Perspectives*, 2(1): 21–48.

Johnson, M.S. and R.P. Rao (1997), 'The impact of antitakeover amendments on corporate financial performance', *Financial Review*, 32(3): 659–690.

Kim J., I. Krinsky and J. Lee (1997), 'Institutional holdings and trading volume reactions to quarterly earnings announcements', *Journal of Accounting, Auditing & Finance*, 12(1): 1–14.

Klapper, L.F. and I. Love (2004), 'Corporate governance, investor protection, and performance in emerging markets', *Journal of Corporate Finance*, 10(5): 703–728.

Kochhar, R. and P. David (1996), 'Institutional investors and firm innovation: a test of competing hypotheses', *Strategic Management Journal*, 17(1): 73–84.

Lang, M. and M. McNichols (1997), 'Institutional trading and corporate performance', Research Paper no. 1460, Graduate School of Business Research, Stanford University, Stanford, CA.

Maher, M. and T. Andersson (2002), 'Corporate governance: effects on firm performance and economic growth', in Joseph A. McCahery, Piet Moerland, Theo Raaijmakers and Luc Renneboog (eds), *Corporate Governance Regimes: Convergence and Diversity*, Oxford: Oxford University Press, pp. 386–419.

Miller, T., and M. del Carmen Triana (2009), 'Demographic diversity in the boardroom: mediators of the board diversity–firm performance relationship', *Journal of Management Studies*, 46(5): 755–786.

Munari, F., R. Oriani and M. Sobrero (2010), 'The effects of owner identity and external governance systems on R&D investments: a study of Western European firms', *Research Policy*, 39(8): 1093–1104.

Newey, W.K. and K.D. West (1987), 'A simple, positive semi-definite, heteroskedasticity and autocorrelation consistent covariance matrix', *Econometrica*, 55(3), 703–708.

O'Connor, M. and M. Rafferty (2012), 'Corporate governance and innovation', *Journal of Financial and Quantitative Analysis*, 47(2): 397–413.

Peneder, M. (2012), 'Competition and innovation: revisiting the inverted-U relationship', *Journal of Industry, Competition and Trade*, 12(1): 1–5.

Peroni, C. and I.S. Gomes Ferreira (2012), 'Competition and innovation in Luxembourg', *Journal of Industry, Competition and Trade*, 12(1): 93–117.

Petersen, M.A. (2007), 'Estimating standard errors in finance panel data sets: comparing approaches', *Review of Financial Studies*, 22(1): 435–480.

Polder, M. and E. Veldhuizen (2012), 'Innovation and competition in the Netherlands: testing the inverted U for industries and firms', *Journal of Industry, Competition and Trade*, 12(1): 67–91.

Potter, G. (1992), 'Accounting earnings announcements, institutional investor concentration and common stock returns', *Journal of Accounting Research*, 30(1): 146–155.

Pugh, W.N., J.S. Jahera and S. Oswald (1999), 'ESOPs, takeover protection, and corporate decision making', *Journal of Economics and Finance*, 48(5): 1985–99.

Reinganum, J.F. (1983), 'Uncertain innovation and the persistence of monopoly', *American Economic Review*, 73(4): 741–748.

Reinganum, J.F. (1985), 'Innovation and industry evolution', *Quarterly Journal of Economics*, 100(1): 81–99.

Sapra, H., A. Subramanian and K. Subramanian (2009), 'Corporate governance and innovation: theory and evidence', Discussion paper published in *Corporate Governance and Capital Markets Ideas*, edited by the Chicago Booth School of Business. http://faculty.chicagobooth.edu/haresh.sapra/docs_WP/GI_01Oct09_SSRN.pdf

Schumpeter, Joseph A. (1934), *The Theory of Economic Development*, Cambridge, MA: Harvard University Press. (First published in German, 1912).

Schumpeter, Joseph A. (1942), *Capitalism, Socialism, and Democracy*, New York: Harper and Brothers. (Harper Colophon edition, 1976.)

Shadab, A. (2008), 'Innovation and corporate governance: the impact of Sarbanes-Oxley', *University of Pennsylvania Journal of Business and Employment Law*, 10(4), 954–1008.

Shleifer, A. and L. Summers (1988), 'Breach of trust in hostile takeovers', in Alan J. Auerbach (ed.), *Corporate Takeovers: Causes and Consequences*, Chicago: University of Chicago Press, pp. 33–56.

Spiess, A.N. and N. Neumeyer (2010), 'An evaluation of R^2 as an inadequate measure for nonlinear models in pharmacological and biochemical research: a Monte Carlo approach', *BMC Pharmacology*, 10(1): 6.

Stein, J.C. (1988), 'Takeover threats and managerial myopia', *The Journal of Political Economy*, 96(1): 61–80.

Thompson, S.B. (2006), 'Simple formulas for standard errors that cluster by both firm and time', Available at SSRN: http://ssrn.com/abstract=914002.

Torchia, M., A. Calabrò and M. Huse (2011), 'Women directors on corporate boards: from tokenism to critical mass', *Journal of Business Ethics*, 102(2): 299–317.

Watson, W.E., K. Kumar and L.K. Michaelson (1993), 'Cultural diversity's impact on interaction process and performance: comparing homogeneous and diverse task groups', *Academy of Management Journal*, 36(3): 590–602.

Zahra, S.A. (1996), 'Governance, ownership, and corporate entrepreneurship: the moderating impact of industry technological opportunities', *Academy of Management Journal*, 39(6): 1713–1735.

APPENDIX

Table 4A.1   Corporate governance, market structure and innovation: R&D/employees ratio as dependent variable

	(1)	(2)	(3)	(4)	(5)	(6)
Board Ind.	2.0460*** (0.7888)					
Board Ind * HHI	0.0140 (0.0191)					
Merger Vote		-0.1443*** (0.0473)				
Merger Vote*HHI		0.0027*** (0.0009)				
Women Director			-0.8329*** (0.2993)			
Women Dir*HHI			0.0116* (0.0061)			
Insider Pct.				-0.0527*** (0.0155)		
Insider Pct*HHI				-0.0002 (0.0003)		
Institution Maj.					-0.5718 (0.3805)	
Institution Maj*HHI					0.0385*** (0.0086)	
Charter Vote						-0.1226*** (0.0416)

	(1)	(2)	(3)	(4)	(5)	(6)
Charter Vote*HHI						0.0019**
						(0.0008)
HHI*100	-0.0708***	-0.2034***	-0.0591**	-0.0491**	-0.0810***	-0.1550***
	(0.0273)	(0.0555)	(0.0239)	(0.0234)	(0.0237)	(0.0468)
HHI*100_Sqd.	0.0006***	0.0007***	0.0006**	0.0006***	0.0006***	0.0006***
	(0.0002)	(0.0002)	(0.0002)	(0.0002)	(0.0002)	(0.0002)
[Turning point]	[59.00]	[145.29]	[49.25]	[40.92]	[67.50]	[129.17]
Comp. Age	-0.0039	-0.0013	-0.0013	-0.0024	-0.0039	-0.0024
	(0.0042)	(0.0044)	(0.0043)	(0.0043)	(0.0044)	(0.0044)
Log(Market Cap)	0.0329	0.0285	0.1200	-0.1304	-0.0070	0.0428
	(0.1033)	(0.1095)	(0.1118)	(0.1061)	(0.1079)	(0.1094)
Return on Assets	-0.0416***	-0.0439***	-0.0446***	-0.0409***	-0.0443***	-0.0451***
	(0.0059)	(0.0063)	(0.0067)	(0.0064)	(0.0066)	(0.0065)
Tobin's_Q	0.8393***	0.8617***	0.8283***	0.9020***	0.8648***	0.8706***
	(0.0928)	(0.0923)	(0.0961)	(0.0924)	(0.0961)	(0.0915)
LT Debt / Capital	-0.4427***	-0.4047***	-0.3750***	-0.4174***	-0.4047***	-0.4185***
	(0.0852)	(0.0871)	(0.0857)	(0.0808)	(0.0848)	(0.0871)
Constant	2.4686	11.9130***	2.8216	8.0848***	5.3530**	10.2823***
	(2.2472)	(3.6420)	(2.3366)	(2.1995)	(2.2433)	(3.0784)
Observations	3707	4443	4712	4705	4712	4443
R-squared	0.12	0.11	0.10	0.13	0.11	0.11
Model d.f.	9	9	9	9	9	9
F-statistic	61.66	66.89	64.10	76.58	67.53	63.02
Firm clusters	1275	1271	1284	1283	1284	1271
Year clusters	7	7	7	7	7	7

Notes: Two-way cluster-robust standard errors in brackets. ***, **, * indicates significance at 1%, 5% and 10% respectively. All independent variables are lagged by one year.

Table 4A.2   Corporate governance, market structure and innovation: log(R&D expenditures) as dependent variable

	(1)	(2)	(3)	(4)	(5)	(6)
Board Ind.	1.0934**					
	(0.4708)					
Board Ind * HHI	0.0278**					
	(0.0113)					
Merger Vote		−0.1139***				
		(0.0415)				
Merger Vote*HHI		0.0024***				
		(0.0008)				
Women Director			−0.6495***			
			(0.2409)			
Women Dir*HHI			0.0124**			
			(0.0051)			
Insider Pct.				−0.0352***		
				(0.0120)		
Insider Pct*HHI				−0.0005*		
				(0.0002)		
Institution Maj.					−0.3028	
					(0.3089)	
Institution Maj*HHI					0.0342***	
					(0.0078)	
Charter Vote						−0.1024**
						(0.0416)
Charter Vote*HHI						0.0016*
						(0.0008)

HHI	-0.0570***	-0.1546***	-0.0348*	-0.0174	-0.0489**	-0.1116**
	(0.0217)	(0.0498)	(0.0203)	(0.0199)	(0.0208)	(0.0460)
HHI_Squared.	0.0004**	0.0004**	0.0003*	0.0003*	0.0004*	0.0004**
	(0.0002)	(0.0002)	(0.0002)	(0.0002)	(0.0002)	(0.0002)
[Turning point]	[71.25]	[193.25]	[58.33]	[29.00]	[62.50]	[137.50]
Comp. Age	0.0001	0.0024	0.0020	0.0010	0.0000	0.0017
	(0.0037)	(0.0039)	(0.0038)	(0.0038)	(0.0038)	(0.0039)
Log(Market Cap)	0.8068***	0.8245***	0.8640***	0.6727***	0.7747***	0.8310***
	(0.0853)	(0.0912)	(0.0935)	(0.0881)	(0.0889)	(0.0913)
Return on Assets	-0.0366***	-0.0365***	-0.0370***	-0.0342***	-0.0374***	-0.0373***
	(0.0046)	(0.0050)	(0.0051)	(0.0050)	(0.0051)	(0.0051)
Tobin's_Q	0.2829***	0.3164***	0.3153***	0.3665***	0.3437***	0.3200***
	(0.0962)	(0.0983)	(0.0958)	(0.0965)	(0.0932)	(0.0989)
LT Debt / Capital	-0.3776***	-0.3576***	-0.3389***	-0.3559***	-0.3464***	-0.3658***
	(0.0679)	(0.0676)	(0.0675)	(0.0645)	(0.0666)	(0.0681)
Constant	-9.5287***	-3.0437	-9.5158***	-5.5731***	-7.9229***	-3.9219
	(1.7527)	(2.9863)	(1.8817)	(1.7710)	(1.8100)	(2.7988)
Observations	4694	5421	5724	5710	5724	5422
R-squared	0.11	0.11	0.10	0.13	0.11	0.10
Model d.f.	9	9	9	9	9	9
F-statistic	68.64	69.42	69.53	96.34	78.29	67.553
Firm clusters	1526	1521	1533	1527	1523	1511
Year clusters	7	7	7	7	7	7

Notes: Two-way cluster-robust standard errors in brackets. ***, **, * indicates significance at 1%, 5% and 10% respectively. All independent variables are lagged by one year.

5. Determinants of policy reforms in the fields of R&D, education and innovation: EU-27 evidence during the Lisbon Decade

Andrea Conte

INTRODUCTION

Improving the innovation performance of European economies is a major challenge for European policy makers and economic analysts. A large set of theoretical and empirical contributions in the economic literature converges on the identification of research and development (R&D) and innovation as the main drivers of economic growth, jobs and social welfare.[1] Over the past decade, also a broad consensus has developed with respect to structural reforms aimed at improving the overall employment, growth and innovation performance of Europe. These issues are at the core of the growth agenda for policy makers, so it is not surprising that many policy initiatives have been registered in the field of R&D, education and innovation at the European level and in many European Member States under the framework and objectives identified by the Lisbon Strategy (2000–10) and afterwards by the Europe 2020 Strategy (2011–20). Latest available data for the EU-27 indicates that Europe is still far from the ambitious target of devoting 3 per cent of GDP to investment in R&D – of which two-thirds is funded by businesses. Therefore, the target is now maintained as part of the renewed Europe 2020 strategy. Overall R&D spending represents 2.03 per cent of EU-27 GDP in 2011 (the latest equivalent figure is 2.87 per cent in the USA and 3.36 per cent in Japan in 2009).

Although extremely important, R&D investments represent only one part of the overall performance of the European innovation system. Indeed, education and other dimensions of innovation such as patenting activity, the number of people employed in the science and technology (S&T) sector and technology transfers represent the other two pillars of the so-called "knowledge triangle", a setting which identifies the interactions and complementarities between different policy areas in support of the broader concept of "knowledge economy". Investing in education is crucial to favoring economic development, technological adoption, a more open and inclusive society and preserving democratic and stable institutions. Innovation policy – beyond R&D – allows maximizing the economic benefit of scientific investments conducted by public and private actors while contributing to a broader diffusion of technological applications which favor economic competitiveness and increase citizens' welfare.

The European gap with the USA is even higher in terms of education expenditure. Indeed, investment in tertiary education represents only 1.3 per cent of EU-27 GDP in 2009 compared to 2.6 per cent in the USA. Although smaller, there is still a gap with respect to expenditures on general education too: 5.7 per cent of GDP in EU-27 and 7.3 per cent in the USA. Although data on other dimensions of innovation is not easily comparable across different countries, the existing evidence indicates that Europe badly needs to increase its effort in sustaining the exploitation and commercialization of its inventions. Among different policy initiatives envisaged under the Europe 2020 strategy,[2] the following are particularly emphasized: reform of the European patent system; better access to finance for young innovative companies; and strengthening of the internal market for innovation.

The current economic downturn has reinforced the idea that major reforms are needed to push Europe out of the crisis. In this context, more attention is devoted to the evaluation of policy reforms – from their design to their implementation. In order to understand the linkages between the reform effort of EU Member States and past economic performance and innovation-related activities, the European Commission and Member States are putting more effort into the monitoring and analysis of the reform process. This has led to the creation of several monitoring tools providing a unique picture of the activity of Member States in several policy areas. For instance, the European Commission's microeconomic reforms database (MICREF) and labor market reforms database (LABREF) provide systematic information on the reform measures in the field of product and labor markets adopted by European Member States. In addition, the European research database (ERAWATCH) records all reforms in the domain of R&D and other innovation activities pursued by Member States and linked to the development of the European Research Area.

By exploiting such a wealth of information, this chapter discusses the determinants of policy initiatives across EU Member States in the domain of R&D and innovation. More specifically, this analysis investigates the linkages between current reform effort and previous economic performance and reforms undertaken in each specific policy field that is identified as important for the knowledge economy in the EU. The aim is to shed light on the underlying factors and complementarities which drive reforms in the area of R&D, innovation and education. This is important since a proper understanding of the determinants of policy reform initiatives – together with the assessment of the correct policy design – is essential for supporting Member States in their reform process at maximizing economic outcomes.

This chapter seeks to extend the understanding of the influences that lead to structural reforms in the domain of the "knowledge economy". In doing so, data on R&D, education and innovation performance are matched with data on reform measures registered in the European Commission's MICREF database, which systematically records product market reforms adopted by Member States.

As a first attempt in this direction,[3] this chapter is essentially an empirical investigation into the determinants of policy reform effort in the area of R&D, education and other innovation dimensions. It controls for specific economic factors beyond the control of governments (such as business cycle) as well as some factors endogenous to the political process itself, such as the debt level or the tax burden in the economy. The empirical results can be summarized as follows: (i) there is an evident increase in the attention that European countries pay towards policy initiatives aimed at supporting the knowledge triangle, with a special emphasis on public and private R&D investment; (ii) the Member States' policy reform effort is responsive to past economic performance and performance in specific areas related to knowledge economy (R&D, education and innovation); (iii) Member States' policy measures are responsive to general business cycle conditions; and (iv) structural country-specific factors play a role in explaining the propensity of EU Member States to engage in policy initiatives. Among these structural factors, specific characteristics related to the governance of national research and innovation systems seems to highlight the importance of sharing best practices among Member States.

The chapter is organized as follows: the next section presents some key analytical references for interpreting the linkages between current policy reforms and past economic and policy performance. The following two sections provide a descriptive analysis of R&D, education and innovation performance and policy reforms across European countries. Thereafter, we describe the indicators used in this study and present the results of the empirical analysis on the linkages between past economic/reform performance and a country's propensity to introduce reform measures. The final section highlights the main conclusions of the chapter and some possible avenues for future analysis.

PUBLIC POLICY IN THE DOMAIN OF R&D, EDUCATION AND INNOVATION

Since Romer's (1986, 1990) seminal contributions, a widespread consensus has emerged on recognizing R&D as the main engine of long-run economic growth. Indeed, R&D activity generates new knowledge (invention) which is then transformed into commercially viable innovations (the development stage of the R&D process). These innovations diffuse in the economy (through adoption by consumers and imitations by firms) and, thus, induce the long-term positive effect on economic growth (Schumpeter, 1934).[4] This is the main reason why public authorities take an active role in stimulating a country's R&D system by providing the infrastructure and the institutional framework for supporting innovation activity.

A second reason refers to the specific features which make R&D different from other types of profit-motivated investments. For example, R&D is characterized by indivisibilities and economies of scale that create strong incentives for firms to monopolize markets. Moreover, the uncertainty inherent in innovation itself makes R&D activities highly risky from a firm's perspective.[5] This uncertainty, together with asymmetric information on the ultimate nature of the R&D investment, makes it more difficult for firms – especially in the current economic conditions – to obtain external finance. Finally, the partial non-excludability of R&D undermines private incentives to invest in R&D (Jones and Williams, 1998; Aghion and Howitt, 1992),[6] which in turn explains why there is a role for government policies in promoting R&D and restoring R&D investments to their socially desirable level.[7]

Indeed, both the current economic slowdown and the gap between the 3 per cent target and the actual R&D performance of European countries makes "R&D and innovation" one of the policy fields where there has been the highest policy activity by governments. The former requires policy initiatives aimed at counteracting the possible slowdown in R&D – due to its cyclical nature, especially in the private sector – and, thus, preserving the knowledge base built in these years. The latter is mirrored in the policy initiatives taken within the context of both the Lisbon Agenda and the Europe 2020 strategy aimed at moving the baseline condition of long-term R&D evolution under the standard TINA argument – There Is No Alternative. In turn, this means that higher policy activity should be registered in those policy areas – such as R&D – where targets are clearly defined and the gap with the actual performance generates incentives for active policy. Financial measures such as the expansion of direct public R&D investments and/or more generous schemes of fiscal incentives for business R&D offer a measurable outcome but become even more difficult when deteriorating economic conditions generate the need of fiscal consolidation. This is the reason why different Member States engage often in a policy mix where financial and institutional reforms go together – with the latter being aimed at increasing the overall efficiency/effectiveness of national research systems (see below).

The arguments for an active government role in supporting education investments follow similar lines. Education externalities are benefits from the education of individuals that benefit others in current and future generations. They are over and above the private benefits that are taken into account by individuals in making their decisions to invest in education. The externality benefits are the main rationale, on efficiency grounds, for public support of education. Increases in the overall level of education can benefit society in ways that are not fully reflected in the wages of educated workers, also due to labor and product market imperfections. Human capital spillovers may increase productivity over and above the direct effect of education on individual productivity.[8]

A large literature has developed in this idea, proposing models where human capital externalities are the main engine of economic growth, especially in new growth theories and recent neoclassical growth theories by Romer and Lucas. Lucas (1988) argues that human capital externalities in the form of learning spillovers may explain long-run income differences between rich and poor countries.

Human capital may continue increasing even without an increase in educational attainment, because human capital adds to a public body of knowledge. Romer (1990) assumes that the growth of productivity depends on the stock of human capital (the existing stock of ideas and the number of people employed in the R&D sector, devoting their time to the accumulation of new ideas). The human capital used in the R&D sector to stimulate innovations is relevant to the countries at the technology possibility frontier, while in other countries, the average level of education available to facilitate the dissemination of technology is likely to be much more relevant. Education has also an indirect effect on productivity and employment through the quality of institutions that may be considered a component of social capital and well-being of individuals and societies (de la Fuente and Ciccone, 2003). Nicoletti and Scarpetta (2003) find that higher skill levels have a positive impact on total factor productivity (TFP) growth, although the effect is not always significant.

All the contributions mentioned above underline the positive linkage between research, education, innovation, and economic growth. This provides the framework for investigating when and why governments intervene in support of the three pillars of the knowledge triangle. Understanding the conditions that lead governments to introduce reforms is a first important step in the direction of supporting the overall reform process undertaken at the European level. Identifying the correct determinants of reforms may lead to a more effective and timely reform process in policy areas highly conducive to growth. The correct design of policies and the evaluation of their impact represent the second pillar of this analysis which, however, goes beyond the scope of this chapter.

Several contributions in the political economy literature investigate the determinants of policy reforms across countries (Fernandez and Rodrik, 1991; Duval and Elmeskov, 2005; Høj et al., 2006). Most of these studies adopt a general approach to the determinants of reforms by testing different sets of economic and political variables. On the contrary, this chapter is one of the few adopting a policy field-specific approach (namely, the knowledge triangle). In turn, this leads to focus the choice of the determinants more on indicators specific to the knowledge triangle rather than on more general institutional aspects (i.e. governance of public funding) which will be discussed only marginally.

EUROPEAN PERFORMANCE IN THE KNOWLEDGE TRIANGLE

R&D intensity (R&D expenditure as a share of GDP) in 2011 stood at 2.03 per cent in the EU, considerably lower than R&D intensity levels in the USA (2.87 per cent) and Japan (3.36 per cent).[9] Over the last five years, Europe has registered a small growth of R&D intensity compared to a more positive trend in the USA, a more marked growth in Japan and a strong catching-up process in China where – although overall R&D intensity is still lower (1.7 per cent) – the volume of R&D investment more than doubled in the last five years.[10]

Figure 5.1 plots R&D intensity in 2011 against R&D performance (variation in the R&D/GDP ratio) between 2006 and 2011 for EU Member States and other major economies. There is a high variation in R&D intensity within Europe. Nine Member States have R&D intensity levels greater than the EU27 average in 2011. Finland, Sweden and Denmark are the only countries with R&D intensity above 3 per cent. Most countries – especially those that joined the EU from 2004 – have been catching up very rapidly in terms of R&D intensity.

The composition of R&D investment is very different across countries (see Table 5.1). 54 per cent of total R&D across the EU27 is funded by private sources (compared to 62 per cent in the USA, 72 per cent in China and 75 per cent in Japan). Values within Europe range from Cyprus and Bulgaria (13 and 17 percent, respectively) to Finland and Germany (above 65 per cent). In 2011, R&D performed by the business sector is at 1.26

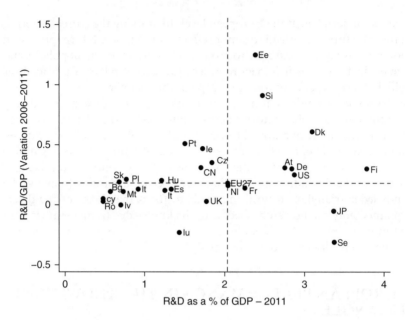

Figure 5.1　　R&D investment as % of GDP: EU27, the USA and Japan

per cent of EU-27 GDP – only slightly higher than the intensity registered in 2000 (1.20 per cent). Moreover, international comparison reveals that the European R&D gap with the US and Japan – as well as the growth in China – is mostly due to its private component rather than to the public one. Indeed, private R&D intensity in China is already very close to the European level. Given the relative importance of private R&D – as discussed above – encouraging private R&D investment is a crucial objective in the context of the Europe 2020 strategy and one of the policy areas where major policy reforms were taken.

In particular, there has been a general trend towards more fiscal incentives than direct subsidies in many European Member States. More specifically, before the crisis, some countries chose to strengthen the whole portfolio of policy instruments by maintaining or even increasing their level of direct funding (e.g., Portugal, Spain, the United Kingdom) while keeping generous R&D tax incentives. On the contrary, some countries with high R&D intensities and a favorable business innovation climate (such as Finland, Sweden or Germany) have both low R&D tax incentives and low direct subsidies for R&D (Steen, 2012). Nowadays, constraints on public finances are reducing the generosity of many fiscal instruments as well as the scope of such policies.[11]

Table 5.1   R&D expenditures across countries: EU-27, the USA, Japan and China in 2011

Country	R&D/ GDP %	% by Business	% Govern- ment	% by Higher Education	% by Private non-Profit	% Abroad	Subsi- dies
CN	1.70	71.70	23.40	–	–	1.30	0.04
EU27	2.03	53.90	34.60	0.90	1.60	8.90	0.07
JP	3.36	75.30	17.70	5.90	0.70	0.40	0.01
SW	2.87	–	–	–	–	–	–
US	2.87	61.60	31.30	3.80	3.40	–	0.14
At	2.75	45.50	38.10	–	0.60	15.90	–
Be	2.04	58.60	25.30	3.20	0.70	12.10	0.07
Bg	0.57	16.90	38.80	0.20	0.20	43.90	0.01
Cy	0.48	12.70	68.30	3.50	0.50	15.00	0.19
Cz	1.84	46.90	37.00	0.80	0.00	15.20	0.13
De	2.84	65.60	30.30	–	0.20	3.90	0.04
Dk	3.09	60.20	27.60	–	3.50	8.70	0.03
Ee	2.38	53.20	34.50	0.30	0.10	12.00	0.09
El	–	–	–	–	–	–	–
Es	1.33	43.00	46.60	3.90	0.70	5.70	0.17
Fi	3.78	67.00	25.00	0.10	1.30	6.50	0.03
Fr	2.25	53.50	37.00	1.00	0.80	7.60	0.09
Hu	1.21	47.50	38.10	–	1.00	13.50	0.15
Ie	1.72	48.10	31.20	1.10	0.50	19.20	0.06
It	1.25	44.70	41.60	0.90	3.10	9.80	0.06
Lt	0.92	28.10	42.30	1.00	0.20	28.50	0.02
Lu	1.43	46.10	33.90	0.10	0.10	19.90	–
Lv	0.70	24.80	22.50	1.60	–	51.00	0.04
Mt	0.73	52.60	30.70	0.20	0.30	16.20	0.01
Nl	2.04	45.10	40.90	0.30	2.80	10.80	0.04
Pl	0.77	28.10	55.80	2.40	0.20	13.40	0.13
Pt	1.50	44.10	44.90	3.20	4.60	3.20	0.04
Ro	0.48	37.40	49.10	1.20	0.20	12.10	0.18
Se	3.37	58.20	27.50	1.10	2.40	10.90	0.05
Si	2.47	61.20	31.50	0.20	0.00	7.00	0.15
Sk	0.68	33.90	49.80	1.80	0.40	14.20	0.10
Uk	1.77	44.60	32.20	1.30	4.90	17.00	0.09

Note: R&D data are disaggregated across countries by four macro-sectors (business, government, higher education, private non-profit).

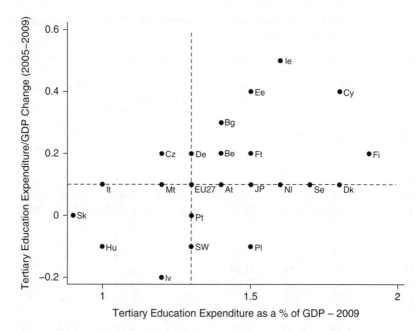

Figure 5.2   Tertiary education expenditure as % of GDP in 2009: EU-27

Beyond the business sector, the composition of Europe's R&D is more dependent on government-funded activity (35 per cent) compared to the USA (31 per cent) and Japan (18 per cent) while the relative weight of higher education funding is lower (0.9 per cent in EU-27 versus 3.8 and 5.9 per cent in the USA and Japan, respectively). However, relative trends indicate a (slow) path of substitution in the last years from the former to the latter source of R&D funding in Europe. The relative institutional and funding balance between government- and higher education-funded R&D illustrates the existence of different governance features of national research systems across EU-27 (see Table 5.1). Second, the relative role of public and private institutions in the higher education sector affects the volume of overall funding and research funding of tertiary education institutions. The increasing internationalization of European R&D is a trend worth mentioning. On average, about 9 per cent of R&D across European Member States is funded by foreign sources. In turn, this is an important step in a more effective development of the European Research Area as well as an important tool for promoting international cooperation and excellence across countries.

Expenditure on higher education as a percentage of GDP is much higher in the US (2.6 per cent) than in the EU-27 (1.2 per cent), largely as a consequence of relatively massive private sector funding of education in the USA due mostly to higher student fees and philanthropic contributions. Also, expenditure on higher education as a percentage of GDP varies considerably across EU-27 (see Figure 5.2). The gap in financing tertiary education has some effects on perceived performance and quality of higher education institutions. Indeed, Europe has fewer universities that act as major research centres of large scientific size and impact compared to the USA and a lower share of contribution to the top 10 per cent of most cited scientific publications.[12]

Among the different technological and non-technological features which characterize European innovation performance, the issue of knowledge creation – namely, the inventive capacity of an economy – generally deserves high political attention (Danguy and van Pottelsberghe, 2011). Indeed, Europe has a lower rate of patent intensity than the USA (see Table 5.2), defined as the number of patent applications in terms of habitants and R&D expenditure. Although data are not fully comparable – because of different institutional settings between the European Patent Office (EPO) and the equivalent US office (USPTO) – the gap indicates the need to intervene to enhance the inventive capacity of the European economy. This is mostly due to an unfavorable sector specialization of the European economy which, in turn, implies lower level of business R&D, lower specialization in high technology (and high patenting) fields such as pharmaceuticals, computers, office machinery, telecommunications and electronics than in medium technology fields such as general machinery, machine tools, metal products and transport (JRC, 2012) as well as lower employment shares in Science and Technology across EU countries (Table 5.2).

Innovation is a multifaceted phenomenon. It encompasses many different policy aspects related to R&D and education; but it involves also finance, firm investments, entrepreneurship, knowledge commercialization and diffusion. The innovation performance of an economy depends therefore on economic factors which go beyond the pure technological dimension, such as market structure and the nature of competition in product and labor markets. These dimensions are integrated and complementary.[13] A broader look at innovation performance in Europe is offered by the European Innovation Union Scoreboard which provides composite indicators of different innovative dimensions.[14]

The ultimate scope of innovation is the exploitation of the results obtained by the pre-market research and development stage. The commercial exploitation of successful innovations is the goal and stimulus of business R&D. The promotion of the single market represents a major tool for opening up business to international competition and generating a wave of market-induced innovations in Europe. Enhancing business R&D in Europe goes, therefore, hand in hand with the advancement of

Table 5.2   Innovation performance across countries: EU-27 and the USA in 2010

Country	% Employed in science and technology	Patents per total R&D	Patents per habitant
US	–	305.57	283.26
EU27	0.72	221.49	108.59
At	0.88	199.87	188.3
Be	0.85	200.72	130.49
Bg	0.36	56.8	1.61
Cy	0.23	120.46	12.97
Cz	0.6	114.86	25.52
De	0.85	311.19	265.57
Dk	1.3	185.59	241.71
Ee	0.71	219.73	38.07
Es	0.71	99.68	6.72
Fi	0.73	167.11	31.62
Fr	1.69	200.32	217.69
Gr	–	83.41	135.11
Hu	0.56	179.87	20.23
Ie	0.78	126.44	79.13
It	0.46	226.39	73.31
Lt	0.62	98.79	6.49
Lu	1.15	126.67	165.91
Lv	0.4	152.63	0.91
Mt	0.36	262.12	1.53
Nl	0.62	297.71	193.42
Pl	0.4	117.05	8
Pt	0.92	39.46	10.19
Ro	0.21	69.78	1.86
Se	1.08	241.38	306.74
Si	0.8	224.16	81.69
Sk	0.66	78.68	6.04
Uk	0.81	157.8	76.51

the single market and the establishment of the European Research Area. Conversely, an important dimension for stimulating growth and to evaluate the correct functioning of the Single Market in Europe is to assess the extent of technological diffusion in Europe.

The share of companies in the EU that demonstrate innovative behavior (via the introduction of new or improved products, processes, services, marketing methods or organizational changes) stood at about 53 per cent in 2010 (see Eurostat, 2010). Enhancing the single market would have a positive effect not only on innovation diffusion but also on the commercial exploitation of the innovations introduced in the markets. Half of the innovative firms in Europe rely on the development of innovation through collaborations with other enterprises/institutions or by acquiring directly from other innovative firms. In other words, innovation diffusion plays a crucial role for enhancing the innovative capacity of many European firms. At the country level, it seems that a positive relationship emerges between the capacity of innovating directly and the "absorption" of innovation developed elsewhere (Cohen and Levinthal, 1990).

POLICIES IN SUPPORT OF THE KNOWLEDGE TRIANGLE

After the analysis of the main indicators in the domain of the knowledge triangle, the analysis moves to the assessment of the policies carried out by Member States in support of the so-called "knowledge economy". In doing so, this section draws on evidence from the MICREF database, which provides information on Member States' policies in the policy domain 'knowledge-based economy'. This policy domain consists of two broad policy fields: 'R&D and innovation' and 'Education'. In turn, the former is disaggregated into three components. The first – public R&D – comprises measures involving national investments on R&D and innovation. The second – private R&D and innovation – includes measures giving incentives to enterprises to invest in research. The last one – public private partnership – describes policies aimed at reinforcing / establishing a form of co-operation between the public authorities and economic agents. Measures in the domain of 'Education' include all reforms aiming to adapt education and training systems to new occupational needs, key competences and future skill requirements as well as measures improving the openness and quality of education.[15]

The policy domain 'knowledge-based economy' represents one of the three broad policy domains around which the MICREF database is thematically organized. The other two domains refer to 'open and competitive markets' and 'business environment and entrepreneurship'. In turn, these domains correspond to seven broad policy fields: market integration; competition policy; sector-specific regulation; start-up conditions; business environment; R&D and innovation; and education. Each policy field is subdivided further into areas of policy intervention which are in turn subdivided into reform areas. Figure 5.3 summarizes reform profiles of different EU Member States based on MICREF taxonomy.[16]

The variability of the reform profiles reflects the different policy mix

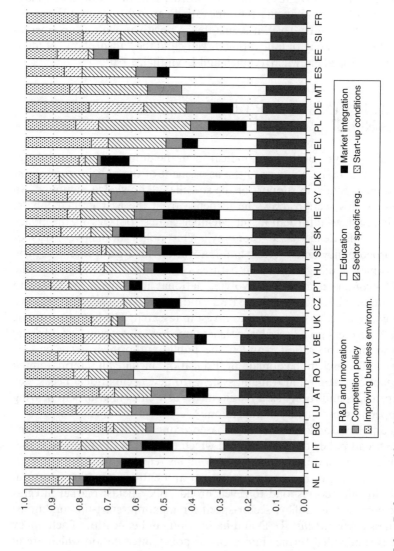

Figure 5.3   Reform profiles of EU-27: 2004–08

across countries. Over the period 2004 to 2008, the Netherlands and Finland have the highest ratio of reforms in the area of R&D and education. Results across countries clearly indicate that the number of reforms is independent from the relative performance of a country in each specific policy domain since – for instance, in the case of R&D – catching-up countries and innovation leaders appear in both tails of the distribution. In fact, this figure seems to suggest that the reform profiles rather reflect the combination of institutional and sector-specific characteristics in each country as well as the identification of bottlenecks and the consequent policy initiatives.

The existence of different institutional settings may influence innovative dynamics across countries as well as the effectiveness of policy measures carried out by governments. The governance of a country's research system represents a potential source of variation in innovation performance across countries. Although governance covers several dimensions, three important factors differ across EU Member States: whether funding decisions are centralized or not, whether there are ad-hoc mechanisms for funding research, and whether there exists an evaluation of public research institutes (Conte et al., 2009).

DATA AND METHODOLOGY

For the purpose of this study, a panel dataset at the country level has been constructed. The final dataset contains annual information on all 27 EU countries over the 2000s. Data on R&D spending, human resources in science and technology (S&T), education and other innovation-specific data are drawn from Eurostat Science and Technology Indicators. Monetary indicators (GDP and R&D expenditure data) have been rescaled in real terms using the GDP Deflator Index available from DG ECFIN Annual Macro Economic Database AMECO. Data on consolidated gross debt and current tax burden are also obtained from AMECO. Annual composite indicators on innovation performance are obtained from the European Innovation Scoreboard.

Annual data on reform measures are drawn from the MICREF database which systematically records product market reforms adopted in EU Member States.[17] The comprehensive structure of the MICREF database allows the investigation of the reform initiatives registered for all 27 EU Member States over the recent years. In particular, the last release of the MICREF database (October 2009) includes 2387 reform measures adopted over the period 2000–08. The time frame for the analysis at the EU-27 level focuses on the period 2004–08 (1727 reform measures) since data for the previous period (2000–03) are only consistently available for EU-15 countries. Over the period 2004–08, 611 reform measures are registered in the broad policy field of the 'knowledge-based economy'.[18] The analysis faces some drawbacks linked to the available information in the MICREF database, the aggregation of the policy reforms and their use in the empirical analysis. First, MICREF registers only significant new reform measures or important changes in the implementation framework since the purpose is to gauge the 'change' ('progress or retreat') in the reform process. Second, MICREF registers measures only once, according to their perceived main reform area or their main characteristic. Therefore, the occurrence of policy measures in a specific area (one or more measures – binary measure) has been considered rather than the number of reforms and/or their scope since these might differ within/across policy areas or similar measures might be replicated at lower administrative levels (i.e. Member States with federal institutions). Finally, the adoption year of a reform measure – rather than the implementation year – is used as a reference point.[19]

The general econometric approach to the determinants of policy reforms is based on the following specification:

$$RM_{ct} = \alpha + L.RM_{ct} + \sum_{i=1}^{S} \beta_i L.\ln(INNOVint)_{ct} + \gamma L.\ln(HRST)_{ct}$$

$$+ \delta \Delta_1 \ln(GDPpc)_{ct} + \theta \Delta_2 \ln(GDPpc)_{ct} + \mu \ln(DEBT)_{ct} + \varphi \ln(TAX)_{ct}$$

$$+ \sum_{c=1}^{C} \omega_c CD_c + \varepsilon_{ct}$$

Here RM_{ct} represents the occurrence of a reform measure in each country (c) and year (t), and it is equal to one if reform is undertaken in the relevant area and zero otherwise. *INNOVInt* indicates innovation intensity; including type of R&D expenditure by sector (i.e. government R&D spending, private R&D) relative to GDP, and other measures of innovation such as patents scaled by R&D or by population, technology balance of payments flows, and intangible assets, etc. *HRST* indicates the share of human resources employed in science and technology as a per cent of total population. *DEBT* refers to 'government consolidated gross debt' while *TAX* indicates 'current tax burden'. The equation also includes the first and second difference (Δ_1 and Δ_2) of per capita GDP to capture the growth performance; as well as a set of country dummies (CD). All explanatory variables are in logarithms and the symbol $L.$ stands for one lag. We used a dynamic specification with lags (L) since we represent the effect of (exogenous) past performance on the political decision to intro-

*Table 5.3   Descriptive statistics of the main indicators: innovation and
policy reforms*

Variable	Mean	Std. Dev.	Minimum	Maximum
Allocation of Public R&D	.46	.50	0	1
Support of Private R&D	.29	.45	0	1
Technology Transfer	.10	.30	0	1
Tertiary educ./ researchers	.45	.50	0	1
R&D Intensity	1.53	.92	.22	4.13
Business R&D Intensity	.94	.73	.01	3.2
Government R&D Intensity	.22	.10	.01	.48
Higher Education R&D Intensity	. 34	.20	0	.92
Eur. Innovation scoreboard EIS 'Throughputs'	.29	.18	.13	.72
GVT Consolidated Gross Debt as % of GDP	49.90	31.10	1.3	175.7
Current Tax Burden on Income as % of GDP	.014	.054	−.1	.8

Source: MICREF, EIS and EUROSTAT Science and Technology Indicators.

duce policy measures. Moreover, we test the hypothesis of persistence of policy initiatives in a specific area through the introduction in the model of the lagged dependent variable. We capture the effect of business cycle on policies by means of a percentage change in GDP (log D) for two periods. Finally, the inclusion of country-specific fixed effects helps to wipe out time-invariant components such as institutional or structural country features.[20] This set of variables is used for all the estimations of the reform measures in the next section. In addition to this group of indicators, a number of variables specific to each policy area are added and tested in the econometric exercise. Finally, given the binary nature of the dependent variable (reform measures), all the models are estimated through means of a probit specification for panel data. Table 5.3 provides descriptive statistics of the indicators used in the analysis.

DETERMINANTS OF POLICY REFORMS IN THE FIELD OF R&D, EDUCATION AND INNOVATION

This section provides an empirical analysis of the determinants of selected policy measures taken in the broad policy domain 'Knowledge-based economy', as defined in the MICREF database. In particular, we focus on the determinants of the probability of reforms (RM) in five reform areas, using the probit econometric specification described above. The reform areas consist of: (1) allocation of public resources for innovation; (2) support for private R&D; (3) tertiary education / supply of researchers; (4) intellectual property rights; and (5) technology transfer.

Each dependent variable is explained by two sets of explanatory variables: (1) knowledge-related and (2) economy-wide indicators. For instance, reforms in the domain of public R&D are regressed on a country's public R&D performance plus additional (more generic) economic indicators. Therefore, we use past performance in government R&D to verify whether there has been the introduction of reforms on the 'R&D public allocation', past performance in business R&D to verify the introduction of reforms in the area of 'private support to R&D' and so on for all the five estimations provided in Table 5.4, which summarizes the main results of the econometric analysis.

In every policy area the occurrence of a reform in the previous year reduces the probability of a new policy initiative in the current year. In other words, governments tend to avoid stretching the reforms in the same policy area over multiple years. This behavior can be explained by the desire to establish legal certainty in a policy area and the need for evaluating the effects of a given reform after it has been introduced.

Governments appear to react to under-performance in input measures of innovation such as R&D expenditures, education expenditures and human resources employed in the S&T sector. For example, the lower (higher) the government-funded R&D intensity, the higher (lower) is the probability of reforms targeting the allocation of public resources for innovation. The same applies to policies that aim to support private R&D: the lower (higher) is the level of business R&D expenditures in the preceding year, the higher (lower) is the probability of reform aimed at supporting business R&D. Similarly, the lower (higher) the intensity of total and tertiary education spending, the higher (lower) is the probability of reforms in this policy field. Finally, the lower (higher) the patent intensity relative to R&D spending, the higher (lower) is the probability of reforms aimed at intellectual property rights protection.

These findings indicate that the Lisbon Strategy has been effective in instigating a catching-up process whereby Member States with low past performance in input measures of innovation (R&D expenditures, education expenditures and in terms of the efficiency with which R&D expenditures are converted into patents) tend to have a higher probability of introducing reforms in related policy areas. In addition, past performance with respect to these innovation indicators tends to have the strongest effects on the probability of reforms – compared to other potential deter-

Table 5.4   Determinants of EU-27 policy reforms related to knowledge triangle – results from Probit estimations (dependent variable: probability of reform)

Reforms for: explanatory variables	Allocation of public resources	Support of private R&D	Tertiary educ./ researchers	Intellectual property rights	Technology transfer
Past reforms (lagged RM)	−2.62*** (0.80)	−1.41*** (0.45)	−1.51* (0.85)	−3.82*** (1.29)	−3.36*** (1.23)
Government R&D as % of GDP (lagged)	−72.1** (28.3)				
Business R&D as % of GDP (lagged)		−7.97*** (2.88)			
Public exp. on education as % of GDP (lagged)			−20.6* (11.5)		
Public exp. on tertiary education as % of GDP (lagged)			−15.9** (7.17)		
Patents per habitant (lagged)				0.22** (0.096)	−0.069 (0.46)
Patents per BERD (lagged)				0.020 (0.012)	0.018 (0.027)
Patents per total R&D (lagged)				−0.089* (0.053)	0.025* (0.013)
EIS 'Throughputs'				55.6** (23.1)	
Government R&D funded by business					
Business R&D funded by government					
Higher ed. R&D funded by business					
HRs in S&T – % of total employment	−2.12*** (0.62)	0.51*** (0.16)	−0.84 (0.62)	−1.63** (0.75)	0.18 (0.20)
First difference of log(GDPpc)	−20.9 (32.1)	39.2** (16.6)	78.8 (110)	84.5 (88.6)	−59.9** (29.0)
Second difference of log(GDPpc)	77.4* (44.2)	−42.0*** (15.7)	−113 (78.2)	28.8 (51.0)	69.1** (29.9)
Government consolidated gross debt	−20.4** (9.83)	−1.33 (2.60)	−19.1 (17.5)	0.60 (12.8)	−1.79 (3.08)
Current tax burden	14.9*** (5.54)	3.70* (2.05)	4.38 (6.69)	−1.21 (8.99)	5.96** (2.51)
Constant	46.0** (19.8)	−22.8*** (8.09)	155 (1646)	3.98 (1280)	−40.1 (12323)
Country dummies	Yes	Yes	Yes	Yes	Yes
Observations	94	141	70	94	123

Notes: Standard errors are in brackets. *, **, and *** indicates significance at 10%, 5%, and 1% respectively.

minants such as public debt or current tax burden. The only exception is the second difference of per capita GDP, which reflects year-on-year expansion or contraction in the economy. However, the effect of the business cycle captured by the second difference of per capita GDP is not consistent across reform areas.

Nevertheless, there are exceptions to the catching-up process identified above. One exception concerns the relationship between patenting intensity per habitant and reforms for protecting intellectual property rights. Here, the evidence indicates that a higher (lower) patents/habitant ratio in the preceding year increases (reduces) the probability of policy reform for intellectual property protection in the current year. We explain this difference by pointing out that the number of patents per capita is an indicator of 'inventive stock' whereas the patent/R&D ratio is a measure of efficiency. As the 'inventive stock' increases, EU governments introduce new reforms not to catch up but to enhance the governance of the 'inventive stock'.

A similar pattern is observed in the relationship between 'EIS throughputs' (i.e., the composite indicator of technology balance of payments flows and intangible assets such as trademarks and designs) and the probability of reforms for protecting intellectual property rights. Here again higher performance in terms of 'EIS throughputs' in the preceding year is associated with higher probability of reforms aimed at protecting intellectual property rights in the current year. This finding increases the relevance of the conclusion derived above – i.e., the higher is the 'inventive stock', the higher is the probability of reforms aimed at governing this stock more effectively.

Also a similar pattern is observed in the area of reforms for governing technology transfers. Here, such reforms are more likely the higher is the relative share of higher education R&D funded by business. The sign in the regression may suggest that reforms in this area are driven more by the need for managing a phenomenon in place – technology transfer – rather than enhancing it. No specific effect is found when looking at the other forms of cross-funding in R&D, namely between the government and the business sector.

The positive relationship between past performance in terms of 'inventive stock' and policy reforms in the relevant area in the current year indicates that the Lisbon Strategy may also be reinforcing the position of the existing 'winners' in the EU. In other words, instead of catching up, we observe a tendency for better-performing Member States to consolidate and reinforce the governance structures related to protection of intellectual property rights and technology transfers.

The combination of findings above indicates that the Lisbon Strategy has been effective in inducing the 'laggards' to introduce policy reforms that may enhance their performance with respect to innovation inputs such as R&D and education expenditures; but it has also instigated a process that may widen the gap between low- and high-performers with respect to the level of 'inventive stock'. High-performing member states with respect to 'inventive stock' may remain a step ahead as the effect of higher reforms for governing the inputs of innovation are likely to take time to have a positive effect on innovation outputs such as patenting intensity, technology transfers and technology trade.

A number of additional factors are common to each regression. The share of human resources in S&T allows controlling for the effect of human capital on the occurrence of different policies. Mixed evidence emerges on the effect of this variable on the different reform measures. Overall, it seems to indicate that countries with a larger share of human resources in S&T – which in turn implies a R&D-prone sector composition of their economies and an overall higher than the average R&D expenditure – focus their policies (almost exclusively) towards the support of private R&D. The business cycle – proxied by the first and second difference of GDP – allows investigating the choice of policies in different business cycle conditions. Indeed, different policy responses emerge in the case of policies supporting public versus private R&D. For instance, more generous support to public R&D is more likely in an expansionary period while support to private R&D is mostly counter-cyclical, as can be seen from the negative sign in the regression. Furthermore, the difference between the signs of the coefficients on the first and second difference of per capita GDP corroborates the counter-cyclical nature of support for private R&D.

Public finance-related variables seem to have an effect on the expected introduction of policies in the area of the knowledge triangle. Indeed, a higher level of consolidated gross debt reduces the room for maneuver of public policies and, therefore, the possibility of sustaining higher level of public R&D investments. On the contrary, countries with a higher current tax burden seem to find it easier to channel resources for supporting public R&D, private R&D as well as programmes of technology transfers.

Further heterogeneous (institutional) country-specific factors (proxied by country dummies) affect the probability of policy measures across countries in each specific vertex of the knowledge triangle. They may need further investigation.

CONCLUDING REMARKS

This chapter has analysed the factors that affect the reform strategies of the EU Member States in support of the 'knowledge economy', namely policies enhancing a country's performance in the area of R&D expenditures, education, governance of intellectual property rights and technology transfers. The descriptive evidence indicates that the EU lags behind the USA and Japan in various indicators of innovation effort. It also reveals significant differences between EU Member States. Hence, there is a strong case for investigating the extent to which the Lisbon Strategy has induced the Member States to engage in policy reforms expected to reduce disparity within the EU and potentially close the gap the between the latter and its major competitors. The case for such investigation is strengthened by the need to explore the scope for more effective policy design in the context of the Europe 2020 strategy that superseded the Lisbon Agenda.

Our findings indicate that the Lisbon Decade has been characterized by both convergence and divergence between EU member states. Convergence is evident in policy areas related to governance of innovation inputs such as government and business R&D expenditures, expenditures on education and the efficiency of converting R&D into patents. In these policy areas, countries with lower performance in the preceding year tend to have a higher probability of introducing reforms in the current year in order to enhance future performance. Indeed, in these policy areas, the effect of past performance on current reforms is stronger than that of other potential determinants such as growth, public debt and tax burden. These findings indicate that the Lisbon Strategy, through its targets and monitoring mechanisms, has been effective in closing the gap between low- and high-performing Member States in terms of building the governance structures necessary to support innovation.

However, the evidence indicates that the Lisbon Strategy is also associated with divergence between EU Member States in policy areas related to governance of the 'inventive stock' reflected in the number of patents per capita, technology trade and protection of intellectual property rights. In these areas, the current reform effort is positively related to past performance, indicating that the governance gap between high- and low-performing Member States is widening. Hence, the challenge for the Europe 2020 Strategy is whether policy reforms introduced in support of R&D and education expenditures during the Lisbon Decade (2000–10) would enable the low-performing Member States to achieve higher levels of 'inventive capital'; and whether this innovation base can then induce them to catch up with the rest of the EU in terms of governance structures necessary for governing the innovation outcomes.

NOTES

1. For a review of the evolution of such literature over time, see Conte (2006).
2. A major step towards a single patent system for Europe happened in December 2012 with the approval of the new unitary patent regime, see http://www.epo.org/law-practice/unitary/unitary-patent.html.
3. To the author's knowledge, there are no other empirical papers dealing with the determinants of reforms specific to the area of R&D, education and innovation.
4. Endogenous growth theory extends Solow's framework (1956 and 1957) by providing a formal link between the creation of knowledge (Romer, 1986), the accumulation of human capital (Lucas, 1988) and economic growth. Among others, the relationship between technological change and growth is discussed by Mankiw et al. (1992), Sala-i-Martin (1997) and Helpman (1998). For a review of the literature on technological change and growth, see Conte (2006).
5. In particular, the additional 'technological uncertainty' embedded in the innovation itself, together with the common 'market uncertainty' faced by firms acting in markets, makes R&D activities highly uncertain and risky from a firm's perspective.
6. A crucial determinant of this outcome is the role played by technological 'spillovers' (Mansfield, 1985; Jaffe, 1986; Acs et al., 1994).
7. Market failures in R&D can be addressed either directly (i.e. by targeting them at their source) or by influencing the incentives (i.e. via the IPR regime) faced by private actors (Goolsbee, 1998; Hall and Van Reenen, 2000; Martin and Scott, 2000).
8. Furthermore, increases in education also may reduce criminal participation and improve voters' political behavior. Higher levels of education may also result in better health for educated individuals and their children. If parental education indeed improves child health, then the total benefits of human capital accumulation are not captured by estimates of the private (monetary) returns.
9. Data for the USA and Japan refer to the latest available year (2009). The descriptive analysis will use latest data while the econometric exercise is constrained to 2008 – due to the time coverage of the latest release of MICREF database.
10. Although R&D intensity may show decreasing returns to scale, a linear extrapolation of EU and CH trends seems to indicate that China may catch up to the level of European R&D intensity by the middle of this decade.
11. Updated country-specific information on the governance of R&D system is provided by the European Commission's ERAWATCH project available at: http://erawatch.jrc.ec.europa.eu/.
12. However, European countries are increasingly reforming their national research systems, opening up to international cooperation, increasing the share of public research expenditure allocated to universities, shifting funding models to more competitive and output-based university funding and increasing institutional autonomy for higher education institutions (European Commission's ERA Key Figures 2009; St. Aubyn et al., 2009).
13. In turn, this makes innovation data more difficult to process and to compare across countries than data on R&D and education. Moreover, some of these aspects are not comparable across countries due to a lack of available data.
14. Innovation performance varies across countries. However, leading innovative countries score well in all these three dimensions and, thus, highlight the high complementarity between different innovation dimensions (see European Commission, 2011).
15. In this domain, the analysis focuses only on reforms in tertiary and post-graduate education.
16. Reform profiles are defined as the shares of reforms in each policy field (over the total number of reforms) of a particular Member State within the given period.
17. The structure of the database is presented in the MICREF user guide available at: http://ec.europa.eu/economy_finance/publications/publication13022_en.pdf.

18. The following reform areas are not included in the analysis: 'pre-school education' and 'secondary education'.
19. The adoption year is a mandatory feature of the MICREF database, the implementation date is optional and it is therefore missing for a large share of measures in the database. The focus on the adoption year stresses more the timing of the political decision rather than the effects of the reform. Exactly this feature of data related to policy measures hampers a comprehensive assessment of the effects of policy measures. Indeed, the combined effect of the lag between adoption and implementation of each specific reform and the lag between its implementation and its effect in the economy implies that the analysis of the effects of policy measures should rely on a much longer time series for the relevant indicators.
20. Indeed, standard variables adopted in the political economy literature – mostly drawn from the World Bank's Database of Political Institution – have been used in the analysis – i.e. the political orientation of the government, the extent of majority seats in the Parliament – but given the specific focus of this study on the determinants of R&D-related policy measures they did not turn statistically significant.

REFERENCES

Acs, Z.J., D.B. Audretsch and M. Feldman (1994), 'R&D spillovers and innovative activity', *Managerial and Decision Economics*, 15(2): 131–138.
Aghion, P. and P. Howitt (1992), 'A model of growth through creative destruction', *Econometrica*, 60(2): 323–351.
Aubyn, M. St., Á. Pina, F. Garcia and J. Pais (2009), 'The efficiency and effectiveness of public spending on tertiary education', European Commission, *ECFIN Economic Papers*, No. 390.
Cohen, W. M. and D.A. Levinthal (1990), 'Absorptive capacity: a new perspective on learning and innovation', *Administrative Science Quarterly*, 35(1): 128–152.
Conte, Andrea (2006), 'The evolution of the literature on technological change over time: a survey', Max Planck Institute of Economics, Discussion Paper No. 107.
Conte, A., P. Schweizer, A. Dierx and F. Ilzkovitz (2009), 'An analysis of the efficiency of public spending and national policies in the area of R&D', *European Economy*. Occasional Papers No. 54.
Danguy, J. and B. Van Pottelsberghe de la Potterie (2011), 'Cost-benefit analysis of the community patent', *Journal of Benefit-Cost Analysis*, 2(2).
de la Fuente, A. and A. Ciccone (2003), 'Human capital in a global and knowledge-based economy', *UFAE and IAE Working Papers*, No. 562.
Duval, R. and J. Elmeskov (2005), 'The effects of EMU on structural reforms in labour and product markets', *OECD Economics Department Working Papers*, no. 438.
European Commission (2011), *Innovation Union Scoreboard 2011*, Luxembourg: Office for Official Publications of the European Communities.
Eurostat (2010), *Seventh Community Innovation Survey*, http://epp.eurostat.ec.europa.eu/portal/page/portal/microdata/cis
Fernandez, R. and D. Rodrik (1991), 'Resistance to reform: status quo bias in the presence of individual-specific uncertainty', *American Economic Review*, 81(5): 1146–55.

Goolsbee, A. (1998), 'Does government R&D policy mainly benefit scientists and engineers?', *American Economic Review*, 88(2): 298–302.

Hall, B.H. and J. Van Reenen (2000), 'How effective are fiscal incentives for R&D? A review of the evidence', *Research Policy*, 29(4–5): 449–469.

Helpman, Elhanan (ed.) (1998), *General Purpose Technologies and Economic Growth*, Cambridge (Mass.): MIT Press.

Høj, J., V. Galasso, G. Nicoletti and Thai-Thanh Dang (2006), 'The political economy of structural reform: empirical evidence from OECD countries', *OECD Economics Department Working Papers*, no. 501.

Jaffe, A.B. (1986), 'Technological opportunity and spillovers of R&D: evidence from firms' patents, profits, and market value', *American Economic Review*, 76(5): 984–1001.

Jones, C.I. and J.C. Williams (1998), 'Measuring the social return to R&D', *Quarterly Journal of Economics*, 113(4): 1119–1135.

JRC (Joint Research Centre) (2012), *Monitoring Industrial Research: The EU Industrial R&D Investment Scoreboard*, Luxembourg: European Commission.

Lucas, R.E. Jr. (1988), 'On the mechanics of economic development', *Journal of Monetary Economics*, 22(1): 3–42.

Mankiw, N.G., D. Romer and D. Weil (1992), 'A contribution to the empirics of economic growth', *Quarterly Journal of Economics*, 107(2): 407–437.

Mansfield, E. (1985), 'How rapidly does new industrial technology leak out?', *Journal of Industrial Economics*, 34(2): 217–223.

Martin, S. and J.T. Scott (2000), 'The nature of innovation market failure and the design of public support for private innovation', *Research Policy*, 29(4–5): 437–447.

Nicoletti, G. and S. Scarpetta (2003), 'Regulation, productivity and growth: OECD evidence', *Economic Policy*, 18(36): 9–72.

Romer, P. M. (1986), 'Increasing returns and long-run growth', *Journal of Political Economy*, 94(5): 1002–1037.

Romer, P.M. (1990), 'Human capital and growth: theory and evidence', *Carnegie-Rochester Conference Series on Public Policy*, 32(Spring): 251–286.

Sala-i Martin, X. (1997), 'I just ran two million regressions', *American Economic Review*, 87(2): 178–83.

Schumpeter, J. (1934), *The Theory of Economic Development*, Cambridge (Mass.): Harvard University Press (1st edition in 1912).

Solow, R.M. (1956), 'A contribution to the theory of economic growth', *Quarterly Journal of Economics*, 70(1): 65–94.

Solow, R.M. (1957), 'Technical change and the aggregate production function', *Review of Economics and Statistics*, 39(3): 312–320.

Steen, J. v. (2012), 'Modes of public funding of R&D: towards internationally comparable indicators', *OECD Science, Technology and Industry Working Papers*, no. 2012/04

PART II

Regulation and innovation

6. The impact of environmental regulation frameworks and firm-level factors on eco-innovations: evidence from DEFRA survey of UK manufacturing firms

Pelin Demirel and Effie Kesidou*

INTRODUCTION

Due to growing concerns about environmental impacts of the industrial society, governments are carefully considering their strategies for sustainable development. Indeed, one can observe the emergence of an increasingly popular stance which posits that the 'environment should no longer be sacrificed to economic growth: rather, the two should be reconciled' (Aggeri, 1999, 706). In easing the unambiguous trade-offs between environmental protection and economic growth, eco-innovations have a central role to play through improving environmental technologies that measure, detect and treat pollution; avoid it at the source; and ensure that the end product has a life span with minimal environmental impact.[1]

An expanding body of empirical and theoretical literature on eco-innovation aims to understand the circumstances which are more conducive to environmental technology investments. The 'ecological, economic and social' dimensions of eco-innovations require an inter-disciplinary approach which combines insights from environmental and innovation economics and is aware of the different methodological lenses of the neoclassical and evolutionary schools of thought (Rennings, 2000, p. 322).

In this chapter, by merging the valuable insights from these disciplines, we examine the determinants of investment into different types of eco-innovations: end-of-pipeline pollution control technologies, integrated cleaner production technologies and environmental R&D. Our findings, based on unique data from DEFRA's firm level survey Environmental Protection Expenditure by Industry, provide important insights on the roles of environmental regulation frameworks and internal firm-level factors that affect the adoption of eco-innovation strategies by incorporating the three types of eco-innovations in the same conceptual framework.

The chapter is structured as follows: the next section discusses the related literature and articulates the conceptual framework of the chapter. The third section presents the data and methodology used for the empirical analysis. The results are discussed in the following section. The final section presents the conclusions and discusses the policy implications of the study.

RELATED LITERATURE AND CONCEPTUAL FRAMEWORK

We begin with a general model of eco-innovation (Table 6.1), which draws upon the framework proposed by OECD (2009). We develop this model further to include a more detailed account of the characteristics specific to each type of eco-innovation, namely, end-of-pipeline pollution control technologies, integrated cleaner production technologies and environmental R&D (Kemp, 1997; Frondel et al., 2007). As indicated in Table 6.1, these eco-innovations range on a spectrum from lower impact (i.e., from incremental innovations in pollution control technologies) to higher impact innovations in environmental R&D.

In the case of end-of-pipeline pollution control technologies, manufacturing firms apply end-of-pipeline solutions in order to treat, handle, measure or dispose of emissions and wastes from production.[2] As the name suggests, these technological solutions are incorporated into existing manufacturing processes at the final stage and are not essential parts of the production process. End-of-pipeline technologies leave the production process mostly unchanged; therefore, they are considered to be incremental innovations. Since end-of-pipeline solutions denote the implementation of non-essential technologies, companies perceive them as costly investments that hamper their competitiveness (OECD, 2009; Porter and van de Linde, 1995a).

Integrated cleaner production technologies refer to new or modified production facilities, which are more efficient than previous technologies; and contribute to pollution reduction by cutting down the amount of inputs used for production and/or by substituting the inputs with more environmentally friendly alternatives[3] (OECD, 2009). Similar to the end-of-pipeline technologies, integrated cleaner production technologies mostly represent environmental process innovations (Rennings et al., 2006). However, integrated cleaner production technologies are designed to ensure that environmental protection is an integral part of

Table 6.1   Categorization of the eco-innovation spectrum

Low-impact – end-of-pipeline innovation: pollution control technologies	Medium-impact – integrated innovation: cleaner production technologies	High-impact – environmental R&D: cleaner product and process innovation
Environmental impact via		
Use of end-of-pipeline solutions	Use of integrated solutions	Use of R&D to generate new or improved products and processes with environmental benefits
Treatment of waste and pollution	Prevention of waste and pollution at source	
	Modification of processes	Increase the stock of knowledge in the field of environmental protection
	Efficiency improvements through input substitution, lower resource input and output	
		Improve products and processes (providing solutions for cleaner production and consumption)
Technological change via		
Implementation of non-essential technologies	Application of new or improved technologies may lead to further adaptations and modifications of products/processes through learning-by-doing and thus generate more significant technological transformations	Potential for more disruptive innovations
Most incremental of all eco-innovations		Product and/or process innovations
Process innovations	Process innovations	
Effects on costs		
Increased costs	Lower investment costs in the long run	High risk and high cost investments with a potential of covering the costs in the long run
Examples		
Waste treatment plants	Installations for reducing the use of water and reuse of waste gas in manufacturing (i.e. closed loop manufacturing systems)	R&D conducted to industrially produce renewable energy, to lower emission vehicles (e.g. catalytic converter), to reduce packaging of products etc
Passive filters such activated carbon	Internal recycling	
Groundwater monitoring sites etc		

manufacturing processes. In other words, unlike end-of-pipeline solutions that attempt to control pollution by adopting an 'after-event, *react and retreat* approach', integrated solutions focus on preventing pollution by adopting a 'forward-looking, *anticipate and prevent* philosophy' (Ashford, 1994, p.4). Compared to the continuous increasing costs of end-of-pipeline technologies, integrated technologies are less costly, since they have the potential to save costs by reducing the use of raw materials, energy and the costs of complying with regulations (Ashford, 1994).

The main aim of environmental R&D is to improve products and processes by providing solutions for cleaner production and consumption. Manufacturing firms that conduct environmental R&D on a systematic basis attempt to increase the stock of knowledge in the field of environmental protection and use this knowledge to devise new applications. Environmental R&D has a higher technological impact compared to the previously discussed categories of eco-innovation because (1) it enhances absorptive capacity as environmental R&D broadens the horizons of the company in environmental matters (Cohen and Levinthal, 1990), and (2) the scope of environmental R&D is not only limited to process innovations but also covers product innovations. Similar to the case of generic R&D, environmental R&D is subject to high risks and high costs.

Since the three types of eco-innovations have different characteristics, we expect that they may have different drivers. In this chapter we consider the role of two broad drivers: environmental regulation frameworks and internal firm-level motivations.

Environmental Regulation Frameworks

Various studies from environmental economics and eco-innovation literatures attempt to decipher whether prescriptive regulatory instruments (such as environmental regulations) or incentive-based regulatory instruments (such as environmental taxes) are more effective and cost efficient in reducing pollution. While incentive-based instruments tend to be superior to prescriptive regulatory policies in areas of cost-efficiency and flexibility[4] (Milliman and Prince, 1989; Requate and Unold, 2003; Requate, 2005), recent developments in eco-innovation studies highlight the value of well-designed prescriptive mechanisms for driving eco-innovations. Specifically, Porter (1991) and Porter and Van Der Linde (1995a, 1995b) have shown that environmental regulations indeed create 'win-win' situations: firms achieve high profits and produce 'green products' because environmental regulations boost R&D activities and thus, stimulate innovation and economic growth (Hart, 2004; Popp, 2005; Rothfels, 2002). An alternative explanation of the 'win-win' situation is offered by Rothfels

(2002) who shows that compliance with environmental regulations can drive firms to become leaders in 'green markets' and thus, become more competitive compared to their foreign peers.

A limited number of studies (of which Frondel et al., 2007 is a prominent example) confirms the need to examine the impact of environmental regulation frameworks on different types of environmental technologies. Their results indicate that prescriptive mechanisms play an important role in stimulating end-of-pipeline solutions but a minimal role in fostering integrated cleaner production technologies. Incentive-based instruments, on the other hand, do not affect either type of eco-innovation. Similar findings regarding prescriptive mechanisms are reported by the OECD survey (Johnstone, 2007) but their results on incentive-based instruments (i.e. taxes) differ, suggesting that taxes stimulate changes in the production process. Cleff and Rennings (2000) also find evidence in favour of incentive-based instruments boosting eco-innovations.

In assessing the relationship between environmental regulation frameworks and environmental technologies, the complexity of environmental technologies requires new socio-technical paradigms which need to combine incentive-based and prescriptive policies (Geels and Schot, 2007). Kemp (1997) argues that there is no single best policy instrument to stimulate clean technology and different instruments play important roles depending on the context they operate in and the type of clean technology that needs to be stimulated. For instance incentive-based mechanisms allow for a wider range of technology choice and innovation; but prescriptive rules may be more beneficial in situations where regulators are faced with a significant problem but lack the information and time to support and design an incentive-based instrument. Similarly, incentive-based instruments may be less effective in dealing with emissions with global impacts, as international cooperation may be difficult to attain. Indeed Jaenicke et al. (2000) find that a combination of instruments performs best in stimulating eco-innovations. Frondel et al. (2007) also agree that the type of instrument is less important but it is important to ensure that these instruments sustain a stringent environmental policy. A recent study by Johnstone et al. (2010) suggests that policy makers should focus on the innovation-inducing characteristics of environmental policies, whether prescriptive or incentive-based, when choosing them. They cite the following qualities of environmental policies as important in boosting the innovation potential of firms:

> '**Stringency** – [i.e. how ambitious is the environmental policy target, relative to the 'baseline' emissions trajectory?], **Predictability** – [i.e. what effect does the policy measure have on investor uncertainty; is the signal consistent,

foreseeable, and credible?], **Flexibility** –[i.e. does it let the innovator identify the best way to meet the objective (whatever that objective may be)?] **Depth** – [i.e. are there incentives to innovate throughout the range of potential objectives (down to zero emissions)?]; and, **Incidence** – [i.e. does the policy target directly the externality, or is the point of incidence a 'proxy' for the pollutant?].(p. 22)'

In the empirical part of this chapter, we investigate the role played by prescriptive regulatory instruments and incentive-based regulatory instruments for boosting the different types of eco-innovations by UK firms.

Internal Firm-level Factors

In this section, we focus on three firm-level motivations that are potential drivers of eco-innovations; namely organizational capabilities, efficiency, and corporate image.

Environmental management systems (EMS) engender important organizational capabilities in the area of environmental protection. EMS are voluntary organizational frameworks that detail the procedures to manage the impacts of the organization on natural environment (Darnall, 2006). EMS are aimed at the continuous improvement of corporate environmental performance with an attempt to get ahead of the existing government regulations to reduce emissions and waste disposal (Kollman and Prakash, 2002). European Union's Environmental Management and Audit Scheme (EMAS) and ISO14001 constitute the most diffused forms of formalized EMS and both schemes require third party certification and investigation. Bansal and Hunter (2003) argue that these two schemes reinforce legitimacy which cannot be claimed through in-house EMS.

There is little consensus on the impact of EMS upon environmental performance or eco-innovation. Russo and Harrison's (2005) findings show that environmental performance does not respond to EMS implementation. Similarly, Boiral (2007) finds that formal EMS fail to improve the environmental performance, yet introduce many cumbersome and bureaucratic procedures. Rondinelli and Vastag (2000) argue that the implementation of EMS cannot ensure that the company will attain environmental sustainability.

On the other hand, some studies find the EMS to be an important determinant of environmental innovations (Hamschmidt and Dyllick, 2001). Dijken et al. (1999) and Biondi et al. (2002) find that the implementation of EMS is an important determinant in the case of SMEs. Other studies pinpoint the importance of different characteristics of EMS that affect the quality of their implementation within the firm and in turn, the organizational changes that occur and subsequently affect environmental performance (Rehfeld et al., 2007; Anton et al., 2004; Arimura et al.,

2008). Rennings et al. (2006) confirm the importance of EMAS certification for environmental innovations among certified facilities in Germany. In particular, their findings indicate the role played by different aspects of EMAS (i.e. maturity and strategic importance of EMAS and the learning processes) for stimulating eco-innovation. They confirm that most features of EMAS (as noted above) affect environmental process innovations but not product innovations because the implementation of EMS is aimed at improving the environmental quality of processes. Anton et al. (2004) also finds that a more comprehensive implementation of EMS (as opposed to a limited implementation) improves the environmental performance. Finally, Wagner (2008) offers empirical evidence, which shows that EMS have a positive effect upon process innovations but no effect upon product innovations.

EMS are also expected to have an indirect effect on the organizational capabilities by boosting environmental awareness and organizational learning (Melnyk et al., 2003). Rennings et al. (2006) highlight the significant role played by learning processes that occur during the implementation of EMS.

We consider two dimensions of efficiency; (1) cost savings arising from expenditures in environmental improvements and (2) equipment upgrades undertaken with the purpose of environmental protection. Eco-innovations that can lead to more efficient means of production may give rise to cost savings that can in return motivate further investments into eco-innovations (Hitchens et al., 2003). Even though many firms report environmental protection activities to be costly for them, Ashford (1994) argues that this is only the case for end-of-pipeline pollution control technologies, and that companies can save costs by investing in cleaner production technologies that reduce pollution and waste at its source:

> When cleaner production and pollution control options that solve the same environmental problems are properly evaluated against one another, the cleaner production options will usually be less costly to implement, operate and maintain . . . because cleaner production technologies reduce cost of raw materials, energy, pollution control, waste treatment and clean-up, and regulatory compliance.' (Ashford, 1994, p. 7)

In line with this statement, a recent OECD study using data from seven OECD countries indicates that there are larger cost savings from investments in cleaner production technologies (Johnstone, 2007). Frondel et al. (2007) provide evidence that cost savings are an important factor that drives cleaner production technologies.

On the other hand, Palmer et al. (1995) argue that cost savings due to environmental innovations are as low as 2 per cent of the environmental compliance costs and are unlikely to provide enough stimuli to drive environmental innovations. They suggest that cost-offsets due to environmental innovations should be rather high in order for cost-savings to be a driver for eco-innovations.

Equipment upgrade activities can similarly lead to more efficient energy use and further cost savings. For example, Yokogawa Electric, a Japanese manufacturer, developed a technology that controls the pumping pressure of air conditioning systems, resulting in large energy savings. Several businesses such as equipment factories, hotels, and supermarkets that upgraded their existing air conditioning systems to Yokogawa's new system were able to reduce their energy consumption significantly (OECD, 2009).

We consider corporate social responsibility (CSR) as an important element of corporate image, which is a recent and controversial concept that embraces environmental issues as one of its three pillars – the other two being the employment/labour practices, and human/social rights. The Earth Summit in Rio (1992) highlighted the importance of environmental issues for CSR and coined the term 'Environmental Social Responsibility' (Hart, 1995; Russo and Fouts, 1997).

The effectiveness of environmental actions motivated by CSR has come under question due to the 'voluntary' basis for compliance under CSR. In other words, are 'voluntary' processes such as CSR effective enough to stimulate eco-innovation? Aggeri (1999) argues that although voluntary agreements provide weaker incentives compared to external policy instruments, they are well adapted to manage uncertainty and coordination issues arising when dealing with sustainable development problems. In particular, innovation-oriented voluntary agreements include a stronger coordination scheme, which is necessary in order to achieve sustainable development.

On the other hand, Williamson et al. (2006) suggest that the voluntary nature of CSR cannot satisfy the need for sustainable production. They argue that the use of regulatory structures that provide the minimum standards for many activities covered by CSR is the only effective way to encourage green activities in companies. Recent empirical evidence on the influence of voluntary programs compared to formal regulation on emissions in the metal-finishing industry indicates that the effectiveness of voluntary programs yielded little, if any, reductions in emissions, while the regulator threat reduced emissions significantly (Brouhle et al., 2009). Hence, the impact and effectiveness of environmental CSR policies on eco-innovation remains unresolved, begging for further research.

Overall, the review of the literature suggests that it is highly unlikely that all types of eco-innovations are stimulated by the same drivers. Our conceptual framework in Figure 6.1 attempts to explore the role played by

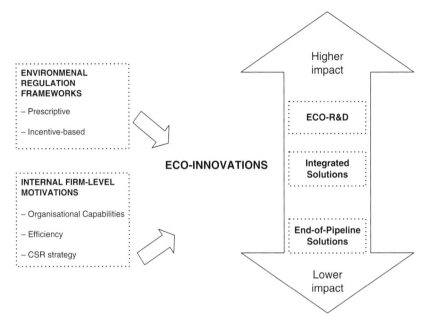

Source: Authors.

Figure 6.1   Conceptual framework

various factors in motivating the different types of eco-innovation by dis-
entangling the effectiveness of the regulatory (external) and firm-specific
(internal) factors. This framework is important to ecological economics
for analytical purposes in guiding empirical research and also for inform-
ing policy makers and businesses regarding the expected environmental,
technological, and economic impact of various regulatory instruments
and internal business activities. Given the existence of mixed evidence on
the roles that regulatory environment and firm-specific factors play in different types of eco-innovations, we apply an empirically oriented strategy
and leave it for the data to reveal the direction and significance of the
impact of these factors in the specific case of the UK.

DATA AND METHODOLOGY

We use a dataset of 289 UK firms that responded to the DEFRA
survey Environmental Protection Expenditure by Industry in years 2005
and 2006. The Department for Environment, Food and Rural Affairs

(DEFRA) conducts the survey with the aim of estimating how much the UK manufacturing sector spends (annually) to protect the environment.[5] The survey represents a unique source of information on the UK environmental spending with a very high level of coverage across all manufacturing industries.[6] With the exception of Kesidou and Demirel (2010), the data has not been used for academic research purposes.

The survey questions give us a valuable opportunity to explore the determinants of different eco-innovations by providing information on firms' investments into (1) end-of-pipeline pollution control technologies (EOP), (2) integrated cleaner production technologies (INT) and (3) environmental R&D (ECORD). As the statistics in Table 6.2 reveal, the majority of UK investments into environmental protection goes into the integrated cleaner production technologies, followed by end-of-pipeline pollution control technologies and environmental R&D. Frondel et al. (2007) and Lanoie et al. (2007) report similar levels of investment for seven OECD countries based on the OECD survey of 3100 establishments.

Additionally, the DEFRA survey provides information on firms' cost savings from environmental activities (CS), their equipment upgrade (Eq_Upgrade), and corporate social responsibility (CSR) motivations, whether or not they subscribe to environmental management systems (EMS), the external validation status of their EMS (i.e. ISO14001) as well as how they perceive environmental regulations (ENV_REG) and environmental taxes (ENV_TAX). Table 6.2 reports the descriptive statistics and a brief definition for all variables used in this study.

Among the 289 firms in the dataset, 70 firms invested in end-of-pipeline technologies (EOP), 66 invested in integrated cleaner technologies (INT) and 73 invested in environmental R&D (ECORD) in 2006. A further breakdown of investment into each eco-innovation variable is presented in Figure 6.2. As indicated; 54.8 per cent of firms in the dataset did not invest into any type of eco-innovation while 45.2 per cent of firms invested in at least one type of eco-innovation. The share of eco-innovators in this study (45.2 per cent) is strikingly similar to that of generic innovators (45 per cent) reported in the UK Community Innovation Survey (Community Innovation Survey, 2009).

We examine the determinants of different types of eco-innovation by using an econometric model where each of the three eco-innovation variables EOP, INT and ECORD (normalized by the total capital of the firm) in year 2006 are independently regressed on a set of lagged internal and external determinants from year 2005 as discussed in detail below.[7] Since the dependent eco-innovation variables (ECOINN) are censored from below at zero (i.e. not all firms invest into eco-innovation), the appropriate estimation technique is a Tobit model (Greene, 2003):

Table 6.2 Description of variables and summary statistics: eco-innovation and regulation

Variables	2005				2006			
	Mean	St. Dev	Min	Max	Mean	St. Dev	Min	Max
Eco-innovation variables								
EOP: end-of-pipeline pollution control technologies (£)	201333	1790586	0	2.41e+07	85879	634398	0	1.00e+07
INT: integrated cleaner production technologies (£)	410167	3652364	0	5.83e+07	753337	1.01e+07	0	1.72e+08
ECORD: environmental research and development (£)	11698	55332	0	530910	33873	333699	0	5448494
Environmental regulation frameworks								
ENV_REG: =1 if the firm invested in environmental protection due to environmental regulation compliance	0.238	0.427	0	1	0.262	0.440	0	1
ENV_TAX: =1 if the firm invested in environmental protection because of environmental taxes	0.041	0.198	0	1	0.044	0.206	0	1

Table 6.2 (continued)

Variables	2005				2006			
	Mean	St. Dev	Min	Max	Mean	St. Dev	Min	Max
Internal firm-level motivations								
CS: total cost savings resulting from environmental improvements (£)	31056	118859	0	1244716	58363	286969	0	3761611
Equ_Upgrade:=1 if the firm invested in environmental protection because of equipment upgrade	0.194	0.396	0	1	0.153	0.360	0	1
EMS: =1 if the firm has implemented environmental management systems	0.384	0.487	0	1	0.446	0.498	0	1
ISO14001: =1 if the firm has and ISO 14001 certified environmental management system	0.296	0.457	0	1	0.282	0.451	0	1
CSR: =1 if the firm invested in environmental protection because of parent company or owner policy/CSR	0.075	0.264	0	1	0.061	0.240	0	1
EMP: number of employees	425	1009	0	12287	434	1065	0	13427
Turnover (£)	2.06E+08	1.05E+09	0	1.10E+10	2.10e+08	1.08e+09	0	1.28e+10
CAP: Total Capital (£)	1.12E+07	6.82E+07	684.3343	9.27E+08	1.46e+07	8.90e+07	1.395973	1.05e+09

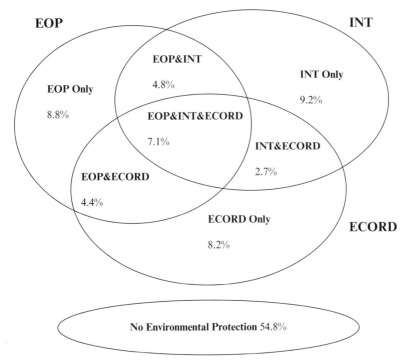

Figure 6.2   Breakdown of firms according to eco-innovation activities

$$ECOINN^*_{i,t} = x'_{i,t-1}\beta + \varepsilon \qquad (6.1)$$

and

$$ECOINN_{i,t} = \begin{cases} ECOINN^*_{i,t} & \text{if } ECOINN^*_{i,t} > 0. \\ 0 & \text{if } ECOINN^*_{i,t} \le 0. \end{cases} \qquad (6.2)$$

where *ECOINN* variable is greater than zero only when the latent *ECOINN** variable exceeds zero which represents cases where firms' willingness to invest into the eco-innovation activities is positive (Sigelman and Zeng 1999). The independent variables, included in the vector *x* correspond to the external and internal determinants of eco-innovation as follows.

Prior work by environmental economists has shown that prescriptive regulatory instruments and incentive-based regulatory instruments are important determinants of eco-innovations (Hart, 2004; Popp, 2005; Rothfels, 2002). We measure prescriptive regulatory instruments with the

ENV_REG variable and we proxy incentive-based regulatory instruments with the ENV_TAX variable. Both are binary variables that respectively assume the value 1 if a firm indicates that environmental regulations or environmental taxes have been effective in their decisions to invest into environmental protection in 2005.

Previous empirical studies have also underlined the role of internal determinants of eco-innovation (Rennings et al., 2006; Frondel et al., 2007; Kollman and Prakash, 2002; Darnall, 2006). Among these firm-level factors, we measure material and energy efficiency gains by considering the cost savings due to environmental improvements (CS) and by taking into account the equipment upgrade motivations (Equ_Upgrade) of firms as reported in 2005.

The environmental organizational capabilities of firms are measured by a binary variable that takes the value 1 if the firm has an environmental management system (EMS) in place in 2005. We further investigate whether the external certification of EMS is an important determinant of eco-innovations using another dummy variable that takes the value 1 if the firm owns an approved ISO 14001 certification. Finally, we explore the role of voluntary activities of companies to protect the environment by including an independent dummy variable, CSR, which indicates whether corporate social responsibility policies have played an important role in the decisions to invest into environmental protection in 2005. The correlation matrix for the dependent and independent variables is presented in Table 6A.1 in the Appendix.

As an additional control, we account for the size (measured by the number of employees) and labour productivity (measured by the output/labour ratio) differences that may lead to different eco-innovation behaviour among firms. We also include dummies for LOW-emission, MEDIUM-emission and HIGH-emission industries.[8] Table 6A.2 in the Appendix presents the emission intensity for each sector.

To have a more comprehensive understanding of the impact of the regulatory and firm-specific factors upon eco-innovations, we decompose the marginal effects attained through the estimation of the Tobit model in equation (6.1) using McDonald and Moffitt's (1980) suggestion of decomposing the slope vector β into:

$$\frac{\partial E[ECOINN_i|x_i]}{\partial x_i} = Prob[ECOINN > 0]\frac{\partial E[ECOINN_i|x_i, ECOINN_i > 0]}{\partial x_i} +$$

$$E[ECOINN_i|x_i, ECOINN_i > 0]\frac{Prob[ECOINN > 0]}{\partial x_i} \quad (6.3)$$

According to equation (6.3), a change in x_i has two effects: (1) the effect on the probability that the observation will fall in the positive part of the distribution (the impact upon convincing the firms to undertake investments in eco-innovations) and (2) the effect on the conditional mean of *ECOINN** in the positive part of the distribution (i.e. the impact upon the level of eco-innovations for those firms with positive spending) (Greene, 2003, p. 766). This decomposition is especially important for understanding the factors that can motivate 54.8 per cent of the firms that do not undertake any kind of eco-innovations. The decomposed marginal effects as in part (1) and (2) of equation (6.3) are reported in all regressions across Tables 6.3, 6.4 and 6.5, which are presented at the end this chapter to minimize the disruption to the discussion below.

RESULTS AND DISCUSSION

As initially anticipated, the results provided in Tables 6.3, 6.4 and 6.5 confirm that different types of eco-innovation indeed have different determinants. Moreover, these determinants have a different impact on the level of eco-innovations and the probability of eco-innovating. These findings have important implications for policy makers who may wish to stimulate a certain kind of eco-innovation by focusing on its specific determinants. Below we discuss the role of internal and external determinants for motivating EOP, INT and ECORD.

Impact of Environmental Regulation Frameworks

With regards to environmental regulation frameworks, our results indicate that prescriptive regulatory instruments such as environmental regulations are effective in driving certain types of eco-innovation, while incentive-based regulatory instruments such as environmental taxes fail to motivate any of the three eco-innovations considered.

Prescriptive regulatory instruments

Our findings go beyond the findings of the existing literature by incorporating three types of eco-innovation in the same framework that allows us to see the presence of a U-type relationship between prescriptive regulations and eco-innovations: prescriptive regulatory rules tend to have significant effects on the low and high ends of the eco-innovation spectrum; namely on the end-of-pipeline technologies (EOP) and on environmental R&D expenditures (ECORD). Their impact is less clear with respect to integrated cleaner technologies (INT), which stand in between EOP and ECORD in terms of environmental and technological significance.

Moreover, decomposing the marginal effects of prescriptive regulations indicates that their impact is large particularly in inducing companies to invest in the end-of-pipeline (EOP) technologies and in environmental R&D (ECORD) expenditures. Their effects on the levels of EOP and ECORD undertaken by firms that are already eco-innovators are smaller but statistically significant. This suggests that prescriptive regulations are more effective in inducing firms to eco-innovate at either end of the eco-innovation spectrum, rather than in 'picking up the winners' within the sample of firms surveyed.

These findings are in line with those of Frondel et al. (2007) who show that regulations are important for the end-of-pipeline technologies, but not for integrated cleaner technologies. According to Frondel et al. (2007, p. 573), because regulations are very prescriptive, and usually 'impose technology standards that can only be met through End-of-Pipeline abatement measures', they stimulate investments in process innovations; specifically in end-of-pipeline technologies, while they have no impact upon integrated cleaner technologies. Hence, our findings confirm the existing literature in the context of the UK.

Simultaneously, our results show that regulations stimulate investments in environmental R&D (ECORD), which gives rise to both process and product environmental innovations. This finding is in line with the 'Porter hypothesis', which states that regulations boost environmental R&D activities and thus stimulate eco-innovation. According to the literature, companies which invest in environmental R&D gain 'strategic advantage' from innovation and become leaders in 'green markets' (Carraro, 2000; Montero, 2002; Hart, 2004; Popp, 2005; Rothfels, 2002).

Incentive-based regulatory instruments
In contrast to prescriptive regulations, environmental taxes do not appear to have a significant impact on any of the three types of eco-innovation. This finding is, again, similar to Frondel et al.'s (2007) results which confirm that incentive-based regulatory instruments do not affect either end-of-pipeline or integrated technologies in Germany. In the specific case of the UK, environmental taxes have not been frequently used as a means of regulating pollution levels since environmental laws have historically been the preferred policy tool in this field (Ashford, 1994; Jordan and Wurzel, 2003). Moreover, environmental taxes are commonly set at a low level and the innovation effects are, therefore, low or insignificant (Kemp, 2000).

Impact of Internal Firm-level Factors

As far as internal factors are concerned, our results indicate that efficiency (equipment upgrade motives and cost savings) and EMS factors have a varied impact on the three types of eco-innovations while CSR is not a significant driver for any type of eco-innovation.

Efficiency

Machinery and equipment upgrades are important means of increasing efficiency for companies and our results indicate that EOP and INT are driven by firms' willingness to upgrade their equipment. This suggests that firms consider the most energy efficient and environmentally friendly technologies when they are renewing existing facilities.

Another indicator of efficiency, cost savings, appears to be an important driver for only the most advanced type of eco-innovations, ECORD, while it has no significant impact on either EOP or INT. This result is understandable for the case of end-of pipeline technologies which are considered to be costly rather than cost-saving investments (Ashford, 1994). The lack of impact in the case of integrated cleaner technologies, on the other hand, gives support to the findings of Palmer et al. (1995) who suggest that cost savings might not be large enough to drive eco-innovations.

Finally, the results suggest that environmental R&D is not only stimulated by regulation but is also market driven, mainly motivated by the cost saving potential of the outcomes that arise from environmental R&D. The decomposition of marginal effects on the cost savings variable confirms that many firms are motivated to invest in environmental R&D due to cost saving possibilities while the impact of cost savings are smaller for those firms that are already investing in environmental R&D.

Environmental Management Systems (EMS)

The impact of EMS, on the other hand, is similar to that of environmental regulations where the most (ECORD) and least (EOP) significant eco-innovations respond to the presence of an EMS in the company. This effect is most clearly visible especially when the impact of ISO14001 certification is considered. EOP and ECORD respond positively to adopting ISO 14001 certification while INT is not stimulated by either maintaining an EMS or subscribing to ISO 14001. A plausible explanation of this finding is related to the innovative heterogeneity of firms where the least innovative firms benefit from having an organizational environmental structure to support them with the minimum compliance requirements through EOP while the most innovative firms use EMS as an innovation platform to build upon for ECORD. The decomposed marginal effects suggest that EMS is especially effective in motivating firms to start investing in EOP and has a significant but smaller effect on increasing the EOP investments of those firms that already invest in EOP. In the case of ECORD, EMS is only effective for persuading firms to invest in ECORD but does not motivate increased ECORD investments by firms that are already active in ECORD activities.

Corporate Social Responsibility (CSR)
CSR fails to be a significant driver of any of the three eco-innovations. This indeed poses questions on how much we can rely on corporate goodwill and voluntary compliance in environmental matters. While environmental awareness and protection is an important foundation for CSR, the costly nature of environmental protection and the externalities associated with these expenditures appear to get in the way of CSR as a powerful driver for environmental protection.

   Finally, we find firm size to be a significant driver for eco-innovation in the case of EOP technology while its impact is not significant in the case of INT or ECORD. Labour productivity, on the other hand, has a small but significant impact in driving EOP and ECORD investments. We do not find any significant industry effects measured by the industry dummies constructed based on pollution intensity.

CONCLUSIONS

This chapter has investigated the determinants of different types of eco-innovation, namely, end-of-pipeline pollution control technologies, integrated cleaner production technologies and environmental R&D expenditures. These three types of eco-innovation differ with respect to their technological significance, costs to companies and their benefits to the environment. By integrating these three different eco-innovation activities in a single framework, we are able to analyse whether and how certain factors stimulate each of these eco-innovations.

   Our findings indicate that environmental regulations affect end-of-pipeline pollution control technologies and environmental R&D while they do not influence integrated cleaner technologies. By setting strict technology standards, regulations stimulate investments in end-of-pipeline technologies, which have the lowest environmental and technological impact while, at the same time, encouraging investments in environmental R&D, which has the highest environmental and technological impact. Consequently, the results of this study suggest that prescriptive regulatory instruments can play an important role in combating pollution not only in the short run, by stimulating investments in process innovations such as end-of-pipeline technologies, but also in the long run by driving investments in process and product innovations through environmental R&D. The latter provides support for the Porter hypothesis and has important implications for the environmental innovation policy. As markets for low-carbon products are estimated to be worth at least $500bn per year by 2050 (Stern, 2006), regulation may play a key role in motivating firms to invest in environmental R&D for the generation of eco-friendly products and services that have significant market potential.

Our results further suggest that the impact of prescriptive regulatory instruments is especially large in motivating companies to adopt eco-innovations while they have a smaller, yet significant impact, upon the intensity of investments on eco-innovations. These results are in line with the literature on the diffusion of generic innovations. In particular, at early stages of diffusion the inter-firm adoption rate dominates the intra-firm intensity of use (Battisti and Stoneman, 2003). Policies tend to focus mainly on the adoption of innovations by firms rather than on their intensity of use. Yet, once beyond the early stages of adoption, the intensity of use becomes extremely important in the generation of benefits from adoption, in general, and of eco-innovations in particular (e.g. in increasing learning and the absorptive capacity of the company) (Battisti and Stoneman, 2003). Therefore, we highlight the necessity for designing prescriptive regulatory instruments that do not only motivate the adoption of eco-innovations but also their intensity of use.

In contrast to prescriptive regulatory instruments, incentive-based regulatory instruments do not affect any type of eco-innovations. The UK is currently adopting a growing number of incentive-based instruments in lieu of the EU. Policy makers should carefully consider the effectiveness of these instruments not only for reducing the immediate pollution but also for stimulating eco-innovations that will lead to a greener economy in the UK. Kemp and Pontoglio (2008) highlight the need for policy instruments that ensure the required policy stringency through appropriate design and effective enforcements. Additionally, our results suggest that incentive-based instruments cannot be relied upon solely and they should be combined with relevant prescriptive instruments. This recommendation is in line with the wider literature on regulation, which tends to report that market-based instruments may be superior under perfect or near-perfect competition; but in the presence of market imperfections the case for prescriptive instruments is stronger even though the ranking of the different policy instruments is not clear-cut (for a review, see Goulder and Parry, 2008).

Our findings also point to the presence of a number of firm-level factors that determine the adoption and/or creation of eco-innovations. First, cost savings resulting from environmental efficiency appear to be only significant in driving investments in environmental R&D which are at the high end of the eco-innovation spectrum. Cost savings come from eliminating or re-using waste. Less advanced eco-innovations, expectedly, have a lower potential for creating such savings for companies. Therefore, it is possible that cost savings are most closely associated with the most advanced eco-innovations. Improvements to the eco-infrastructure play a significant role in ensuring that even firms with less advanced eco-innovations can reap cost benefits. For example, ensuring that firms have accessible outlets for the sale of their by-products can be highly effective in encouraging cost savings and increasing eco-innovations.

Eco-innovations at the low end and the middle of impact spectrum (i.e. EOP and INT), on the other hand, are motivated by increased environmental efficiency due to equipment upgrades, which allow firms to shift to more energy efficient means of production. We note the benefits of policy incentives, such as 'scrappage' style programs, that will make it easier for firms to trade-in their machinery for more energy efficient alternatives.

The second category of firm-level factors, the environmental organizational capabilities, also affect the innovation effort at low and high ends of eco-innovations, possibly providing the new starters with the required organizational structure on their first attempt to eco-innovate and also the most capable innovators with a sound framework to enable them to apply their innovation skills and knowledge to environmental matters. We find that ISO14001 certification is effective in strengthening the positive impact of environmental management systems on both end-of-pipeline technologies and environmental R&D.

The third firm-level factor, CSR, is interestingly not a significant driver of any type of eco-innovation. This casts doubt on the effectiveness of voluntary agreements by companies to reduce their environmental impact. CSR policies can most effectively be used as a supporting mechanism to environmental policies which underline the minimum basis for environmental compliance.

Table 6.3   Determinants of end-of-pipeline (EOP) innovations

Dependent variable	EOP	Marginal effects for the decision to conduct EOP	Marginal effects for EOP>0	EOP	Marginal effects for the decision to conduct EOP	Marginal effects for EOP>0	EOP	Marginal effects for the decision to conduct EOP	Marginal effects for EOP>0
In (Employees)(t-1)	0.042**	0.043**	0.009***	.044***	.044***	.010***	.055***	.055***	.012***
	0.017	0.012	0.004	.017	.012	.004	.019	.012	.004
Productivity (t-1)	.000***	.000***	.000***	.000***	.000***	.000***	.000***	.000***	.000***
	.000	.000	.000	.000	.000	.000	.000	.000	.000
Environmental regulation frameworks									
ENV_REG (t-1)	.133***	.134***	.029***	.141***	.143***	.031***	.174***	.176***	.038***
	.043	.042	.009	.046	.045	.010	.048	.039	.011
ENV_TAX(t-1)	−.130	−.130	−.029	−.127	−.127	−.028	−.180*	−.181**	−.040*
	.097	.092	.021	.092	.088	.020	.104	.091	.023
Internal firm-level motivations									
ln (CS)(t-1)	.174	.175	.038	.180	.181	.040	.207*	.209*	.046*
	.122	.122	.027	.118	.119	.026	.110	.109	.025
Equ_upgrade(t-1)	.156**	.157***	.035**	.156**	.157***	.034**	.160**	.162***	.035**
	.061	.048	.014	.061	.048	.013	.063	.049	.014
EMS(t-1)	.115**	.116***	.026**						
	.050	.038	.011						
ISO14001(t-1)				.103**	.103**	.023**			
				.052	.041	.011			

Table 6.3 (continued)

Dependent variable	EOP	Marginal effects for the decision to conduct EOP	Marginal effects for EOP>0	EOP	Marginal effects for the decision to conduct EOP	Marginal effects for EOP>0	EOP	Marginal effects for the decision to conduct EOP	Marginal effects for EOP>0
Internal firm-level motivations									
CSR(t-1)							.147 *.091*	.148* *.077*	.032 *.020*
MEDIUM-Pollution	.143 *.133*	.143 *.126*	.032 *.029*	.151 *.134*	.153 *.127*	.034 *.029*	.163 *.139*	.165 *.130*	.036 *.030*
HIGH-Pollution	.173 *.134*	.174 *.126*	.038 *.029*	.182 *.136*	.183 *.127*	.040 *.030*	.180 *.138*	.182 *.130*	.040 *.030*
Constant	-.702*** *.228*			-.705*** *.228*			-.588*** *.157*		
F	2.23**			2.20**			2.18**		
Log Likelihood	-64.053			-67.839			-65.142		
Pseudo R2	0.306			0.298			0.294		
Left-censored observations	73			73			73		
Uncensored observations	216			216			216		
Number of obs	289			289			289		

Note: Significance *0.1, **0.5, ***0.01. Robust standard errors in italics.

170

Table 6.4 Determinants of integrated technology (INT) innovations

Dependent variable	INT	Marginal effects for the decision to conduct INT	Marginal effects for INT>0	INT	Marginal effects for the decision to conduct INT	Marginal effects for INT>0	INT	Marginal effects for the decision to conduct INT	Marginal effects for INT>0
In (Employees)(t-1)	.043* *.023*	.027* *.014*	.010* *.005*	.039* *.023*	.025* *.015*	.009* *.005*	.054** *.023*	.034** *.014*	.012** *.005*
Productivity (t-1)	.000 *.000*	.000 *.000*	.000 *.000*	.000 *.000*	.000 *.000*	.000 *.000*	.000 *.000*	.000 *.000*	.000 *.000*
Environmental regulation frameworks									
ENV_REG(t-1)	.093 *.071*	.059 *.046*	.021 *.016*	.096 *.070*	.061 *.045*	.022 *.016*	.133* *.069*	.084* *.044*	.030* *.016*
ENV_TAX(t-1)	.153 *.169*	.096 *.107*	.035 *.098*	.160 *.165*	.102 *.106*	.037 *.038*	.121 *.167*	.076 *.106*	.028 *.038*
Internal firm-level motivations									
ln (CS)(t-1)	.213 *.137*	0.134 *.085*	.049 *.031*	.214 *.139*	.136 *.119*	.049 *.032*	.241* *.131*	.152* *.080*	.055* *.030*
Equ_upgrade(t-1)	.293*** *.099*	.185*** *.054*	.067*** *.023*	.291*** *.098*	.186*** *.054*	.067*** *.023*	.297*** *.101*	.187*** *.055*	.068*** *.024*
EMS(t-1)	.111 *.075*	.070 *.045*	.025 *.017*						
ISO14001(t-1)				.136 *.079*	.087* *.048*	.031* *.018*			

Table 6.4 (continued)

Dependent variable	INT	Marginal effects for the decision to conduct INT	Marginal effects for INT>0	INT	Marginal effects for the decision to conduct INT	Marginal effects for INT>0	INT	Marginal effects for the decision to conduct INT	Marginal effects for INT>0
Internal firm-level motivations									
CSR(t-1)							.189 *.115*	.119* *.071*	.043 *.026*
MEDIUM-Pollution	-.042 *.177*	-.026 *.112*	-.010 *.041*	-.037 *.177*	-.024 *.112*	-.008 *.040*	-.015 *.180*	-.009 *.113*	-.003 *.041*
HIGH-Pollution	.019 *.171*	.012 *.108*	.004 *.040*	.027 *.170*	.017 *.109*	.006 *.039*	.026 *.173*	.017 *.109*	.006 *.040*
Constant	-.704*** *.144*			-.704*** *.141*			-.753*** *.219*		
F	2.70***			2.68***			2.78***		
Log likelihood	-119.360			-118.91			-119.076		
Pseudo R2	0.104			0.107			0.106		
Left-censored observations	70			70			70		
Uncensored Observations	219			219			219		
Number of obs	289			289			289		

Notes: Significance *0.1, **0.5, ***0.01. Robust standard errors in italics.

Table 6.5 Determinants of environmental R&D expenditures (ECORD)

Dependent variable	ECORD	Marginal effects for the decision to conduct ECORD	Marginal effects for ECORD > 0	ECORD	Marginal effects for the decision to conduct ECORD	Marginal effects for ECORD > 0	ECORD	Marginal effects for the decision to conduct ECORD	Marginal effects for ECORD > 0
ln (Employees)(t-1)	.016	.015	.003	.013	.012	.003	.025*	.023*	.005*
	.014	*.013*	*.003*	*.014*	*.014*	*.003*	*.013*	*.012*	*.003*
Productivity (t-1)	.000***	.000***	.000***	.000***	.000***	.000***	.000***	.000***	.000***
	.000	*.000*	*.000*	*.000*	*.000*	*.000*	*.000*	*.000*	*.000*
Environmental regulation frameworks									
ENV_REG(t-1)	.108**	.101**	.023**	.110**	.103***	.024**	.129**	.123***	.029**
	.048	*.040*	*.010*	*.048*	*.040*	*.010*	*.051*	*.039*	*.011*
ENV_TAX(t-1)	.107	.100	.023	.113	.106	.024	.087	.083	.019
	.106	*.099*	*.010*	*.105*	*.097*	*.023*	*.102*	*.097*	*.022*
Internal firm-level motivations									
ln (CS)(t-1)	.151***	.142***	.032***	.148***	.138***	.032***	.171***	.162***	.037***
	.054	*.051*	*.011*	*.053*	*.050*	*.011*	*.050*	*.045*	*.011*
Equ_upgrade(t-1)	-.005	-.005	-.001	-.005	-.004	-.001	-.005	-.005	-.001
	.049	*.046*	*.011*	*.049*	*.045*	*.010*	*.049*	*.046*	*.011*
EMS(t-1)	.081*	.076**	.017*						
	.049	*.038*	*.010*						

Table 6.5 (continued)

Dependent variable	ECORD	Marginal effects for the decision to conduct ECORD	Marginal effects for ECORD > 0	ECORD	Marginal effects for the decision to conduct ECORD	Marginal effects for ECORD > 0	ECORD	Marginal effects for the decision to conduct ECORD	Marginal effects for ECORD > 0
Internal firm-level motivations									
ISO14001(t-1)									
CSR(t-1)				.102* *.054*	.095** *.039*	.022* *.011*	.046 *.062*	.043 *.059*	.010 *.013*
MEDIUM-Pollution	-.145 *.149*	-.136 *.100*	-.031 *.030*	-.143 *.139*	-.133 *.099*	-.031 *.030*	-.131 *.136*	-.125 *.101*	-.028 *.029*
HIGH-Pollution	-.114 *.131*	-.106 *.100*	-.024 *.028*	-.110 *.130*	-.102 *.099*	-.024 *.028*	-.106 *.128*	-.101 *.100*	-.022 *.028*
Constant	-.284*** *.088*			-.274*** *.088*			-.311*** *.086*		
F	2.24**			2.35**			2.74***		
Log likelihood	-80.47			-79.78			-81.59		
Pseudo R2	0.119			0.126			0.106		
Left-censored observations	66			66			66		
Uncensored observations	223			223			223		
Number of obs	289			289			289		

Notes: Significance *0.1, **0.5, ***0.01. Robust standard errors in italics.

NOTES

*   This chapter is an edited version of Pelin Demirel and Effie Kesidou, 'Stimulating different types of eco-innovation in the UK: government policies and firm motivations', *Ecological Economics*, 70(8): 1546–1557, Copyright (2011), with permission from Elsevier. The authors would like to thank Rocky Harris and Steve Wellington from DEFRA for providing us access to the dataset and clarifications on the data collection methods. We are grateful to Giuliana Battisti, Peter Swann, Sourafel Girma, Mehmet Ugur and two anonymous referees of *Ecological Economics* for useful comments and suggestions on earlier drafts. We also thank Eskandar Rashid Mohamed for excellent research assistance. All errors, of course, remain our own.

1. Environmental technologies cover a broad range of different technology applications aimed at alternative energy production or providing solutions to environmental problems (Cooke, 2008). Eco-innovation is defined as 'the creation or implementation of new, or significantly improved, products (goods and services), processes, marketing methods, organizational structures and institutional arrangements which – with or without intent – lead to environmental improvements compared to relevant alternatives' (OECD, 2009, p. 19).

2. Examples of end-of-pipeline technologies include effluent treatment plant and exhaust air scrubbing systems.

3. Examples of integrated technologies include the following (Ashford, 1994): (a) improved housekeeping, which refers to improvements in management practices, monitoring, and maintenance; (b) changes to process technologies, through optimization, which conserves raw materials and energy; (c) changes to products with the use of new technologies, which reduces the consumption of resources, waste and emissions; (d) changes to inputs by substituting toxic materials with environmentally friendly alternatives.

4. Environmental economists use models, which treat pollution as a negative externality; the generators of these externalities are induced through a set of Pigouvian taxes and/ or tradable permits to pay for the full range of social costs that their activities entail (Baumol and Oates, 1988).

5. A stratified random sample of companies (based on SIC code and firm size) from the Inter Departmental Business Register (IDBR) held by the Office for National Statistics (ONS) was targeted by the survey in years 2005 and 2006. Note that firms with less than 10 employees were not covered in the sampling process.

6. In particular, the response rates are respectively 18.7% and 20.4% in 2005 and 2006. 1466 firms responded to the survey in 2005 and 1599 firms responded to the survey in 2006. 289 firms that are included in the following analysis responded in both years.

7. Our rationale for using lagged independent variables mainly rests on the fact that there would be an expected lag between implementation of CSR, EMS, environmental regulations, taxes etc., and their impact on eco-innovations. While using lagged observations results in a loss of data, we consider this to be an appropriate sacrifice given the yearly variation in the data and potential lag effects.

8. The set of industries covered in the sample correspond to UK SIC (2003) codes 10, 11, 14, 15, 17, 18, 19, 20, 21, 22, 23, 24, 25, 26, 27, 28, 29, 30, 31, 32, 33, 34, 35, 36, 40 and 41. We have classified these industries in three groups with respect to their pollution intensity: low, medium and high emission. This classification is based on DEFRA's greenhouse gas (GHG) emissions data for 93 UK economic sectors between 1990 and 2008. We have taken an average for the GHG emissions for each sector in the UK across the years and ranked these values in ascending order. In what follows, the industries classified as LOW emission are those that are at the lowest quartile of the UK pollution intensity, those classified as MEDIUM emission are those that are within the 2nd and 3rd quartile of the range and finally, the industries classified as HIGH emission are those in the top quartile of the UK pollution intensity.

REFERENCES

Aggeri, F. (1999), 'Environmental policies and innovation: a knowledge-based perspective on cooperative approaches', *Research Policy*, **28** (7), 699–717.

Anton, W.R.Q., G. Deltas and M. Khanna (2004), 'Incentives for environmental self-regulation and implications for environmental performance', *Journal of Environmental Economics and Management*, **48** (1), 632–654.

Arimura, T.H., A. Hibiki and H. Katayama (2008), 'Is a voluntary approach an effective environmental policy instrument? A case for environmental management systems', *Journal of Environmental Economics and Management*, **55** (3), 281–295.

Ashford, N.A. (1994), *Government Strategies and Policies for Cleaner Production*, New York: United Nations Environment Programme, Industry and Environment Centre.

Bansal, P. and T. Hunter (2003), 'Strategic explanations for the early adoption of ISO 14001', *Journal of Business Ethics*, **46** (3), 289–299.

Battisti, G., and P. Stoneman (2003), 'Inter- and intra-firm effects in the diffusion of new process technology', *Research Policy*, **32** (9), 1641–1655.

Baumol, W.J., and W. E. Oates (1988), *The Theory of Environmental Policy*, Second edition. Cambridge, UK: Cambridge University Press.

Biondi, V., F. Iraldo and S. Meredith (2002), 'Achieving sustainability through environmental innovation: the role of SMEs', *International Journal of Technology Management*, **24** (5–6), 612–626.

Boiral, O. (2007), 'Corporate greening through ISO 14001: a rational myth?', *Organization Science*, **18** (1), 127–146.

Brouhle, K., C. Griffiths and A. Wolverton (2009), 'Evaluating the role of EPA policy levers: an examination of a voluntary program and regulatory threat in the metal-finishing industry', *Journal of Environmental Economics and Management*, **57** (2), 166–181.

Carraro, C. (2000), 'Environmental technological innovation and diffusion: model analysis', in J. Hemmelskamp, F. Leone and K. Rennings (eds), *Innovation-Oriented Environmental Regulations: Theoretical Approaches and Empirical Analysis*, Heidelberg, New York: Physica Verlag, pp. 269–297.

Cleff, T., and K. Rennings (2000), 'Determinants of environmental innovation-empirical evidence from the Mannheim Innovation Panel and an additional telephone survey', in J. Hemmelskamp, F. Leone and K. Rennings (eds), *Innovation-Oriented Environmental Regulations: Theoretical Approaches and Empirical Analysis*, Heidelberg and New York: Physica Verlag, pp. 269–297.

Cohen, W. and D. Levinthal (1990) 'Absorptive capacity: a new perspective on learning and innovation', *Administrative Science Quarterly*, **35** (1), 128–152.

Cooke, P. (2008), 'Cleantech and an analysis of the platform nature of life sciences: further reflections upon platform policies', *European Planning Studies*, **16** (3): 375–393.

Darnall, N. (2006), 'Why firms mandate ISO 14001 certification', *Business & Society*, **45** (3), 354–381.

Dijken, K.V., Y. Prince, T. Wolters, M. Frey, G. Mussati, P. Kalff, O. Hansen, S. Kerndrup, B. Sondergard, E.L. Rodrigues and S. Meredith (1999), *Adoption of Environmental Innovations*, The Netherlands: Kluwer Academic Publishers.

Frondel, M., J. Horbach and K. Rennings (2007), 'End-of-Pipe or cleaner production? An empirical comparison of environmental innovation decisions across OECD countries', *Business Strategy and the Environment*, **16** (8), 571–584.

Geels, F.W., and J.W. Schot (2007) 'Typology of sociotechnical transition pathways', *Research Policy*, **36** (3), 399–417.

Goulder, L.H. and I.W. Parry (2008), 'Instrument choice in environmental policy', *Review of Environmental Economics and Policy*, **2** (2), 152–174.

Greene, W.H. (2003), *Econometric Analysis*, 5th edn, New York: Prentice Hall.

Hamschmidt, J. and T. Dyllick (2001), 'ISO 14001: profitable? Yes! But is it eco-effective?' *Greener Management International*, 43–54.

Hart, O. (1995), *Firms, Contracts, and Financial Structure*, Oxford: Clarendon Press.

Hart, R. (2004), 'Growth, environment and innovation – a model with production vintages and environmentally oriented research', *Journal of Environmental Economics and Management*, **48** (3), 1078–1098.

Hitchens, D., M. Trainor, J. Clausen, S. Thankappan and D. De Marchi (2003), *Small and Medium Sized Companies in Europe – Environmental Performance, Competitiveness and Management*, Heidelberg: Springer Verlag.

Jaenicke, M., J. Blazejczak, D. Edler and J. Hemmelskamp (2000), 'Environmental policy and innovation – an international comparison of policy frameworks and innovation effects', J. Hemmelskamp, F. Leone and K. Rennings (eds), *Innovation-Oriented Environmental Regulations: Theoretical Approaches and Empirical Analysis*, Heidelberg and New York: Physica Verlag, pp. 269–297.

Johnstone, N. (2007) *Environmental Policy and Corporate Behaviour*, Cheltenham,UK and Northampton, MA, USA: Edward Elgar Publishing, in association with OECD.

Johnstone, N., I. Hascic and M. Kalamova (2010), 'Environmental policy design characteristics and technological innovation', *Journal of Analytical and Institutional Economics*, 27(2), 275–299.

Jordan, A., and R.K.W. Wurzel (2003), 'Comparative conclusions – "new" environmental policy instruments: an evolution or a revolution in environmental policy?', *Environmental Politics*, **12** (1), 201–224.

Kemp, R. (1997), *Environmental Policy and Technical Change*, Cheltenham, UK and Northampton, MA, USA: Edward Elgar Publishing.

Kemp, R. (2000), 'Technology and environmental policy: innovation effects of past policies and suggestions for improvement', *Innovation and the Environment*, OECD Proceedings, 35–61.

Kemp, R., and Pontoglio, S. (2008), 'The innovation effects of environmental policy instruments – a typical case of the blind men and the elephant', paper for DIME WP 2.5 Workshop on Empirical Analyses of Environmental Innovation, Fraunhofer Institute for Systems and Innovation Research (ISI), Karlsruhe, January 17–18.

Kesidou, E., and P. Demirel (2010), 'On the drivers of eco-innovations: empirical evidence from the UK', NUBS Research Paper Series No. 2010-03. Nottingham University Business School, Nottingham, UK.

Kollman, K. and Prakash, A. (2002), 'EMS-based environmental regimes as club goods', *Policy Sciences*, **35** (1), 43–67.

Lanoie, P., J. Laurent-Lucchetti, N. Johnstone and S. Ambeck (2007), 'Environmental policy, innovation and performance: new insights on the Porter hypothesis', Working Paper GAEL; 2007-07.

McDonald, J.F. and R.A. Moffitt (1980) 'The uses of Tobit analysis', *The Review of Economics and Statistics*, **62** (2), 318–321.

Melnyk, S.A., R.P. Stroufe and R. Calantone (2003), 'Assessing the impact of environmental management systems on corporate and environmental performance', *Journal of Operations Management*, **1** (3), 329–353.

Milliman, S.R. and R. Prince (1989), 'Firm incentives to promote technological change in pollution control', *Journal of Environmental Economics and Management*, **17** (3), 247–65.

Montero, J.-P. (2002), 'Permits, standards, and technology innovation', *Journal of Environmental Economics and Management*, **44** (1), 23–44.

OECD (2009) *Sustainable Manufacturing and Eco-Innovation: Framework, Practices and Measurement– Synthesis Report*, Paris: OECD.

Palmer, K., W.E. Oates and P.R. Portney (1995), 'Tightening environmental standards: the benefit-cost or the no-cost paradigm?', *The Journal of Economic Perspectives*, **9** (4), 119–132.

Popp, D. (2005), 'Uncertain R&D and the Porter hypothesis', *Contributions to Economic Analysis and Policy*, **4** (1), Article 6.

Porter, M.E. (1991), 'America's green strategy', *Scientific American*, **264** (4), 168.

Porter, M.E. and C. van der Linde (1995a), 'Toward a new conception of the environment–competitiveness relationship', *Journal of Economic Perspectives*, **9**(4), 97–118.

Porter, M.E. and C. van der Linde (1995b), 'Green and competitive: ending the stalemate', *Harvard Business Review*, **73** (5).

Rehfeld, K.-M., K. Rennings and A. Ziegler (2007), 'Integrated product policy and environmental product innovations: an empirical analysis', *Ecological Economics*, **61** (1), 91–100.

Rennings, K. (2000), 'Redefining innovation – eco-innovation research and the contribution from ecological economics', *Ecological Economics*, **32** (2), 319–332.

Rennings, K., A. Ziegler, K. Ankele and E. Hoffman (2006), 'The influence of different characteristics of the EU environmental management and auditing scheme on technical environmental innovations and economic performance', *Ecological Economics*, **57** (1), 45–59.

Requate, T. (2005), 'Dynamic incentives by government policy instruments – a survey', *Ecological Economics*, **54** (2–3), 175–195.

Requate, T. and W. Unold (2003), 'Environmental policy incentives to adopt advanced abatement technology: will the true ranking please stand up?', *European Economic Review*, **47** (1), 125–146.

Rondinelli, D. and G. Vastag (2000), 'Panacea, common sense, or just a label? The value of ISO 14001 environmental management systems', *European Management Journal*, **18** (5), 499–510.

Rothfels, J. (2002), 'Environmental policy under product differentiation and asymmetric costs: does leapfrogging occur and is it worth it?', in L. Marsiliani, M. Rauscher and C. Withagen (eds), *Environmental Economics and the International Economy*, Dordrecht: Kluwer Academic Publishers.

Russo, M.V. and P.A. Fouts (1997), 'A resource-based perspective on corporate environmental performance and profitability', *Academy of Management Journal*, **40** (3), 534–559.

Russo, M.V. and N.S. Harrison (2005), 'Organizational design and environmental

performance: clues from the electronics industry', *Academy of Management Journal*, **48** (4), 582–593.
Sigelman, L. and L. Zeng (1999), 'Analysing censored and sample selected data with Tobit and Heckit models', *Political Analysis*, **8** (2), 167–182.
Stern, N. (2006), *Stern Review: The Economics of Climate Change*, Office of Climate Change, UK.
Wagner, M. (2008), 'Empirical influence of environmental management on innovation: evidence from Europe', *Ecological Economics*, **66** (2–3), 392–402.
Williamson, D., G. Lynch-Wood and J. Ramsay (2006), 'Drivers of environmental behaviour in manufacturing SMEs and the implications for CSR', *Journal of Business Ethics*, **67** (3), 317–330.

APPENDIX

Table 6A.1   Correlation matrix: eco-innovation and regulation

	1	2	3	4	5	6	7	8	9	10	11	12
1. EOP	1.0000											
2. INT	0.1383*	1.0000										
3. ECORD	0.2017*	0.4564*	1.0000									
4. Ln(emp) (t-1)	0.0702	–0.0526	–0.0757	1.0000								
5. Prod (t-1)	0.0247	–0.0210	0.0635	–0.0518	1.0000							
6. Regulations (t-1)	0.0719	–0.0077	0.0611	0.1203	–0.0370	1.0000						
7. Taxes (t-1)	0.0477	0.0531	0.0954	0.0302	–0.0148	0.0461	1.0000					
8. ln(CS)(t-1)	0.1717*	0.1353	0.1087	–0.0725	–0.0127	0.0390	0.2376*	1.0000				
9. Equipment Upg (t-1)	0.1319	0.2449*	–0.0312	0.0264	–0.0368	–0.1731*	0.0293	0.1100	1.0000			
10. EMS (t-1)	0.1536*	0.0433	–0.0161	0.3951*	0.0665	0.2642*	0.0137	0.0985	0.0016	1.0000		
11. ISO14001 (t-1)	0.1317	0.0840	–0.0017	0.4028*	0.0853	0.2149*	–0.0208	0.0695	0.0025	0.8205*	1.0000	
12. CSR(t-1)	0.0928	0.0573	–0.0279	0.0869	–0.0199	–0.0679	0.0067	–0.0016	–0.0087	0.1473	0.1555*	1.0000

Table 6A.2   Classification of industries with respect to pollution intensity

SIC	Industry	Pollution intensity
40	Electricity, Gas, Steam and Hot Water Supply	HIGH
27	Manufacture of Basic Metals	HIGH
11	Extraction of Crude Petroleum and Natural Gas; Service Activities Incidental to Oil and Gas Extraction	HIGH
41	Collection, Purification and Distribution of Water	HIGH
23	Manufacture of Coke, Refined Petroleum Products and Nuclear Fuel	HIGH
24	Manufacture of Chemicals and Chemical Products	HIGH
26	Manufacture of Other Non-Metallic and Mineral Products	HIGH
15	Manufacture of Food Products and Beverages	HIGH
10	Mining of Coal and Lignite; Extraction of Peat	HIGH
21	Manufacture of Pulp, Paper and Paper Products	MEDIUM
25	Manufacture of Rubber and Plastic Products	MEDIUM
20	Manufacture of Wood And Products of Wood And Cork, Except Furniture; Manufacture of Articles of Straw and Plaiting Materials	MEDIUM
28	Manufacture of Fabricated Metal Products, Except Machinery and Equipment	MEDIUM
17	Manufacture of Textiles	MEDIUM
36	Manufacture of Other Products	MEDIUM
29	Manufacture of Machinery and Equipment	MEDIUM
34	Manufacture of Motor Vehicles, Trailers and Semi-trailers	MEDIUM
22	Publishing and Printing	MEDIUM
14	Other Mining and Quarrying	MEDIUM
35	Manufacture of Other Transport Equipment	MEDIUM
31	Manufacture of Electrical Machinery and Apparatus	MEDIUM
33	Manufacture of Medical, Precision and Optical Instruments, Watches and Clocks	MEDIUM
32	Manufacture of Radio, Television and Communication Equipment and Apparatus	LOW
18	Manufacture of Wearing Apparel; Dressing and Dyeing of Fur	LOW
30	Manufacture of Office Machinery and Computers	LOW
19	Tanning and Dressing of Leather; Manufacture of Handbags, Saddlery, Harness And Footwear	LOW
16	Manufacture of Tobacco Products	LOW

7. Regulation and ICT capital input: empirical evidence from 10 OECD countries

Simon Porcher

INTRODUCTION

Over the past twenty years, European governments have clearly aimed at increasing growth by encouraging innovation, which is assumed to be positively related to product-market deregulation and resulting competition. This approach has been evident both in the Single Market program of the early 1990s which aimed to harmonize national regulations and in the so-called Lisbon Strategy (2000) which aimed at increasing the share of research and development (R&D) expenditures in GDP. Both projects have considered deregulation and market-opening reforms as means to foster innovation.

One of the assumptions that underpin the Lisbon Strategy is that economic competitiveness depends on increased investments in information and communications technologies (ICT). This assumption is justified by referring to the experience of the United States, where economic growth was underpinned by high sectoral productivity gains that, in turn, were related to successful adoption of ICT. Indeed, labour productivity growth in the United States escalated from 1.1 per cent in 1990–95 to 2.5 percent in 1995–2000 while it slowed down or remained stable in most European countries (van Ark et al., 2003). This observation has generated excessive enthusiasm and often unrealistic expectations about the new economy, leading governments to assume that investments in ICT capital would raise the economic performance of Europe. The telltale story was that slower growth in Europe was linked to a comparatively small ICT diffusion at the industry level, which was due to higher levels of regulation in European countries. ICT is expected to bring substantial productivity and welfare gains as a result of lower information and search costs and simplified long-distance business services in accountancy, banking and information processing via outsourcing for example. More specifically, ICT diffusion is often used as a proxy for the 'new economy' which defines a new long-term growth trajectory based on these technologies and fostered by some institutional infrastructures.

While a lot of studies link ICT investments with growth (Jorgenson and Stiroh, 1999; Oliner and Sichel, 2000), the relationship between regulation and ICT diffusion has remained a relatively under-researched issue. This is all the more important because, at the same time, many governments have been keen on implementing deregulation and ICT-increasing policies. The idea is straightforward: an efficient use of ICT generally requires firm reorganization and institutional flexibility, which can be restricted by excessively stringent regulations. In product markets, rigid regulations can reduce competitive pressure and thus lower the incentives to use the most efficient production techniques. In addition, stringent regulation hinders the performance of the labour market by reducing the skill acquisition of the work force.

Yet, the existing literature indicates that product-market regulation may have different effects on innovation depending on the distance to the technological frontier. The received argument following Aghion et al. (2005) is that the cost of product market regulation is higher the closer is an economy to the technology frontier. The aim of this chapter is to assess the validity of the argument according to which deregulation spurs investments in ICT (Bartelsman et al., 2002; Arnold et al., 2008), and that this effect is more important when economies are close to the technological frontier (Aghion et al., 2005).

We estimate an empirical model with variables for the distance to the technology frontier, regulation, as well as interaction terms between them. We estimate the model at the industry level and report evidence that the marginal effect of regulation on ICT intensity does not become more adverse even at the technological frontier. Our results show that regulation can even spur investments in ICT, especially for countries that are close to the technological frontier. Hence, we argue that deregulation policy cannot be considered as a substitute for active science and technology policies.

This chapter contributes to the literature in several ways. First, it is one of the rare empirical investigations that account for differences in ICT diffusion across countries and industries. Second, it provides an explanation for cross-country differences in ICT diffusion in 10 OECD countries, drawing attention to a positive relationship between regulation and ICT intensity when countries are close to the technology frontier. Finally, it demonstrates that the impact of regulation on ICT intensity is not uniform and depends on the distance to the technological frontier, raising doubts about the simple links established between deregulation and increased

ICT intensity. The chapter is organized as follows. In the next section, we provide a brief review of the related literature. Then, we present the empirical strategy and the problems related to estimations. In the following sections, we first introduce the data used in the empirical analysis and then present the results of the baseline model. Finally, we conclude by summarizing the main findings and highlight the policy implications.

RELATED LITERATURE

Although the policy discourse in the European Union tends to establish a causal link between deregulation and competition on the one hand and innovation on the other, the theoretical work on the relationship between regulation/competition and innovation does not provide a clear-cut answer to whether deregulation and competition can lead to higher innovation at the microeconomic or macroeconomic levels. For example, Schumpeter (1934) argues that market concentration increases firms' incentives to innovate as it enables firms to obtain post-innovation monopoly profits as rewards for their innovation efforts. In other words, the monopoly deadweight loss is the price we have to pay in order to stimulate firms to undertake research and development (R&D) expenditures. Furthermore, R&D investment is a major factor driving technological change and economic growth. Therefore rising competition decreases not only innovative rents but also incentives to innovate.

On the other hand, given perfect appropriability, product market competition encourages efficiency (Arrow, 1962). Leaders would keep innovating to preserve their market power while potential entrants may hope to capture market share by surpassing the incumbents with new and better products. In this framework, competition is a necessary condition for innovation. These conflicting findings have led to a large set of empirical studies – dating back at least from Nickell (1996) – on the relationship between competition and certain measures of economic performance such as productivity or innovation.

Extensions of the Schumpeterian innovation-based endogenous growth model allow for differentiated effects from competition on to innovation. The landmark study by Aghion et al. (2005) combines the Schumpeterian and Arrow-like perspectives to derive an inverted-U relationship between competition and innovation. The mechanism behind this curve is the following: firms compare the expected profit of pre- and post-innovation rents. When competition is limited but increases, firms might escape competition by innovating. However, if competition is fierce, the negative Schumpeterian effect of competition on R&D dominates the positive escape-competition effect. The positive effect of competition on innovation and R&D is strongest in leveled industries characterized by neck-to-neck firms with similar technological level and unit costs. The intuition is that in leveled industries, an incremental increase in productivity helps the firm to reap market shares from a large number of competitors. Hence, in leveled industries the positive escape-competition effect of competition on R&D is stronger than in unleveled industries. The authors also found robust evidence for an inverted-U shaped relation between the Lerner index and the number of patents granted in a sample of 330 UK firms between 1968 and 1997. The 'Schumpeterian effect' of competition should dominate when the level of competition is high, whereas the 'escape-competition effect' should be prominent at low levels of product market competition. Moreover, following the prediction of the theoretical model, the inverted-U shaped relationship was found to be steeper for firms that are closer to the technology frontier in their industry.

A thin literature on the relationship between regulation and innovation reports a negative relationship between the two and thus emphasizes the positive impact of lower product-market regulation on innovation and productive efficiency. This is the case in a series of studies on the potential impact of regulation on various measures of economic performance in OECD countries. For example, Nicoletti and Scarpetta (2003) considered a sample of 23 industries for 18 OECD countries over the period 1984–98. They tested a model of total factor productivity (TFP) growth, using product-market regulation indicators devised by the OECD both alone and in interaction with a technology gap variable, which is measured as the log difference between the factor productivity level of the country-industry and the factor productivity of the leader. Their results indicate that economy-wide product market regulations that curb competition have a negative effect on productivity. Even if regulation itself has a positive but non-significant impact on productivity, a statistically significant positive coefficient is found for the interacted variables. As the technology gap variable is always negative, a positive coefficient for the interaction terms means a negative regulation effect on productivity. This result is interpreted as a slow-down in the catching-up process, whereby a country with the same technological gap as another country experiences slower productivity growth as a result of higher levels of regulation.

A somewhat similar result is reported in Bartelsman et al. (2002), who provide evidence that stringent regulations in the product markets reduce competitive pressures and thereby have a negative effect on innovation and adoption of new technologies, including ICT. The authors conclude that strong regulation can lead to less-intensive ICT adoption in European industries. A more recent paper by Arnold et al. (2008) finds a similar result to that of Bartelsman et al. (2002) and Nicoletti and Scarpetta (2003). The authors used firm-level data for the 1998–2004 period and found that anti-competitive service regulations hamper productivity growth in ICT-using sectors, with a particularly pronounced effect on firms that are catching up with the technology frontier and on those that are close to international best practice. Their results thus show that regulation particularly hurts firms that have the potential to excel in domestic and international markets. Hence, regulation should be lowered in order to increase innovation and productivity.

Such results are also confirmed in Griffith et al. (2010), who utilize the Business Enterprise Research and Development Expenditures (BERD) for 12 industries and 9 countries from 1987 to 2000 and the countries' deregulation efforts within the Single Market project to demonstrate that reduced product market regulation is conducive to increased innovation, all else equal.

However, other empirical evidence suggests that regulation can have a positive impact on innovation at the industry level. Amable et al. (2010) devised a model similar to that of Aghion et al. (2005) but include the possibility that leaders carry out R&D; and by so doing, complicate the laggards' catching up process. It is assumed that the engagement of the 'leader' in a new discovery induces a change in the technological paradigm: even if the quality difference is still one step, the leader's innovation makes this last step harder to climb for the follower. This model takes into account firms' strategies. There are asymmetries between the leader and its potential competitors: the former uses a relative advantage to bias the technological paradigm while the competitive fringe anticipates their investment in R&D as non-profitable. Thus, market regulation can have a positive impact on the competitive fringe's innovation by making the leader's position less profitable. The impact of regulation can also be positive and growing in high-tech industries. The empirical test, based on a panel of manufacturing industries in 17 OECD countries over the period 1979–2003, shows that regulation has an increasing positive impact on industries' efficiency when getting closer to the technological frontier.

A different strand of the literature on the relationship between environmental regulations and eco-innovations (see Demirel and Kesidou in chapter 6 of this volume) also indicates that both prescriptive and incentive-based environmental regulations can be conducive to eco-innovation. For example, whilst Milliman and Prince (1989), Requate and Unold (2003) and Requate (2005) report that incentive-based instruments are superior to prescriptive regulation, Hart (2004), Popp (2005) and Rothfels (2002) demonstrate that compliance with prescriptive environmental regulations can drive firms to become leaders in 'green markets' and thus become more competitive compared to their foreign peers. These findings can be explained by the presence of market imperfections that prescriptive or incentive-based regulation can address to a certain extent (Goulder and Parry, 2008).

EMPIRICAL STRATEGY

The purpose of this chapter is to test the impact of regulation on innovation with a time series cross-section data at the industry level for ten OECD countries. This leads us to consider a variable *panelvar*, which combines industries and countries that are considered as individual cases. We also consider year dummies to take into account fixed time effect, i.e. macroeconomic shocks that are homogeneous through individuals, and thus make the results more robust. The following Within-group regression is considered:

$$ICT_{it} = \beta_1 REG_{it} + \beta_2 FRONT_{it} + \beta_3 REG*FRONT_{it} + \beta_4 REG^2_{it} + \gamma_0 X_{it}$$
$$+ \lambda_t + \varepsilon_{it} \tag{7.1}$$

Here ICT_{it} is ICT capital intensity in a given industry-country i at time t; REG_{it} is the value of the regulation indicator; $FRONT_{it}$ is the extent of closeness to the technology frontier and X_{it} is a set of control variables that include the capital/labor ratio, externalities, and import penetration. This is a non-linear model that includes the squared values of regulation to strengthen the concavity of my model and test whether there is a non-linear relationship between regulation and ICT capital input. We estimate the model four times, using four different measures of regulation as described below.

As we included an interaction term in the model and a squared variable of the market regulation, the marginal effect of regulation on ICT capital intensity depends on the value of market regulation itself and of the closeness to the frontier. The tables of regression will be followed with computed marginal effects of the regulation on innovation and its significance at the mean value of REG_{it} for different values of $FRONT_{it}$. The marginal effect of regulation takes the form of $\beta_2 + \beta_3 FRONT + 2\beta_4 REG$.

To measure *ICT intensity*, we use industry-country-level ICT capital input (ICT_{it}), computed by the Groningen Growth and Development Center (GGDC) in the EU *Klems Database*. This variable is available from 1980 to 2005 for 10 OECD countries (Austria, Denmark, Finland, Germany, Italy, Netherlands, Portugal, Sweden, UK, US) and 11 manufacturing industries (Food products, Textiles, Wood products, Paper,

Chemicals and chemical products, Rubber and plastics, Other non-metallic mineral products, Metals and fabricated metals, Machinery and equipments, Electronic and optical machinery, and Motor vehicles – see Table 7A.1 in the Appendix).

Here, we consider the ICT capital input share in the value-added to measure ICT capital intensity. Value-added is taken from the Groningen Growth and Development Centre – International Comparisons of Output and Productivity (GGDC-ICOP) database for each country and each industry. All nominal series were deflated to 1997 in their national currency and then 'cross-section' deflated using the industry purchasing power parities provided by Timmer et al. (2007). The authors considered a mix between purchasing power parities based on two points of the productive process: consumer expenditure and production. This method allows obtaining transitivity in multilateral comparisons.

Closeness to the frontier $(FRONT_{it})$ is calculated using productivity levels for each industry in each country from 1980 until 2005. Closeness to the productivity frontier is measured as the ratio between the productivity in industry i in country j at time t and the highest productivity level in the same industry i at the same time t. For example, in 1980, the closeness to the frontier for Germany in the paper industry (ISIC-REV 21) is the ratio between German and Finnish productivity in the paper industry in 1980, as Finland is the more productive country in the paper industry in that year. Hence, the lower the value of $FRONT_{it}$ the closer is the industry/country to the technological frontier.

As proxies for *regulation* (REG_{it}), we use four regulation indicators provided by the OECD, which allow for comparing different regulatory environments on a long-time basis. The regulatory environment indicator for non-manufacturing sectors $(REGREF_{it})$ is available for the whole period at the national level. It gives us information about the degree of regulation in network industries (telecoms, electricity, gas, post, rail, air passenger transport, road freight) that are highly related to manufacturing sectors. It is documented by Conway and Nicoletti (2006). The higher the value of the indicator, the higher is the level of regulation.

The impact of *REGREF* on the manufacturing sector is measured by *REGIMP*, which is available from 1980 until 2003 at the industrial level for the OECD countries. This indicator measures the extent to which industries are constrained by administrative burdens, entry regulation and other market barriers in key non-manufacturing sectors such as network services, retail distribution, financial services and professional business services. The underlying idea is that these sectors are in constant interaction with manufacturing so that their regulation also constrains the operation of manufacturing firms. The OECD connects the regulatory practices in these input sectors using input-output matrices, showing their role as suppliers for the whole industry.

The *product market regulation*, PMR_{it}, is provided by the OECD and documented by Conway et al. (2005). It provides an estimation of barriers to entry for each country. This indicator has been calculated for two years, 1998 and 2003. We consider the value of 1998 for the period 1980–99 and the value of 2003 for the period 2000–05. Finally, *the size of the public enterprise sector*, $PMRP_{it}$, is a component of *PMR* that focuses on state control in the product markets. This measure can capture the differences of R&D investments in the private and the public sectors. It is also available for 1998 and 2003 and we apply the same method as for the *PMR*.

The regressions also include explanatory variables capturing alternative mechanisms influencing the intensity of ICT capital input. The main control variable is the capital/labor ratio KL_{it}, measured as the ratio of capital stock to the number of hours worked, calculated using investment series provided by the GGDC's EU Klems Database. Externalities, EXT_{it}, is measured as the international intensity of the ICT capital input, i.e. as the ratio of ICT capital input to value-added for the rest of the world. We use EXT_{it} as a proxy to measure spillover effects of the ICT intensity. We also include the import penetration, $MPEN_{it}$, which is provided by the OECD and available at the industry level in the OECD-STAN Database. This is an indicator of import product penetration and can be a proxy for 'openness' at the industry level. The summary statistics for all variables are given in Table 7A.2 in the Appendix.

RESULTS

Table 7.1 reports the results for within-group regressions, where the dependent variable is ICT intensity regressed on four different measures of regulation: *REGREF*(1), *REGIMP*(2), *PMR*(3) and *PMRP*(4). For each regression, we also report in a sub-table the marginal effects of regulation on innovation for different levels of the closeness to the technology frontier. The first line presents the marginal effect of regulation on ICT intensity at the technology frontier – i.e., when closeness to the frontier is maximum (i.e, distance to the frontier is minimum). The third line reports the marginal effect of regulation on ICT intensity when closeness to the frontier is at mean value of the closeness in the panel. The last line shows the marginal effect when the closeness to frontier is at its minimum (i.e., when distance to the frontier is maximum). Thus, the bottom half of Table 7.1 enables us to follow how the marginal effects of regulation on ICT intensity evolve when distance to the frontier is increasing.

Table 7.1   Effects of regulation on ICT intensity in OECD countries

Regulation proxy >	(1) REGREF	(2) REGIMP	(3) PMR	(4) PMRP
REGULATION	−0.109**	−8.149**	−0.281	−0.394
	(0.0433)	(3.770)	(0.457)	(0.266)
FRONT	−0.657**	−0.647**	−0.524**	−0.610**
	(0.283)	(0.262)	(0.253)	(0.275)
REG*FRONT	**0.114***	**3.719***	0.193	**0.159***
	(0.0607)	(1.838)	(0.119)	(0.0902)
REG²	0.00341	25.18**	0.0853	0.0518
	(0.00309)	(11.71)	(0.0896)	(0.0314)
KL	1.315***	1.370**	1.514**	1.462**
	(0.489)	(0.556)	(0.604)	(0.570)
EXT	0.00111	0.00178	0.000815	0.000835
	(0.00120)	(0.00147)	(0.00121)	(0.00120)
MPEN	0.000997**	0.000899**	0.00103***	0.00103**
	(0.000425)	(0.000436)	(0.000366)	(0.000424)
Constant	0.441**	0.608**	0.230	0.678
	(0.185)	(0.252)	(0.497)	(0.447)
Time fixed effects	Yes	Yes	Yes	Yes
Within R-squared	0.407	0.381	0.367	0.385
Number of cases	110	110	110	110

Marginal effects of regulation on ICT intensity
Value of closeness:

Maximum	0.0311*	1.6558*	0.2128***	0.0419
	(0.0165)	(0.8770)	(0.0737)	(0.0346)
0.75	0.0027	0.7259	0.1645*	0.0022
	(0.0097)	(0.5169)	(0.0850)	(0.0441)
Mean	−0.2564	−0.204	0.1161	−0.0376
	(0.01943)	(0.4333)	(0.1039)	(0.0608)
0.25	−0.0540	−1.1337	0.0678	−0.0774
	(0.0335)	(0.7286)	(0.1270)	(0.0805)
Minimum	−0.0824*	−2.0635*	0.0195	−0.1172
	(0.0482)	(1.1386)	(0.1524)	(0.1013)

Note: The dependent variable is the ICT capital intensity. All models are estimated as Within Fixed Effects regressions. Industry-country-clustered robust standard errors are reported in parentheses with ***p<0.01, **p<0.05 and *p<0.10. The marginal impact of regulation on ICT intensity is reported in the second part of the table for different levels of closeness to the technology frontier.

We comment briefly on the results of the regressions. Considering all models, we find that the coefficients on the dependent variables are stable in the different specifications. Regulation has significant negative effects on ICT intensity in models (1) and (2) and a negative but insignificant effect in models (3) and (4). This result is somewhat similar to the conventional wisdom that regulations curbing competition are responsible for the low intensity of ICT capital input in OECD industries and countries. Furthermore, closeness to the technological frontier enters negatively and is significant at conventional levels in all specifications, suggesting that, within each industry, countries that are further behind the technological frontier have relatively higher levels of ICT capital input to catch up with their peers.

The interaction of regulation and closeness to the frontier (*REG*FRONT*) has a significant positive effect in all models except model (3). It means that for a given level of closeness to the technological frontier, within a given industry, increasing the level of regulation increases the relative investment in ICT capital input. This finding indicates that regulation may have negative partial effects on ICT intensity, but it also offsets the negative effects of the closeness to the frontier. Stated differently, regulation is more likely to slow down the catching-up process when industries are far from the technology frontier, but it is less likely to do so when industries are close to the technology frontier. This finding has an important policy implication in that policy prescriptions that assume a uniform effect from regulation on to innovation are likely to be counterproductive – especially when industries are close to the frontier.

The signs for the capital/labour ratio (*KL*) and import penetration (*MPEN*) are positive and significant in all models, but the magnitude of the openness coefficient is small. These results indicate that capital-intensive industries and industries with higher levels of import penetration tend to invest more in ICT, all else being equal. The sign of externalities is positive but insignificant, indicating absence of spillover effects.

According to Aghion et al. (2005), the marginal effects of competition on innovation should be negative far from the technological frontier but should be positive close to the frontier. If we accept the received interpretation of regulation as a measure of low competition, their findings would imply that the effects of regulation on innovation (which we measure by ICT intensity here) should be negative closer to the technological frontier but positive when industries are far from the technological frontier. The marginal effects we report in Table 7.1 do not support the findings of Aghion et al. (2005). When closeness to the frontier is maximum, the marginal effect of regulation on ICT intensity is positive and significant in all regressions except (4), where the measure of regulation is the level of public sector presence in the industry. The marginal effect is negative only when closeness to the frontier is minimum and it is significant only when *REGREF* and *REGIMP* measures of regulation are used (estimations 1 and 2).

Therefore, far from obtaining an increasingly negative effect of regulation on innovation as one approaches the technological frontier, we obtain the opposite. Even if regulation can have a negative effect on the laggards, it has a significant positive effect on the level of ICT capital input when industries are at the technological frontier. This result is all the more important as it is quite robust and similar in magnitude, when the marginal effect of regulation is measured by *REGREF*, *REGIMP* and *PMR*. We thus conclude the effect of regulation on innovation not only depends on the industries' distance to the frontier, the latter causes the effect to follow a U-shaped rather an inverted-U shaped trajectory.

Our results can be compared with those obtained in the previous empirical literature linking regulation policy, technology gap and a measure of economic performance at the industry level. The results presented in this chapter contradict the findings reported by Aghion et al. (2005) but are similar to Amable et al. (2010), who use a similar dataset but another measure of innovation – namely, the number of patents per hours worked. They are also compatible with the results reported by Nicoletti and Scarpetta (2003) and Arnold et al. (2008), who decompose the effects of regulation at different levels of the technology gap. Lack of evidence for a negative relationship between regulation and productivity is also reported in Griffith and Harisson (2003), who investigate the effect of the Single Market Program on innovation, measured as expenditures in R&D. The authors find that regulatory reforms that have reduced the level of economic rents are associated with a reduction in R&D and growth rates when looking at changes over time within countries. Cross-countries' differences support the opposite – countries with lower average levels of rents are those that have higher productivity and R&D investments.

In line with this literature, we propose two explanations for our results. First, the assumption that product-market regulation limits competition may not be necessarily valid. Instead of limiting competition, regulation may impose a specific competitive environment where firms are induced to use ICT for product innovation rather than cost-cutting advantages as a means of maintaining market shares. Secondly, regulation may also induce firms to innovate with the aim of enhancing quality instead of reducing production costs. Hence, blanket proposals that product-market deregulation is a necessary condition to spur innovation, as is the case in the EU's Lisbon Strategy, may be effective in inducing innovation aimed at cost reductions rather than enhancing quality of product variety. Product-market deregulation may encourage convergence between European industries by inducing the laggards to invest in innovation, but it may be counterproductive in securing convergence between EU industries and their counterparts in the USA.

CONCLUSIONS

In this chapter, we have investigated the relationship between different measures of regulation and industry-level ICT intensity as a measure of innovation in 10 OECD countries. In line with the literature on the relationship between competition/regulation and innovation, we have examined the relationship between regulation and ICT intensity paying attention to the non-linear nature of the competition-innovation relationship and the closeness to the technology frontier. Unlike Aghion et al. (2005), we have found that the marginal effect of regulation on innovation tends to follow a U-shape trajectory as industries get closer to the technology frontier. The marginal effect is negative when industries are further away from the technology frontier and becomes positive when industries are at the technology frontier, with no significant effects when the distance to the frontier is between the two extremes. We propose two explanations for these results. First, regulation may induce firms to engage in innovation aimed at improving quality standards instead of cutting costs as a means of maintaining market share. Secondly, regulation may encourage firms to undertake drastic rather than piecemeal innovation.

Although our results contradict the existence of an inverted-U curve between competition and innovation, they are compatible with theoretical work and micro empirical studies that report the existence of a Schumpeterian effect in the relationship between market structure and innovation. Policy prescriptions in Europe where industries are close to or at the technological frontier, should take into account the positive effects of regulation on innovation, at least in the form of ICT intensity. Hence, product market deregulation strategies suggested by some recommendations of the Lisbon Agenda are not substitutes for an ambitious science and technology policy coupled with product market regulation. The combination of science and technology policy with regulation that encourages quality and product variety may not secure convergence between the laggards and leaders of the European industries, but may be effective in securing convergence between EU and USA industries – which is the declared aim of the EU's Lisbon Strategy.

REFERENCES

Aghion, P., N. Bloom, R. Blundell, R. Griffith and P. Howitt (2005), 'Competition and innovation: an inverted-U relationship', *Quarterly Journal of Economics*, 120 (2), 701–728.

Amable, B., L. Demmou and I. Ledezma (2010), 'Product market regulation, innovation and distance to frontier', *Industrial and Corporate Change*, 19 (1), 117–159.

Arnold, J., G. Nicoletti and S. Scarpetta (2008), 'Regulation, allocative efficiency and productivity in OECD countries: industry and firm-level evidence', *OECD Economics Department Working Papers*, 616.

Arrow, K. (1962), 'Economic welfare and the allocation of resources for invention', in H.M. Groves (ed.), *The Rate and Direction of Inventive Activity: Economic and Social Factors*, NBER, 609-626. http://papers.nber.org/books/univ62-1

Bartelsman, E., A. Bassanini, J. Haltiwanger, R. Jarmin, S. Scarpetta and T. Schank (2002), 'The spread of ICT and productivity growth: is Europe really lagging behind in the new economy?', *CEPN Working Paper*.

Conway, P. and G. Nicoletti (2006), 'Product market regulation in the nonmanufacturing sectors of OECD countries: measurements and highlights', *OECD Economics Department Working Paper*, 530.

Conway, P., V. Janod and G. Nicoletti (2005), 'Product market regulation in OECD countries, 1998 to 2003', *OECD Economics Department Working Paper*, 419.

Goulder, L.H. and I.W. Parry (2008),'Instrument choice in environmental policy', *Review of Environmental Economics and Policy*, 2(2), 152–174.

Griffith, R. and R. Harisson (2003), 'The link between product market reform and macro-economic performance', *European Commission – European Economy – Economic Papers*, 209.

Griffith, R., R. Harisson and H. Simpson (2010), 'Product market reform and innovation in the EU', *Scandinavian Journal of Economics*, 112 (2), 389–415.

Hart, R. (2004), 'Growth, environment and innovation: a model with production vintages and environmentally oriented research', *Journal of Environmental Economics and Management*, 48 (3), 1078–1098.

Jorgenson, D.W. and K.J. Stiroh (1999), 'Information technology and growth', *American Economic Review*, 89 (2), 109–115.

Milliman, S.R. and R. Prince (1989), 'Firm incentives to promote technological change in pollution control', *Journal of Environmental Economics and Management*, 17 (3), 247–65.

Nickell, S. (1996), 'Competition and corporate performance', *Journal of Political Economy*, 61 (1), 631–652.

Nicoletti, G. and S. Scarpetta (2003), 'Regulation, productivity and growth: OECD evidence', *Economic Policy*, 36, 9–72.

Oliner, D. and S. Sichel (2000), 'The resurgence of growth in the late 1990s: is information technology the story?', *Journal of Economic Perspectives*, 14 (4), 3–22.

Popp, D. (2005) 'Uncertain R&D and the Porter hypothesis', *Contributions to Economic Analysis and Policy*, 4 (1), Article 6.

Requate, T. (2005), 'Dynamic incentives by government policy instruments: a survey', *Ecological Economics*, 54 (2–3), 175–195.

Requate, T. and Unold, W. (2003), 'Environmental policy incentives to adopt advanced abatement technology: will the true ranking please stand up?', *European Economic Review*, 47 (1), 125–146.

Rothfels, J. (2002), 'Environmental policy under product differentiation and asymmetric costs: does leapfrogging occur and is it worth it?', in L. Marsiliani, M. Rauscher and C. Withagen (eds), *Environmental Economics and the International Economy*, Dordrecht: Kluwer Academic Publishers.

Schumpeter, J.A. (1934), *The Theory of Economic Development*, Cambridge: Harvard University Press.

Timmer, M., G. Ypma and B. van Ark (2007), 'PPPs for industry output: a new dataset for international comparison', Research memorandum GD-82, Groningen Growth and Development Centre.

van Ark, B., R. Inklaar, and R.G. McGuckin (2003), 'ICT and productivity in Europe and United States: where do the differences come from?', *CESifo Economic Studies*, 49 (3), 295–318.

APPENDIX

Table 7A.1   List of industries

ISIC-REV Classification	Industries
15–16	Food products, beverages and tobacco
17–19	Textiles, textile products, leather and footwear
20	Wood and products of wood and cork
21–22	Pulp, paper, paper products, printing and publishing
24	Chemicals and chemicals products
25	Rubber and plastic products
26	Other non-metallic
27	Basic metals
28	Fabricated metal products, except machinery and equipment
29	Machinery and equipment, n.e.c.
30	Office, accounting and computing machinery
31	Electrical machinery and apparatus, n.e.c.
32	Radio, television and communication equipment
33	Medical, precision and optical instruments, watches and clocks
34	Motor vehicles, trailers and semi-trailers

Table 7A.2   Descriptive statistics

Variable	Observations	Mean	Stand. Dev.	Min	Max
ICT	2552	0.1103	0.2166	0.0003	2.8358
REGREF	2860	3.8099	1.4270	0.9385	5.9214
REGIMP	2640	0.1234	0.0377	0.0484	0.2220
PMR	2860	1.7612	0.4636	0.8243	2.5940
PMRP	2860	2.6978	0.9140	1.1926	4.2001
FRONT	2841	0.5326	0.2670	0.0042	1
KL	2567	0.0431	0.0271	0	0.1793
EXT	2552	0.0849	0.0711	0.0075	0.4509
MPEN	2613	40.1517	29.9851	2.37	400.48

Note: This table gives the descriptive statistics for the ten countries/eleven industries over 26 years from 1980 to 2005. The number of observations in the regressions differs because of some missing observations for some years.

8. Does regulation affect innovation and technical production efficiency? Evidence from the global pharmaceutical industry

Eshref Trushin*

INTRODUCTION

There is growing evidence that the European pharmaceutical industry is lagging behind that of the United States in terms of research and development (R&D) expenditures, biotech innovations, and number of blockbuster drugs. Three decades ago about two-thirds of all pharmaceutical innovations took place in Europe, whereas it accounts for less than 40 per cent at the present time (Schwitzer 2006: 167, 239). The average share of new molecular drugs in total increased from 30 per cent in 1995 to 53 per cent in 2005 in the USA, while in Western Europe this share decreased from 30 per cent to 10 per cent over the same period (Pammolli and Riccaboni, 2007: 130,133). Some authors blame pharmaceutical regulations, especially in Europe, for the productivity decline in the industry. For example, Reuben and Burstall (2005: xi, v) warn that 'negative attitudes prevail toward science' in Europe, that the 'decline in products from Europe is the source of the discovery deficit' and that the European industry may move to the USA.

The relationship between pharmaceutical regulation and innovation is becoming especially interesting in the new era of austerity as governments around the world are trying to save extra on pharmaceutical procurement by introducing new cost-containing drug regulation. Will such budget cuts lead to stagnation in the drug R&D or affect efficiency of production? Can this new regulation have a long-lasting effect as a drug development takes many years and costs hundreds of million dollars?

Regulations are supposed to remedy market failures or be normative for the purpose of safety or equality in access. Major market failures in the industry include asymmetry of information on drug quality between firms and users, monopoly rights granted by patents, and moral hazard problems as patients and doctors do not face the full costs of drugs due to insurance. There is no silver bullet to address these failures and each country introduces own drug price regulations, which are also affected by political factors. The list of typical regulation includes reference pricing in line with similar drugs on sale in other markets, positive or negative lists for reimbursement, price caps, cost-sharing requirements, generic substitution with off-patent drugs, prescribing budgets for physicians, the government-industry price-volume agreements, and profit controls. Given the multiplicity of regulatory rules, industry regulation differs significantly between European Union (EU) countries and between the latter and other countries.

RELATED LITERATURE

Companies often have to build extra production capacity to establish a market presence or to comply with reimbursement regulations. In some countries like Australia, Belgium, France, Hungary, and Spain, ethical drug prices are often negotiated ad hoc between the national health insurance and the firms, depending on their contributions to the national economy (Puig-Junoy, 2005). Price WaterhouseCoopers (2007: 37) stated that 'the industry is already suffering from overcapacity, with utilization rates of less than 50 per cent at some plants' and the current contraction in the aggregate demand due to the global financial crisis exacerbates this problem.

Various types of price and indirect profit controls employed by European governments might divert incentives for pharmaceutical innovation. Danzon (1997: 45, 49, 51) argues that price controls in France and Japan stimulate cost-saving imitative drug research strategy, leading to minor innovations. The cap on the rate of return on new drugs in the United Kingdom (UK) provides incentives for overinvestment in capital and R&D (Mrazek and Mossialos, 2004). Finkelstein and Temin (2008: xi) argue that the experiences of Europe and Canada have shown that pharmaceutical price controls 'kill innovation'. Vernon and Golec (2008:4) state that 'Pharmaceutical price regulations reduce pharmaceutical R&D spending', which is supported by works of other authors (Giaccotto et al. 2005; Schwitzer, 2006; Civan and Maloney, 2009).

However, some authors also argue that regulation may have a positive effect on drug innovation. For example, Munos (2009) suggests that countries with more demanding regulation encourage firms to invest in R&D

and innovate more. For example, Light (2009) finds that the European level of R&D expenditures per new chemical entity was similar to or even higher than that of the US in the period 1993–2003. Regulatory standards can force firms to target better quality R&D (Jacobzone, 2000) and increase trust and demand for drugs (Katz, 2007). Finally, current regulation may be simply ineffective as firms and doctors might adjust their behaviour to reduce the restrictions.

An important aspect of innovation is monopolization through patents. Patents guarantee monopoly rights on invention and are viewed as the necessary limited harm to reward inventors. However, some regulators seek to constrain returns on patented drugs through price regulations, which are the most controversial measures given high costs of new drug development. Many drugs require 10–12 years to develop and present opportunity costs, which Paul et al. (2010) estimate at $1.8 billion per new drug. According to PAREXEL (2004: 83), the estimated cost of developing a new drug in the USA varies from $608 million in 1996 according to Lehman Brothers estimations, to $802 million in 2000 by the Tufts Centre for the Study of Drug Development, $880 million in 2001 by the Boston Consulting Group, and $948 million in 2003 by the Tufts Centre for the Study of Drug Development. To protect future cash streams from new drugs and recover the R&D costs, the pharmaceutical industry is crucially dependent on patents, brands, reputation, and access to distribution channels – i.e. intangible assets (Schwitzer, 2006).

Pharmaceutical regulations can affect the levels of R&D expenditures and the value of the intangible assets in general, leading to production inefficiency. Although the existing literature on the regulation of the pharmaceutical industry is well developed, there are some gaps that need to be addressed. For example, there is a tendency to focus on the relationship between regulation and firm performance or healthcare costs instead of the effects of regulation on innovation effort or productive efficiency in different regulatory jurisdictions. Even when the relationship between regulation and R&D expenditures is investigated, the investigation seldom extends to cover the effects of market concentration on either innovation or productive efficiency. Finally, the empirical literature provides mixed findings, indicating that further research is required to verify whether regulation and/or market concentration are related to innovation and/or productive efficiency.

This chapter aims to address these gaps by utilizing a panel dataset for more than 1,000 pharmaceutical firms in 11 countries for the period 1997–2007. First, I conduct independence tests to verify if R&D intensity (R&D/sale and R&D/assets ratios) is related to the stringency of price regulation and market concentration in 11 countries. Then

I estimate average technical efficiency levels for firms within each country. Technical production inefficiencies are estimated with stochastic frontier modelling using three major inputs: intangible assets as a result of accumulated innovation activities, tangible assets, and labour. In the third stage, I conduct independence tests to verify if technical inefficiency is related to the stringency of price regulation and market concentration in 11 countries. The tests in stages 1 and 3 are conducted as Pearson chi-squared and likelihood-ratio tests for association between R&D intensity and production inefficiency on the one hand and the stringency of pharmaceutical price regulations and market concentration on the other.

The chapter is organized as follows. In the next section, I discuss the effect of intangible assets on technical efficiency. This is followed by discussion of the stochastic frontier analysis methodology I use to estimate technical inefficiency in each country – i.e., in each regulatory jurisdiction. The results are presented and discussed in the penultimate section, which is followed by concluding remarks.

THE ROLE OF INTANGIBLE ASSETS

Intangible assets are one of the production factors used for estimation in this chapter. Such assets include legally protected rights such as patents, licences, copyrights, royalty agreements, goodwill, industrial designs, trademarks, trade names, customer lists, etc. The most important intangible assets in the pharmaceutical industry are patents: about two-thirds of all pharmaceutical inventions would not have been commercialized in the absence of patent protection (Mansfield, 1986). Patents are a leading factor in research management and are often filed to block rivals by building a 'patent wall' around firms' own drugs. They are also used as collateral and as leverage in research partnerships, but it is very difficult to value them with lack of trading in patents (Rivette and Kline, 2000).

Patents may look like bricks in the wall, which appear not to be actively used. A 1998 survey by British Technology Group (BTG) International (cited by Rivette and Kline, 2000: 59) found that more than two-thirds of intellectual property rights were not exploited by the US firms. 'About half, probably more, of all patented inventions in the United States are never commercially exploited' (Sichelman, 2010: 341). The specifics of patenting in the pharmaceutical industry are that drug candidates are patented before they are tested in clinical trials for many years. In this regard it is difficult to measure pharmaceutical innovations because a majority of patents issued are based on failed drug candidates or drugs with little chemical innovation or therapeutic impact. According to a report for the EU Commission (Gambardella et al. 2006: II-IV), about one-third of the European patents are not used for any industrial or commercial purpose and about half of the unused patents are 'blocking' patents to prevent rivals from using the technology. This report finds chemical and pharmaceuticals industries have one of the highest shares of unused patents.

Companies tend to overinvest in patent protection, which may appear irrational. A 1998 survey of 150 technology-intensive firms and research universities in the United States, Western Europe and Japan conducted by BTG found that 12 per cent of the organizations had more than one thousand unutilized patents and only 15 per cent of the entities reported no unutilized patents. Approximately 30 per cent of Japanese firms reported having more than 2,000 unused patents (cited by Kamiyama et al., 2006: 9). A survey of about 6,700 Japanese firms found that more than 60 per cent of Japanese patents were not being used at all (Japan Patent Office, 2004).

One of the more comprehensive surveys of business patenting by American and Japanese firms found that the top reasons for patenting innovations were preventing of copying and lawsuits, whereas licensing revenue was mentioned by less than one-third of respondents (Cohen et al., 2002). According to PAREXEL's (2004: 47) reference to a Merck study, the share of revenues derived from patent licensing by leading pharmaceutical companies varied from 0 to 40 per cent. Firms hesitate to sell or license unexploited patents as this could be an advantage to their competitors. A larger share of patents in total assets can also signal for larger entry barriers as patents might increase costs up to 40 per cent for pharmaceutical firms, which may want to invent around a patent (Mansfield et al., 1981).

The problem of underutilized patents and excess capacity is exacerbated by price regulations. In some countries, regulation of inputs, e.g. rate of return on capital in the UK, distorts cost-minimizing choices and facilitates overinvestment (Danzon, 1997: 65). Ekelund and Perrson (2003) compare prices of new chemical entities (NCEs) in Sweden and the US between 1987 and 1997, and conclude that price regulations limit price competition of branded drugs. In the segmented drug markets price can be a signal of quality and companies optimally choose their prices to send the proper signal to customers. Price caps limit such signals and difference in drug prices may not reflect the corresponding difference in therapeutic benefits of drugs, thus limiting operating profits of innovators and also distorting innovation planning.

THE STOCHASTIC EFFICIENT FRONTIER METHODOLOGY

The pharmaceutical industry is global and run by multinational companies that can employ transfer pricing to minimize tax liabilities and strategically locate their enterprises. However, it is usually the case that subsidiaries are run by their own relatively independent management who optimize production inputs given local national regulations. Transportation costs of drugs, especially in the EU, are small in comparison to the unit price so that production location is determined mainly by access to the local markets. With the exception of China, the difference in production infrastructure, wage, and production skills in the sample of countries is not large. For a detailed discussion on comparative advantage of major countries, see Pammolli and Riccaboni (2007).

To estimate technical production inefficiency I assume that all firms located in a country employ the same production technology and can use similar corporate management tactics under common national regulations. I estimate technical inefficiency at firm level for each country assuming a similar production function and using several econometric specifications for the stochastic frontier analysis. The estimated inefficiency levels are then tested for independence from the national level of stringency of price regulations.

This chapter relies on stochastic frontier modelling, which is simplified to the following scheme. It is assumed that pharmaceutical production has a common frontier set by a concave production function and such input factors of production as tangible and intangible assets and labour measured by the number of employees. Given some fixed technology frontier these production factors transform the inputs into an output measured by companies' operating revenue, i.e. revenue from the firms' profile operations. However, companies differ by distance to this frontier, which is a sum of two components: a random idiosyncratic noise with mean zero and the technical inefficiency part, in which stochastic distribution is assumed for econometric estimations. The technical inefficiency at firm level for each country is estimated with several distributional specifications of the technical inefficiency term: truncated normal, half-normal, exponential, and Battese-Coelli (1992) time varying parameter. In all specifications the idiosyncratic error term is assumed to be normally distributed.

The data represent a panel of firms' financial statements for the period 1996–2007 and the random effect specification is used for the panel frontier estimations. Following the literature, the specification of the production frontier function of inputs is taken as the second order Taylor series approximation in form of the translog production function.

The regulation indicators are inputted at country level based on expert rankings of stringency of price regulations. It is expected that less inefficiency is achieved in the least price regulated markets and the highest inefficiencies tend to characterize countries with the most regulated markets. The estimated inefficiency levels are then tested for independence from the national price regulations ranking and from concentration of sales with unconditional independence Pearson chi-squared and likelihood-ratio tests. The null hypothesis is that there is no systematic dependency between these series and that any relationship is just random.

Fried et al. (2008) have reviewed over 200 industrial applications of production efficiency analysis in just a few years. Indeed, variation in productivity between observed and an optimal (frontier) output is an important industry indicator. Unfortunately, I did not find research addressing technical inefficiency in the global pharmaceutical industry in connection with national regulations. The idea is that stringent pharmaceutical regulations can reduce the productive ability of assets and limit the ability of firms to achieve production efficiency due to the regulatory environment.

The mathematical programming approach of data envelopment analysis (DEA) is not used here as it produces large inefficiency measures in the presence of productivity outliers, which might be caused by drug price shocks. Such shocks are possible under oligopolistic competition and the entrance of generic drugs after expiration of patents that usually lead to rapid price decline. The use of DEA technique is then constrained as the data on detailed price and commodity compositions are not available for every firm and year. Consumer segmentation and market power encourage companies to use price discrimination strategies to maximize profits so that detailed information about prices and volumes is often a commercial secret.

The stochastic frontier models were first developed by Aigner et al. (1977). In this approach the disturbance term consists of two components: usually symmetrically distributed idiosyncratic error component v_i and strictly positive technical inefficiency component u_i. The distributions of both components are stipulated to enable estimations based on the maximum likelihood approach.

Following the literature (Greene, 2008), the technical efficiency (TE_i) for i-th firm is defined as a ratio of the actual output y of the firm to production possibility frontier [$f(x)$] for the industry. Hence, denoting factor inputs for firm i by x, we can write:

$$TE_i = y/f(x) \leq 1 \tag{8.1}$$

In the logarithmic form:

$$logy_i = log f(x_i) + log TE_i + v_i = log f(x_i) + v_i - u_i \qquad (8.2)$$

Here, $u_i \geq 0$ and it is a measure of *technical inefficiency*. If u_i is zero then *TE* equals one, and the firm is assumed to be technically efficient. Technical efficiency of the i-th firm is therefore a relative measure of its output to the maximum achievable output of the given technology (Lovell, 1993). In other words, a firm produces less than it could given its inputs if the firm were not located on the technological frontier and the distance to the frontier is defined as technical inefficiency. In the specification above, the technical inefficiency term is scaled such that $0 < TE_i \leq 1$. If $u_i = 1$, the firm is located on the technological frontier. All firms cannot locate on the frontier so that some of them operate with technical inefficiency, i.e. below the production frontier $f(x)$. To emphasize this mathematically, the technical inefficiency term u_i is written with negative sign in the equation (8.2) and assumed to be non-negative, whereas v_i can take any value. Both idiosyncratic v_i and technical inefficiency u_i terms are presumed to be independently and identically distributed (i.i.d) and uncorrelated with factor inputs (x) in the model. In the literature, the technical inefficiency term is often truncated at zero and normally distributed, and the idiosyncratic term is assumed with zero mean and often symmetrically distributed.

Following Greene (2005), the production at firm level can be written for the panel as follows:

$$y_{it} = \beta' x_{it} + \mu z_i + v_{it} - u_{it} \qquad (8.3)$$

where y_{it} is production of the i-th firm at time t, v_{it} is a disturbance with normal distribution $N(0,\sigma_v^2)$, and $u_{it} = |U_{it}|$. U_{it} shows deviation from the efficient frontier and is often assumed to be normally distributed $N(0,\sigma_u^2)$. x_{it} are factors of production, which might depend on time to account for technical change, and the time invariant component z_i accounts for unobservable heterogeneity not related to production. The u_{it} is referred to as the inefficiency term and v_{it} is the idiosyncratic error and they both are also assumed to be i.i.d. It is conventional in the specification of production function that it is monotonically increasing in all factors of production with non-negative marginal products.

The estimation is based on the maximum likelihood method, which estimates the conditional expectation of the inefficiency $E[u_{it}|\varepsilon_{it}]$, as proposed by Jondrow et al. (1982) and where $\varepsilon_{it} = v_{it} - u_{it}$. Usual assumptions on distribution of the technical inefficiency term are truncated normal $u_{it} = |U_{it}|$, $U_{it} \sim N(\mu,\sigma_u^2) > 0$ and exponential, although other distributional specifications such as *gamma* or half normal are also widely used in the literature.

I have conducted the estimations with panel data for over one thousand pharmaceutical firms in 11 countries, which consist of leading pharmaceutical producers and China. In the time-invariant models, the inefficiency term u_{it} is considered to be independent of time. In all models considered here, the idiosyncratic v_{it} is assumed to be normally distributed.

Greene (2005) notes that in time invariant models u_i can absorb cross-firm heterogeneity and this might cause some biased estimation for the inefficiency. In time effect models, technical inefficiency is postulated with some time dependent coefficient $\delta(t)$, sometimes called the decay parameter. There is a variety of models depending on specification of $\delta(t)$ multiplier and results depend on this choice. In the popular Battese-Coelli (1992) model, which, however, does not incorporate varying inefficiencies due to business cycles, the inefficiency term u_{it} is a truncated-normal random variable multiplied by an exponentially changing function of time $\delta(t) = e^{-\delta(t-T)}, i.e.\ TE_{it} = U_i e^{-\delta(T-t)}$ and the idiosyncratic term v_{it} is assumed to be i.i.d. and normally distributed. If $\delta(t) < 0$, inefficiency increases over time and reaches its highest (base) level in the last period. If $\delta(t) > 0$, inefficiency is subject to decay.

Omitting time and firm subscripts (t and i) for the sake of simplifying the notation in the formula below, the stochastic production frontier function with the operating revenue (y) is represented as translog function of factor inputs of tangible fixed assets (*ltanas*), intangible fixed assets (*linas*), and number of employees (*lemp*); together with time trend and interaction terms between the inputs:

$$\ln(y) = C_0 + C_1 \ln(employees)$$
$$+ C_2 \ln(tangible\ assets) + C_3 \ln(intangible\ assets) +$$
$$C_4 \ln^2(employees) + C_5 \ln^2(tangible\ assets) + C_6 \ln^2(intangible\ assets)$$
$$+ C_7 \ln(employees)\ln(tangible\ assets) + C_8 \ln(intangible\ assets)\ln(employees)$$
$$+ C_9 \ln(tangible\ assets)\ln(intangible\ assets) + time + time^2 + v_{it} - u_{it} \quad (8.4)$$

The translog production function is popular in the literature as it represents the second-order Taylor series approximation of the function and allows changing partial elasticities of substitution between factors of production. The right-hand side regressors are checked for multicollinearity before all coefficients from C_1 to C_9 are estimated.

If $C_1 + C_2 + C_3 = 1$ and other coefficients are zero, the production function has constant returns to scale. The outcome and all factors are in a natural logarithm of their original level. For concave functions the Hessian matrix is negative semidefinite, which means that every principal minor of odd order is less than or equal to zero and every principal minor of even order is greater than or equal to zero, which is satisfied in all estimations. This ensures that the production function has the properties required by the microeconomic theory, especially the diminishing marginal returns. The estimated frontier production functions are then used to estimate the mean of technical inefficiency terms u_{it} for each country based on assumed distributions of the inefficiency term u_{it} and the idiosyncratic term v_{it}.

DATA AND EXPECTED RESULTS

Data in this chapter is compiled from financial statements of more than one thousand pharmaceutical firms for the period 1997–2007, obtained from the *Orbis* database (Table 8.1). This database provides comprehensive financial information about companies and it is assembled from various expert sources by Bureau van Dijck.[1] The share of intangible assets in total assets in the selected pharmaceutical producing countries is significant and ranges between 20 – 25 per cent.

Most companies registered in a country usually produce for the domestic market. The average share of the pharmaceutical firms' domestic sales is usually dominant: 89.94 per cent for Austria, 89.47 per cent for China, 77.28 per cent for France, 64.13 per cent for Germany, 94.44 per cent for Japan, 87.32 per cent for Spain so that local price regulations matter. The exception is the USA, where the share of domestic sales in total was about 35 per cent from 1997 to 2009 (PhRMA, 2010: 44,50). The USA is the world's largest pharmaceutical market with the highest R&D expenditures and with the most liberal drug price regulations. Hence, it can be viewed as the strategic priority for major pharmaceutical companies. In other words, firms may prefer to stay in the US market even when experiencing short-term losses.

Companies are assumed to be less constrained in optimizing inputs in less regulated jurisdictions. Therefore, it is expected to observe less inefficiency in less price-regulated markets and more inefficiency in countries with more price-regulated markets. National regulation (Table 8.2) is approximated by a simple rank for stringency of price regulations, which ranges from 1 (less stringent) to 3 (the most stringent). This regulation index is used by experts of the Pharmaceutical Industry Competitiveness Task Force (2005).

Drugs compete in their own niches, which are often characterized by therapeutic class addressing a particular condition. The top three drugs dominate sales for most large therapeutic classes, which is the characteristic of oligopolistic markets supported through patents. Companies are attracted to such markets by the potential of high oligopolistic rents by

Table 8.1   *Descriptive statistics of the logarithm of factor inputs*

Country	Statistics	log (operating revenue)	log (intangible assets)	log (tangible assets)	log (number of employees)
Australia	Observ.	191	191	191	191
	Mean	9.365	8.406	7.222	4.613
	St.Dev.	3.453	2.905	2.833	2.172
France	Observ.	1034	1034	1034	1034
	Mean	12.012	7.451	8.775	5.834
	St.Dev	1.661	2.847	2.351	1.605
Germany	Observ.	534	534	534	534
	Mean	12.412	8.625	9.997	7.011
	St.Dev	2.210	3.174	2.655	2.060
Japan	Observ.	415	415	415	415
	Mean	17.775	12.859	16.712	7.205
	St.Dev	1.820	2.440	1.842	1.261
Netherlands	Observ.	397	397	397	397
	Mean	12.368	8.839	9.457	5.861
	St.Dev	1.512	2.875	2.404	2.056
Spain	Observ.	597	597	597	597
	Mean	18.187	13.289	15.318	5.576
	St.Dev	2.184	3.045	2.475	1.298
Sweden	Observ.	208	208	208	208
	Mean	13.093	10.494	10.557	5.196
	St.Dev	2.781	2.774	2.953	1.796
Switzerland	Observ.	123	123	123	123
	Mean	12.983	10.881	12.342	7.608
	St.Dev	2.792	3.153	2.181	2.106
UK	Observ.	1138	1138	1138	1138
	Mean	11.401	9.034	9.393	5.885
	St.Dev	2.291	2.579	2.674	1.988
USA	Observ.	2020	2020	2020	2020
	Mean	10.182	9.601	8.916	5.574
	St.Dev	2.903	2.872	2.739	2.3202
China	Observ.	539	539	539	539
	Mean	13.013	10.144	12.387	7.282
	St.Dev	1.296	1.529	1.147	1.011

Note: In each cell the first quantity is the number of observations, the second is the mean, and the third one is the standard deviation.

Source: Orbis dataset of firms for the period 1997–2007.

Table 8.2 Characteristics of the pharmaceutical industry and regulation by country

	Concentration of top three product sales in the top hundred therapeutic classes, %	Stringency of price regula- tions index	Median R&D to assets	Median R&D to sales
Australia	Not known	3	0.087	0.297
Canada	79.4	3	0.164	0.524
France	78.18	2	0.158	0.207
Germany	58.87	2	0.077	0.096
Italy	71.49	2	0.085	0.103
Japan	78.25	1	0.057	0.084
Netherlands	86.24	2	0.064	0.052
Sweden	91.60	1	0.182	0.714
Switzerland	Not known	1	0.067	0.127
UK	90.20	2	0.115	0.179
USA	85.56	1	0.169	0.431

Note: Stringency of price regulations index ranges between 3 (the most stringent) and 1 (the least stringent);

Sources: 'Stringency of price regulations index' is adopted from the Pharmaceutical Industry Competitiveness Task Force (2005: 14); 'Concentration of top three product sales in the top hundred therapeutic classes' is adopted from Pammolli and Riccaboni (2007: 175); R&D intensity indicators are calculated for each country from *Orbis* dataset of firms for the period 1997–2007.

offering new patented drugs, but high risks and costs of drug R&D and access to the distribution channels can sustain high rents in the long run.

EMPIRICAL RESULTS AND DISCUSSION

We begin with simple testing of the hypotheses on relationship between median R&D intensity on the one hand and stringency of price regulation and market concentration on the other. The median values are chosen for their stability in presence of outliers. The tests can be performed with already available data provided in Table 8.2. The null hypothesis is that the stringency of price regulation and median R&D to sales and median R&D to assets ratios are independent or only randomly related. The results in Table 8.3 below indicate that we fail to reject the null hypotheses as the p-values are greater than the critical values at 5 per cent or 10 per cent significance. This is the case for the Pearson chi-squared and likelihood ratio tests and indicates that R&D intensity and stringency of price

Table 8.3   Tests of independence of the median R&D intensity from the regulation index and from concentration of sales

Test	Ratio of R&D to sales and regulation	Ratio of R&D to assets and regulation	Ratio of R&D to sales and concentration of sales	Ratio of R&D to assets and concentration of sales
Pearson chi-squared	33.00 (0.32)	33.00 (0.32)	72.00 (0.23)	72.00 (0.23)
Likelihood ratio	29.53 (0.49)	29.53 (0.49)	39.55 (0.99)	39.55 (0.99)

Note: Corresponding p-values are in brackets.

regulations are related only randomly. This result does not change even if the UK price regulation is categorized at level 1, similar to the stringency of regulation in the US. Although the sample is small and the power of the test is low, it is unlikely that stricter price regulation of pharmaceuticals is negatively associated with the median R&D intensity.

I also fail to reject the null hypothesis that R&D intensity is not related to market concentration, which I calculate on the basis of the top three product sales in the top one hundred therapeutic classes. Again, this is the case in the Pearson chi-squared and likelihood ratio tests. Nevertheless, these tests are appropriate only for linear relationships. Some previous studies (e.g., Aghion et al., 2002, 2005) and the chapters by Ugur and Hashem and Ugur in this volume indicate that the relationship between market concentration and innovation is non-linear. Hence, the failure to reject the absence of a linear relationship in our sample of pharmaceutical firms may be due to the existence of non-linear relationship between concentration and R&D intensity.

The second step in our analysis is to estimate the mean technical inefficiency (i.e., the mean distance to the efficiency frontier) for the pharmaceutical industry in each regulatory jurisdiction. This estimation is based on equation 8.3 and model 8.4 above, with results given in Table 8.4 below. When the assumed distribution of the distance to frontier is time-invariant truncated normal, the most liberal pharmaceutical price regulation in the UK and the USA is associated with the smallest distance to the frontier (0.835 and 0.727 respectively). However, this result is not robust across other distribution assumptions for the inefficiency term. For example, under the Battese-Coelli time effects assumption, the most efficient industry is in France, followed by the USA and UK. When the assumed distribution is half-normal, the most efficient industry is in Spain,

Table 8.4　Summary of the mean technical inefficiency estimations: pharmaceutical industry in sample countries

	Truncated normal time invariant	Battese-Coelli time effects	Half-normal distribution of inefficiency	Exponential distribution of inefficiency	Stringency of price regulations	Concentration of top three product sales, %
Australia	na	.419 (.283)	na	.593 (.299)	3	na
France	.879 (.160)	.003 (.003)	.587 (.245)	.631 (.264)	2	78.2
Germany	.928 (.078)	.363 (.251)	.577 (.321)	.647 (.269)	2	58.9
Japan	.937 (.091)	.139 (.084)	.701 (.235)	.629 (.339)	1	78.3
Netherlands	.916 (.089)	.135 (.121)	.551 (.268)	.629 (.269)	2	86.2
Spain	.904 (.127)	.061 (.087)	.236 (.278)	.254 (.298)	3	75.9
Sweden	.877 (.063)	.184 (.212)	.987 (.000)	na	1	91.6
Switzerland	0.938 (.050)	.006 (.047)	Na	.182 (.244)	1	na
UK	.835 (.202)	.006 (.047)	.549 (.180)	.638 (.193)	1	90.2
USA	.772 (.207)	.052 (.076)	.638 (.199)	.721 (.171)	1	85.6
China	.897 (.132)	.022 (.029)	.995 (.000)	na	na	67.6

Note:　na – not available. Technical inefficiency estimated with random effect panel models. The means of the inefficiency terms and the corresponding standard errors are displayed in brackets. Truncated normal model assumes that the technical inefficiency u_{it} is i.i.d. normally distributed with mean μ and truncation at zero; in the Battese-Coelli model, the inefficiency term u_{it} is a truncated-normal random variable multiplied by the exponentially changing function of time $\delta(t) = e^{-\delta(t-T)}$; half-normal distribution of inefficiency u_{it} is i.i.d. normal with mean zero with truncation at zero; the exponential distribution of inefficiency u_{it} is i.i.d. exponentially distributed. In all models, the idiosyncratic disturbance v_{it} is i.i.d. normally distributed with mean zero.

Sources:　The stringency of price regulations is adapted from the Pharmaceutical Industry Competitiveness Task Force (2005: 14). The concentration of sales is compiled from Pammolli and Riccaboni (2007: 169, 175) for the top three products in the top hundred ATC4 therapeutic classes for the period 1994–2004.

followed by France, the UK and the USA. Lower levels of inefficiency in American and British industries could be related to the liberal pharmaceutical price regulation, which leads to greater price difference between brand (patented) and generic (off-patented) drugs. This price difference

Table 8.5   Tests of independence: mean technical inefficiency versus regulation and concentration of sales

Test	Regulation and technical inefficiency with truncated normal specification	Regulation and technical inefficiency with time effect specification	Concentration of sales and technical inefficiency of the truncated normal specification	Concentration of sales and technical inefficiency with time effect specification
Pearson chi-squared	2.64 (0.85)	7.38 (0.28)	11.88 (0.45)	10.0 (0.26)
Likelihood ratio	3.54 (0.73)	7.27 (0.29)	12.5 (0.41)	7.49 (0.48)

Note: Corresponding p-values are in brackets.

then translates into greater revenue (hence less inefficiency) for firms that hold the relevant patents.

The question is whether this expected relationship between the leniency of the price regulation and the level of inefficiency holds across the sample of countries. Conducting Pearson Chi-squared and likelihood independence tests, I fail to reject the null hypothesis that the relationship between regulation and technical inefficiency is only random (Table 8.5). Similarly, I fail to reject the null hypothesis that technical inefficiency is not related to market concentration, measured with the shares of the top three product sales in the top hundred therapeutic classes. These results do not change if one considers the relationship between estimated inefficiencies and the interaction term for regulation stringency and concentration of sales.[2]

Hence, the evidence from our sample of more than 1,000 firms in 11 countries indicates that neither innovation effort (ratio of median R&D to sales or assets) nor technical inefficiency (the mean distance to the efficiency frontier) is related to the stringency of the regulation in each country. Stated differently, price regulations do not seem to determine the firms' ability to achieve the highest level of sales revenue given the level of factor inputs.

This result may be due to two reasons. First, the power of the tests we conduct is low due to low number of countries. Secondly, the production function we estimate is based on tangible and intangible assets. The problem with the latter is that their quality is not observable. This is the case even for patents. Evaluation of the patent quality for each firm is a quite complex task and requires a lot of detailed information such as market shares for each drug, patent novelty and possibilities for reverse engineering by rivals. The typical patent quality indicators such as forward and backward citations may not reflect their contribution to operating profit of the firm.

Furthermore, time discounting pattern of patents is also uncertain. The value of patents can sharply decrease if rivals innovate around and discover a better drug. For example, a survey of about 50 European commercial banks (Kamiyama et al., 2006, p. 20) found that none of them routinely accepts intangible assets as collateral for loans to new firms as the realization value of these assets is uncertain.

One well-known accounting method to estimate intangible assets is to subtract the book value of tangible assets from the firms' capitalization, but capitalization depends on many factors, which may not relate to intangible assets. Customers' brand loyalty is another elusive variable. Accounting for unobserved heterogeneity in the quality of intangible assets would be very fruitful in the evaluation of technical inefficiency of the pharmaceutical industry, which is a direction for further research.

It is also possible that price controls do not really work. Price controls failed to control drug expenditures growth in France, Germany, Italy, and the UK in 1970–90. In countries where physicians had incentives to prescribe, price controls were unlikely to work, which also led to significantly higher physical drug consumption in France, Italy and Germany (Danzon, 1997). Price controls might not be effective in achieving generic substitution. For example, generics represented 43 per cent of all prescriptions in the United States in 1998, 40 per cent in Canada in 1996–97, about half of all prescriptions in Denmark and Finland, 40 per cent in Germany and the Netherlands, and 69 per cent in the United Kingdom. Their share is still low in France (just over 3 per cent), Belgium and Switzerland (Pazderka and Stegemann, 2006).

CONCLUSIONS

There is no evidence indicating that the stringency of drug price regulations is systematically associated with R&D intensities and/or technical production inefficiency. The same result is obtained when I test for the relationship between market concentration and R&D intensities and/ or technical production inefficiency. There is partial evidence indicating that the most liberal pharmaceutical price regimes in the UK and the US have the lowest inefficiency in the truncated normal time invariant random effect panel specification, but this result is not robust across other specifications for the inefficiency term. Tighter cost-containment regulations appear not to be associated with technical efficiency, national market concentration or R&D intensity of companies, which can be explained by the specific global nature of the industry's production and innovation. The policy implication of this result is that price regulations do not seem to constrain firms from achieving the highest output given factor inputs.

The strong limitation of the findings is that the small sample of only eleven countries reduces power of the tests. Another major problem is the difficulty involved in accounting for the quality of intangible assets. Time discounting of patents and quality of patent portfolios can be major confounding factors, which must be taken into account in further research.

NOTES

*   I sincerely thank Brigitte Granville and Mehmet Ugur for their support and encouragement; all shortcomings are my own. This chapter is partly based on a subsection of my PhD dissertation.
1. Orbis data are checked for quality and accuracy by Bureau van Dijck. For more information, see http://www.bvdinfo.com/Products/Company-Information/International/ORBIS.aspx
2. Independence test results for relationship between inefficiency and the interaction term are not presented here, but can be provided on request.

REFERENCES

Aghion, P., W. Carlin and M. Schaffer (2002), 'Competition, innovation and growth in transition: exploring the interactions between policies', William Davidson Working Paper Number 501 (March).

Aghion, P., N. Bloom, R. Blundell, R. Griffith and P. Howitt (2005), 'Competition and innovation: an inverted-U relationship', *The Quarterly Journal of Economics*, **120**(2), 701–728.

Aigner, D., K. Lovell and P. Schmidt (1977), 'Formulation and estimation of stochastic frontier production models', *Journal of Econometrics*, **6**, 21–37.

Battese, G. and T. Coelli (1992), 'Frontier production functions, technical efficiency and panel data: with application to paddy farmers in India', *Journal of Productivity Analysis*, **3**(1), 153–169.

Civan, A. and M. Maloney (2009), 'The effect of price on pharmaceutical R&D', *The B.E. Journal of Economic Analysis & Policy*, **9**(1), 15.

Cohen, M., A. Goto, A.Nagata, R.Nelson, J.Walsh (2002), 'R&D spillovers, patents and the incentives to innovate in Japan and the United States', *Research Policy*, **31**, 1349–1367.

Danzon, P. (1997), *Pharmaceutical Price Regulation: National Policies Versus Global Interests*, Washington, D.C.: The American Enterprise Institute for Public Policy Research.

Ekelund, M. and B. Persson (2003), 'Pharmaceutical pricing in a regulated market', *The Review of Economics and Statistics*, **85**(2), 298–306.

Finkelstein, S. and Temin, P. (2008), *Reasonable Rx: How to Lower Drug Prices*, London: Pearson Education.

Fried, H.O., Lovell, C.A.K., and Schmidt, S.S. (2008), 'Efficiency and productivity', in H. Fried, K. Lovell and S. Schmidt (eds), *The Measurement of Productive Efficiency and Productivity Growth*, Oxford: Oxford University Press, pp. 3–91.

Gambardella, A., P. Giuri, and M. Mariani (2006), 'Study on evaluating the knowledge economy: what are patents actually worth? The value of patents for today's economy and society', Siena: European Commission research report ETD/2004/IM/E3/77.

Giaccotto, C., R. Santerre, and Vernon J. (2005), 'Drug prices and research and development investment behaviour in the pharmaceutical industry', *Journal of Law and Economics*, **XLVIII**, 195–214.

Greene, W. (2005), 'Fixed and random effects in stochastic frontier models', *Journal of Productivity Analysis*, **23**, 7–32.

Greene, W. (2008), 'The econometric approach to efficiency analysis', in H. Fried, K. Lovell and S. Schmidt (eds), *The Measurement of Productive Efficiency and Productivity Growth*, Oxford: Oxford University Press, pp. 92–250.

Jacobzone, S. (2000), 'Pharmaceutical policies in OECD countries: reconciling social and industrial goals', Labour Market and Social Policy, Occasional Paper 40, Paris: OECD.

Japan Patent Office (2004), 'Results of the survey on intellectual property-related activities', 2003, Tokyo: Japan Patent Office.

Jondrow, J., C.A. Lovell, I. Materov and P. Schmidt (1982), 'On the estimation of technical inefficiency in the stochastic frontier production function model', *Journal of Econometrics*, **19**(2/3), 233–238.

Kamiyama, S., J. Sheehan, and C. Martinez (2006), 'Valuation and exploitation of intellectual property. statistical analysis of science, technology and industry', Working Paper 2006/5, Paris: Organisation for Economic Cooperation and Development (OECD).

Katz, A. (2007), 'Pharmaceutical lemons: innovation and regulation in the drug industry', *Mich. Telecomm. Tech. L. Rev.*, **14**(1), 1–41.

Light, D. (2009), 'Global drug discovery: Europe is ahead', *Health Affairs*, **28**(5): w969–w977.

Lovell, K. (1993), 'Production frontiers and productive efficiency', in H. Fried, K. Lovell and S. Schmidt (eds), *The Measurement of Productive Efficiency: Techniques and Applications*, Oxford: Oxford University Press.

Mansfield, E. (1986), 'Patents and innovation: an empirical study', *Management Science*, 32(2), 173–181.

Mansfield, E., M. Schwartz and S. Wagner (1981), 'Imitation costs and patents: an empirical study', *The Economic Journal*, **91**, 907–918.

Mrazek, M. and E. Mossialos (2004), 'Regulating pharmaceutical prices in the European Union', in E. Mossialos, M. Mrazek and T. Walley (eds), *Regulating Pharmaceuticals in Europe: Striving for Efficiency, Equity and Quality*, Berkshire, England: Open University Press, pp. 114–128.

Munos, B. (2009), 'Lessons from 60 years of pharmaceutical innovation', *Nature Reviews Drug Discovery*, **8**, 959–968.

Pammolli, F. and M. Riccaboni (2007), *Innovation and Industrial leadership: Lessons from Pharmaceuticals*, Washington, D.C.: Centre for Transatlantic Relations, The Johns Hopkins University.

PAREXEL (2004), *PAREXEL's Pharmaceutical R&D Statistical Sourcebook 2004/2005*, Waltham, MA: PAREXEL International Corporation.
Paul, S., D. Mytelka, C. Dunwiddie, C. Persinger, B. Munos, S. Lindborg and A. Schacht (2010), 'How to improve R&D productivity: the pharmaceutical industry's grand challenge', *Nature Reviews Drug Discovery*, **9**, 203–214.
Pazderka, B. and K. Stegemann (2006), *Patent Policy and the Diffusion of Pharmaceutical Innovations, Intellectual Property and Innovation in the Knowledge-based Economy*, Ottawa: Industry Canada.
Pharmaceutical Industry Competitiveness Task Force (2005), 'Competitiveness and performance indicators', available at http://www.abpi.org.uk/Details.asp?ProductID=258 (accessed 8 June 2008).
PhRMA (2010), *Pharmaceutical Industry: Profile 2010*, Washington, D.C.: The Pharmaceutical Research and Manufacturers of America.
PriceWaterHouseCoopers (2007), 'Pharma 2020: The vision – which path will you take?', available at http://www.pwc.com/gx/en/pharma-life-sciences/pharma-2020/pharma-2020-vision-path.jhtml (accessed 1 May 2009).
Puig-Junoy, J. (2005), 'Price regulation systems in the pharmaceutical market', in J. Puig-Junoy (ed.), *The Public Financing of Pharmaceuticals*, Cheltenham, UK: Edward Elgar Publishing, pp. 35–58.
Reuben, B. and M. Burstall (2005), 'Pharmaceutical R&D productivity: the path to innovation (executive summary)', *Cambridge Healthtech Institute Insight Pharma Reports*, Cambridge, MA: Cambridge Healthtech Advisors, a division of Cambridge Healthtech Institute, available at http://www.insightpharmareports.com/reports/2005/55_RDProductivity/Exec_sum.pdf, (accessed 6 March 2009).
Rivette, K. and D. Kline (2000), 'Discovering new value in intellectual property', *Harvard Business Review* (January–February), 55–66.
Schwitzer, S. (2006), *Pharmaceutical Economics and Policy*, NY: Oxford University Press Inc, USA.
Sichelman, T. (2010), 'Commercializing patents', *Stanford Law Review*, **62**(2), 341–413.
Vernon, J. and J. Golec (2008), *Pharmaceutical Price Regulation: Public Perceptions, Economic Realities, and Empirical Evidence*, Washington, D.C.: The American Enterprise Institute for Public Policy Research.

9. Innovation and regulatory outcomes: evidence from the public-private contracts for water supply in France

Freddy Huet and Simon Porcher

INTRODUCTION

Many scholars advocate that competition for the market can effectively substitute for competition on the market in network industries characterized by natural monopoly characteristics (Demsetz, 1968; Posner, 1972). However, the literature also emphasizes that a lot of potential pitfalls arise when public authorities implement auctions for the award of public-private partnership (PPP) contracts in monopolistic sectors (Crocker and Masten, 1996). One of the most important problems lies in the fact that it is difficult to replace the firm winning the very first auction at the end of the contract. The transaction cost literature (Williamson, 1976; Klein, 1998) suggests that when the incumbent is in charge with the realization of specific investments, a bilateral dependency arises between the firm and the public authority. The problem lies in the fact that the value of these assets would be lost if the firm is replaced. The existence of specific assets then creates a 'lock-in' situation that makes it difficult for the public authority to switch to another supplier. As a consequence, the incumbent enjoys a 'first mover' advantage over rivals at contract renewals (Williamson, 1975). Whether this advantage is due to opportunistic behaviour or reputational bonus remains an open question.

To the extent that incumbents may be aware that it is difficult to challenge their monopoly position, they may have incentives to behave opportunistically. Several types of opportunistic behaviours are analysed in the empirical literature. The firm may renege on its contractual promises after the contract is signed (Zupan, 1989; Prager, 1990). For instance, it may deliberately overestimate demand or underestimate costs to obtain the market, and then ask for a price increase pretending that it did not anticipate the bad market conditions. Although the empirical evidence indicates that the incumbent's advantage at contract renewal is not a myth, the incumbents do not necessarily take advantage of their monopoly position to behave opportunistically. This is usually due to reputation concerns that may restrain the firms' opportunistic conduct. The problem with such findings is that they do not provide a satisfactory explanation as to why firms would have reputational concerns if they know that they have a first-mover advantage and what factors may tilt the balance in favour of reputational concerns and opportunistic behaviour.

The literature on relational contracting addresses these questions. According to Kim (1998), a principal renews the contract with a well-performing agent when the value of future cooperation is greater than the one-shot gain from reneging on the promised rent. Reputation building can make the agent work harder: investments in innovative capital are a measurable input of these reputational concerns. In the theory of the firm, reputation is viewed as an asset or a resource providing the firm with a competitive advantage (Rao, 1994; Dowling, 2004). Consequently, a large part of the literature on reputation is devoted to the link between corporate social responsibility and financial returns. Within the setting of relational contracting, contract renewal acts as an implicit incentive mechanism to motivate the agent to invest in its reputation in order to create a business asset that can substitute for detailed contractual controls (Gulati, 1998).

The literature on innovation and its impact on the firm shows that investing in innovative capital increases the quality of products and corporate reputation (Branco and Rodrigues, 2006) while product differentiation through innovation helps reputation building (Fombrun and Shanley, 1990). Hoppe et al. (2012) link innovation to reputation in a PPP framework. In their model, the agent provides the basic version of the infrastructure and can exert unobservable effort to come up with an innovation, which may reduce the costs of adapting the public service to future needs. Such innovation can be rewarded with a suitable bonus payment. Under renewable contracts, the incentive to innovate is the renewal of the contract and the innovation can be considered as a measure of reputation. Naturally, investments in innovation create a lock-in situation in which the incumbent increases asset specificity and thus the winners' curse.

Focusing on the British railway industry, Affuso and Newberry (2002) find that train operating companies tend to increase their investments when the contract's duration shortens, i.e. when competitive pressure increases. However, they fail to determine whether the investments realized are really specific and aim to create a 'lock-in' or if they merely represent a signal sent by incumbent operators to the regulator in order to prove their commitment and then, to enhance their chance to be awarded the subsequent franchise. Theoretical and empirical studies in contract theory also point out a possible increase in the performance of franchise bidding agreements before contract's renewal (Yvrande-Billon and Gautier, 2008; Iossa and Rey, 2010). Whether this time constraint can mitigate or exacerbate the impact of asset specificity on reputational behaviours remains an open question.

In this chapter, we focus on strategic actions that may be pursued by incumbents precisely in the perspective to raise rivals' entry costs and then to increase their 'first mover' advantage. More precisely, we study incumbents' incentives to withhold information during PPP contracts in the water industry. The level of specific investments in innovative capital can break the information gap between the principal (usually, a municipality) and the agent (usually, a private operator). However, firm behaviour is affected by the degree of competition for the market at the local level and the life cycle of the contract. In contracts that are characterized by a limited duration, the time to the end of the contract is an important determinant of the strategic behaviour of the firm.

Using a dataset on the French water industry compiled by the French Environment Institute (IFEN), the French Health Ministry (DGS) and the National Statistics Institute (INSEE) and based on more than 4,000 French municipalities with water services under private management in 2004 and 2008, we show that incumbent firms that invested in innovative leak detection systems diffuse more information about the network. Indeed, a large part of the information asymmetry might be due to a lack of investments in information systems. Investing in innovative technologies then breaks the potential opportunistic behaviour of the firm. However, in France past investments in innovative leak detection systems are negatively correlated with the potential challenge of the rivals and increase the 'lock-in' situation. This result can be interpreted as strategic market protection behaviour. However, when competition intensity increases, the level of information transmitted decreases, a situation that helps the incumbent to preserve his informational advantage over potential challengers. As rivals are not properly informed about the state and various characteristics of the network, they may be discouraged to bid so as to avoid the winner's curse problem (Wilson, 1967).

To sum up, then, our results are consistent with the three following ideas. First, past innovations impact the regulatory outcomes. Second, incumbent firms tend to withhold information in order to maintain their competitive advantage at contract renewal or when the degree of competition is important. Third, the interaction of the level of innovation with the degree of competition is negative, i.e. competitive pressure mitigates the positive impact of innovative capital input on the level of information transmitted to the public authority. These results however contrast with previous empirical findings emphasizing the role of reputation effects as an efficient way to deter opportunism in PPP contracts.

The remainder of the chapter is organized as follows. The first part is devoted to a brief description of the French water industry and our dataset. We then describe the analytical framework and derive the testable propositions before showing the results of the empirical analysis. A brief conclusion follows.

THE FRENCH WATER INDUSTRY: GOVERNANCE, COMPETITION AND INNOVATION

In France, as in most European countries, municipalities must provide local public services that have public good characteristics. However, if the responsibility for service provision is public, its management can be either public or private. In this case, municipalities may choose between alternative contractual arrangements that differ according to the operator's investments in the service and the allocation of risk across the two parties.

Governance of Water Services

There are several types of organizational modes for local public services. Direct public management implies that the public authority undertakes all operations and investments needed for the provision of the service. Alternatively, the local public authority may choose to involve an outside firm in the operation of the service choosing a PPP contract. Most contracts involving a private firm are lease contracts. In those agreements, the firm is in charge of the day-to-day service operation (water production and distribution, network maintenance, bill collection, water pressure supervision etc.). What is more, the firm is directly remunerated by consumers' bills, exposing it to some operating risks. However, the most important investments, and notably the investments concerning network renewals and extensions, are generally realized by municipalities.

There are however other types of PPP contracts that French municipalities also use. These arrangements differ according to the importance of the investments and financial risks borne by the firm. Alternatively, the local public authority may choose to involve an outside firm in the operation of the service, choosing a '*gérance*' contract in which it pays an external operator a fixed fee, or an 'intermediary management' contract that is similar to the *gérance* contract except that a small part of the operator's revenues depend on its performance. These contracts proffer few incentives to reduce costs and transfer no (or few) risks and decision rights to a private operator. Finally, under a 'concession' contract, the external operator also undertakes construction risk, as it must finance a large part of investments over the duration of the contract. Moreover, the infrastructure is typically transferred to the local public authority at the end of the contract, most often without financial compensation. These contractual agreements differ from the previous ones in that they give operators incentives to reduce costs, and operators share risk in exchange for greater decision rights and claims on revenues.

The firm managing the water service through a public-private contract accumulates over time some strategic information about demand characteristics, the state of the network and more generally about the operating costs. Naturally, it may have incentives to withhold its private information in order to make it more difficult for outsiders to compete on its market at contract renewal. Facing an opportunistic incumbent, municipalities may face important difficulties to obtain information about the water service. This is especially true if we consider the acquisition of network information to the extent that in the water industry, the pipes are underground and not easily observable. Of course, municipalities may engage in auditing procedures by hiring independent consultants to improve their network knowledge. But these procedures may be costly so that many municipalities may be reluctant to bear such costs.

Nevertheless, when reputation mechanisms do exist, incumbents' incentives to disclose information may be enhanced. For instance, they may decide to behave fairly when they think that such a strategy can be useful for obtaining new contracts in other regions. This situation can be referred to as 'reputation effects external to the existing relationship' because the incumbent behaves fairly so as to increase his chance to extend his market to other municipalities (Zupan, 1989). Of course, in situations when the incumbent has incentives to cooperate, the municipality may obviously be able to obtain information about the water service at a lower cost compared to the alternative of conducting costly audits.

Organization of Competition

Since the 'Sapin law' (1993), the public authority can select its partner following a two-step procedure. In the first step, the public authority launches a classic invitation to tender opened to all interested operators. At the end of the tendering procedure, the public authority shortlists the candidates allowed to take part in the second phase of selection. This second step involves a negotiation process between the public authority and the shortlisted candidates. At the end of the negotiation, the public authority chooses its final partner for the duration of the contract.

In inviting tender, the local public authority is not legally constrained in setting the criteria according to which it shortlists and ultimately chooses an operator. Moreover, it needs not publicize its subjective criteria, creating an informational asymmetry between the local public authority and prospective operators and giving the local public authority greater latitude in selecting a partner. This could reduce competition for the field and facilitate collusion among operators or between the local public authority and some operators. But giving municipalities freedom in the choice of their final partner may also induce some desirable outcomes. For instance, when the selection process is flexible, the municipality may be able to threaten the incumbent with nonrenewal of the contract even though the incumbent's bid is advantageous but is also characterized by strategic decisions that prevent challengers from competing on a fair basis. If the municipality's threat is perceived as credible, the incumbent may finally prefer to disclose his private information in order to preserve some chance to keep his ongoing market at the rebidding stage. This situation can be referred to as 'reputation effects internal to the existing relationship' because the fear of losing the current contract may dissuade firms from behaving opportunistically. In a rigid auction procedure, the municipality would be obliged to simply choose the lowest bid, and then to renew the opportunistic incumbent.

Therefore, in the French institutional context characterized by a flexible selection process, there is some place for internal reputation effects to play a role. But these reputation effects will exist only if municipalities can credibly commit to terminating opportunistic incumbents despite the political costs implied by such decisions. Indeed, when the incumbent decides to withhold information, the bidding parity is not ensured anymore and the probability increases that the bid proposed by the best challenger is higher than the incumbent's bid. This is due to the fact that the challengers' winner's curse problem induces them not to bid aggressively. Nevertheless, selecting a challenger who submits a less interesting bid than the one proposed by the opportunistic incumbent may not be politically sustainable. Therefore, if the incumbent anticipates that the non renewal sanction is not credible his incentives to withhold information may not be curbed.

Innovation as Investment in Specific Assets

Innovation in water industries is characterized by two facts. On the one hand, water is a cheap good: the cost of producing tap water lies mainly in its treatment and its transportation. In France, leaks represent around

20 per cent of the stock of water introduced in pipes. Even if water is cheap, it is however not free and it can be costly in the end for private operators or for the customers themselves if they have to pay for the leaks in their bills. On the other hand, investments in leak detection systems are costly and may have an immediate impact on prices. This could be one of the reasons why few operators invest in this kind of monitoring system: investments should be done at the beginning of the contract to avoid a 'hold-up' of their investments. In order to protect operators or public actors from the 'hold-up' dilemma, contracts make the difference between private and public domains. Some investments might be done by private firms and remain in the public domain at the end of the contract while investments made on purpose of the private domain will be removed at the termination of the contract.

How does investment in innovation affects firms' behaviour? One would expect firms investing in strategic assets to behave opportunistically at the renewal: the threat of withdrawing private investments in case of operator change is an important explanation of path dependency, i.e. the fact that there are few switches from an operator to another at the end of the contract (see Chong et al., 2012 for a discussion of 'switchers'). In our framework, we use past investments in innovative capital input as a predictor of firm behaviour. The use of a modern technology to deter leaks is a signal for reputational concerns and thus we expect the level of transferred information to be more important when such investments are implemented. However, such behaviour should be mitigated by the level of competition for the market. When competition is high, firms' past investments in innovative capital input may not increase the probability of reputational behaviour and hence the level of network information transferred to the municipality.

EMPIRICAL STRATEGY

Our dataset consists of 4,351 observations at the municipality level for two different years (2004 and 2008), representing a total of 2,647 municipalities with PPP contracts. Each observation represents a PPP contract signed between a municipality and a private firm. The dataset is nationwide so the distribution of observations covers the whole French territory. In what follows, we present the variables and provide detailed descriptions for each variable.

Our *dependent variable* captures the reputational concerns of the incumbents and it is proxied by updates of the network maps which, in turn, reflect the information transmitted by the incumbent firm to the municipality. In a PPP agreement, the incumbent firm is expected to update the network maps if the incumbent is in charge of operating the service. Network map updates can provide structural information (date when the pipe was installed, kind of material used for the pipe, topographic information etc.). But they can also provide information about the interventions realized on the network during the year (locations of mains repairs for example). Frequent updates enable the municipality to constantly have new information that may be useful to plan future investments on the network and to enhance bidding parity at contract renewal. These aspects explain why the French legislation requires updating the network maps at least once a year.

Our data allowed us to construct a dummy variable (*INFO*), which is equal to 1 when network map updates are observed in the municipality in 2004 and 2008. In contrast, the value of the *INFO* is 0 if no update is realized. Of course, our proxy does not enable us to assess the quality and the extent of the updates, but we can be confident about the fact that more network information is available to the municipality when *INFO* equals 1 compared to when *INFO* equals 0. As can be seen in Table 9.1, 76.9 per cent of the municipalities have at least partial updates of the network maps.

As indicated above, investments in leak detection systems are costly and specific. Investments in such systems are expected to be positively related to the dependent variable (*INFO*), which captures the network map update information transferred to the principal by the agent. Leak detection systems can be non-existent, manual or computer-based. The more complex system is the one that uses geo-referring systems (GIS), as this system automatically targets and localizes leaks. Hence, we construct a *GIS* dummy as a measure of innovative investment and expect this variable to have two effects on the level of information that the incumbent provides to the municipality.

On the one hand, GIS investment may be followed with concealment of network update information because such investments strengthen the 'lock-in' situation that makes the incumbent more likely to win the contract at the renewal stage. The 'lock-in' situation is associated with high costs for the municipality that wishes not to renew the contract with the incumbent and with high entry cost for the potential entrants as the latter would have to buy the incumbent's fixed capital. In this case, the incumbent is acting opportunistically and the effect of *GIS* on *INFO* is negative. On the other hand, large investments made by an operator are a signal similar to increased effort by the agent in a principal-agent framework. In this case, investments in GIS leak detection systems will be associated with higher probability of transmitting information, but the motive is

Table 9.1   Descriptive statistics: innovation and reputational behaviour

Variable	Definition	Mean	Std. Dev.	Min	Max
INFO	Takes the value 1 if a network map update is observed in 2004 and 2008	0.769	0.422	0	1
GIS	Takes value 1 if the local authority has geo-referring information system to localize leaks	0.582	0.493	0	1
PCOMP	Proxy for the potential competition intensity at the department level	0.862	0.068	0.489	0.972
SHAREDM	Percentage of the municipalities in the department that chose in-house provision	0.038	0.089	0	0.877
EXPIRY	Time to the end of the contract measured in years (year of contract termination − 2004)	6.541	4.335	0	25
DENSITY	Population per kilometer of pipe	0.022	0.029	0	0.882
INTER-AUTHORITY	Takes value 1 if the local authority is organizing water distribution in cooperation with other local authorities	0.777	0.417	0	1
AUTARCHY	Produced volume/(produced volume + imported volume)	0.879	0.237	0	1
OPERATOR1	Takes 1 if the local authority has a PPP contract with this operator	0.407	0.491	0	1
OPERATOR2	Takes 1 if the local authority has a PPP contract with this operator	0.229	0.421	0	1
OPERATOR3	Takes 1 if the local authority has a PPP contract with this operator	0.230	0.421	0	1

now to signal reputation concerns rather than increase the cost of contract renewal for the municipality or the potential entrant. In our sample, 58.2 per cent of municipalities are partly or fully equipped with GIS. The remaining municipalities are not equipped with geo-referring systems but with simple information systems or manual detection systems.

However, the relationship between innovation investment and the level of information disclosed (hence the level of opportunistic or reputational behaviour) unfolds in the presence of a wide range of competition and contractual factors that also affect the probability of opportunistic and reputational behaviour. One such factor is the level of competition between operators within a department (region). To measure competition, we calculate a Herfindahl-Hirshman index (*HHI*) at the departmental level. We then derive a competition variable (*PCOMP*) that captures the level of potential competition between firms in the region as follows:

$$PCOMP_j = 1 - HHI_j$$

Here, HHI_j is the Herfindahl-Hirshman index for a given department j and is calculated with market shares of the operators in the department. This indicator captures the prospect for an incumbent to conquer new markets in the area where they operate. Intuitively, the higher is $PCOMP_j$ (or equivalently the lower is HHI_j), the higher is the prospect for the incumbent to conquer new markets. On the contrary, when $PCOMP_j$ equals 0 (or when HHI_j equals 1), this means that there is only one firm operating in the region, which means that this firm has presumably few possibilities to conquer new markets. In our dataset, *PCOMP* is on average equal to 0.862, i.e. the level of competition is presumably high. Therefore, in geographical areas where several firms are present, incumbents may have more incentives to provide network information. Behaving fairly may enable them to build a good reputation that may be helpful to extend their market shares at the expense of their rivals. We then expect a positive sign for $PCOMP_j$ if reputation concerns matter.

However, the presence of other firms in a region may also represent a threat for the incumbent. As the incumbent may prefer to give priority to the protection of their current market, we cannot exclude the possibility that the presence of other operators in the neighbourhood fosters his strategic behaviours instead of lowering them. In other words, a negative sign for $PCOMP_j$ may be consistent with the idea that incumbents disclose less network information in areas where the number of other suppliers is high so as to protect their market from competition. Hence, the impact of competition intensity on the level of information disclosed (i.e., on the level of reputational behaviour) is negative.

The same logic applies if we consider competition among organizational modes instead of inter-firm competition. More precisely, a second proxy measuring for each region the market shares of in-house public provision is introduced ($SHAREDM_j$). The higher this variable, the more the region is dominated by direct public management services. In particular, a high value for $SHAREDM$ means that the municipalities involved in a PPP contract in these regions are likely to be located near other municipalities providing water in-house. On average $SHAREDM$ equals 0.038, meaning that the intensity of competition coming from public actors is rather low. However when a municipality involved in a PPP agreement is located in the neighbourhood of municipalities that opted for direct management, it can easily associate with them at the end of the PPP and benefit from their experience in the case that they are not satisfied with the performance of their incumbent. In other words, the proximity of municipalities providing water in-house makes the transition to direct management easier for municipalities in PPP at the end of the contract.

The variable $SHAREDM$ then proxies the degree of potential competition between PPP and in-house provision, and in the same way as $PCOMP$, we expect this variable to have an ambiguous impact on incumbents' incentives to disclose network information. On the one hand, the proximity of other municipalities that operate their water service in-house may induce the incumbent to behave less opportunistically in order to send a good signal to these municipalities and convince them to switch for a PPP contract. On the other hand, the dominance of in-house provision in the department may also represent a threat for the current markets detained by the incumbent to the extent that the municipalities they contract with may switch more easily from a PPP to direct management at the end of the contract. As a consequence, when $SHAREDM$ is high, the incumbent may have incentives to disclose less network information in order to make the transition to in-house provision more costly for the municipality.

To summarize, a positive sign for the two competition variables described above would reflect incumbents' incentives to behave fairly in order to conquer new markets (reputation). However, a negative sign would reflect a strategic behaviour of market protection (opportunism).

In our database, we also make use of variables reflecting the contractual characteristics of the service. In particular, we account for the influence of the contract's expiring date on the incumbent's incentives to disclose information. For this purpose, we created a variable called $EXPIRY$. It represents the difference between the year when the contract expires and the year of observation. Hence, the smaller $EXPIRY$, the closer is the PPP contract to its renewal date.

Some studies in contract theory report that an incumbent's performance may increase towards the end of contract (Iossa and Rey, 2010; Yvrande-Billon and Gautier, 2008). One reason is that the principal (i.e., the municipalities in our case) may suffer from bounded rationality problems such as limited memory or myopia. Under this assumption, municipalities may forget or forgive opportunistic past behaviour and focus on recent performances to decide about renewing the contract with the incumbent. A second argument relies on the assumption that the incumbent becomes more concerned with contract renewal as the contract's expiry date gets closer. In both cases, the incumbent can be expected to disclose more information about the network towards the end of the contract. This is to enhance their reputation and increase the probability of winning the contract.

However, we also expect the incumbent to disclose less information (i.e., to engage in opportunistic behaviour) towards the end of the contract. There are two reasons why this might be the case. First, the nature of the contract may provide incentives to the incumbent to disclose information in the early years of the contract rather than towards the end. Indeed, the institutional feature of the French water services provides such incentives because municipalities are responsible for network maintenance in the majority of the PPP agreements. Obviously the more reliable and timely the information they have about the network, the more efficient they can be in reducing water leakages and thereby the operating costs of the incumbent. Hence, at the beginning of the PPP contract, the incumbent may find an interest in disclosing their private information. Of course, disclosing information may reduce their informational rents but this reduction may be more than compensated by a decrease in the operating costs thanks to municipalities' more efficient investments in network maintenance.

The second reason relates to the effect of disclosed information on potential entrants and the municipality. The incumbent cannot be sure that information disclosure towards the end of the contract will enable them to secure the contract at the renewal stage. However, they know that the disclosed information will be useful for potential bidders. Indeed, the more the contract approaches its end, the more the information disclosed by the incumbent can be used by rivals to compete for the market at the forthcoming auction. Similarly, the disclosed information may induce the municipality to switch for in-house provision. In such cases, the incumbent withholds information towards the end of the contract to deprive the potential rivals of the information they can use to optimize their bids; or to deprive the municipalities of the information they need to decide in favour of in-house supply.

Given the analysis above, the variable *EXPIRY* may have a positive or negative effect on the level of information disclosed (i.e., on the level of

*Table 9.2   Expected effects and implications for opportunistic versus
           reputational behaviour*

Variable	Opportunistic considerations	Reputational considerations
PCOMP	−	+
SHAREDM	−	+
EXPIRY	+	−
GIS	−	+

reputational behaviour). A positive coefficient on the *EXPIRY* variable
would signal opportunistic behaviour since lower values for *EXPIRY*
would be associated with lower values for *INFO*. Ipso facto, a negative
sign would signal reputational behaviour.

A summary of the expected effects of the variables above on the probability of disclosing network update information is given in Table 9.2. In
the table, four variables (*GIS, PCOMP, SHAREDM*, and *EXPIRY*) have
either negative or positive effects on the probability of disclosed information. The negative (positive) sign of *GIS, PCOMP* and *SHAREDM* indicates opportunistic (reputational) concerns; whereas the implication is the
opposite with respect to *EXPIRY*.

A question that arises here is whether investments in innovative capital
(*GIS*) interact with competition and contractual variables and with what
consequences for the probability of disclosing information about the
network. We address this question by including three interaction terms
in our model to be estimated: *GIS*PCOMP; GIS*SHAREDM*; and
GIS*EXPIRY. As we hypothesize that the impact of the constituent
variables could be either way, we also hypothesize that the interaction
effects can be either positive or negative. In other words, inter-operator
competition (*PCOMP*), competition between private and in-house provision (*SHAREDM*), and closeness to the end of the contract (*EXPIRY*)
may have substitution or complementary effects when they are interacted
with the innovation effort (*GIS*). Whether the effect is complementary
or substitute depends on the signs of the coefficients on the partial terms
and the combined terms. We shall revisit this issue when we interpret the
results below.

We also included in the model a set of *control variables* that might
impact on the firm's incentives to disclose information. The *DENSITY*
variable, measured as the ratio of the population of the municipality with
the length of the network, can impact the level of information disclosed
by the firm. Indeed, municipalities with a large density probably have a
higher capacity and higher incentives to get detailed network maps from

the operators because they have more skilled staff and deeper financial resources to hire technical experts that can control the nature of the information disclosed by the firm.

AUTARCHY is a ratio that measures the degree of a municipality's dependence on import of water from other municipalities. Lower values of *AUTARCHY* indicate the municipality is obliged to import water from other municipalities to meet users' demand. If *AUTARCHY* is close to 0, the firm running the water service totally depends on the imports of water from another municipality. Higher levels of *AUTARCHY* imply abundance of water resources in the municipality, which we expect to increase the bargaining power of the 'autarchic' municipalities and attract new entrants at the contract renewal stage. This combination induces incumbents to disclose information to the municipality so as to increase their chance of winning at the contract renewal stage.

We also consider whether a municipality that is part of a group of municipalities to provide water has bigger market power. A dummy *INTER-AUTHORITY* is equal to 1 if the municipality provides water jointly with others and 0 otherwise. This is due to the fact that a group of municipalities may have higher experience and financial power than municipalities alone. We expect a positive impact of this dummy on the level of information disclosed by the incumbents to public authorities.

Dummies for the three big operators are finally used as controls with independent operators as the reference variable. We account for the possibility that some operators can be more reluctant to provide information than others.

MODEL AND RESULTS

The general model we intend to estimate takes the following form:

$$INFO_{it} = \alpha_1 GIS_{it} + \alpha_2 INTER_{it} + \alpha_3 PCOMP_{jt} + \alpha_4 SHAREDM_{jt} + \alpha_5 EXPIRY_{it} + \beta X_{it} + \varepsilon_{it}$$

where $INFO_{it}$ is a proxy for information in the form of network map updates; GIS_{it} is a dummy equal to 1 if the operator has invested in geo-referring leak detection systems; $INTER_{it}$ is the interaction term between GIS_{it} and one of the indicators of competition ($PCOMP_{jt}$, $SHAREDM_{jt}$ or $EXPIRY_{it}$); $PCOMP_{jt}$ is the reported value of potential competition for the municipality i located in the department j; $SHAREDM_{jt}$ is the reported percentage of the municipalities in the department that chose in-house provision in department j, $EXPIRY_{it}$ is the number of years before the

Table 9.3   Innovation and reputational behaviour: results from probit estimations

Variables	(1) INFO	(2) INFO	(3) INFO
GIS	1.368** (0.623)	0.699*** (0.0580)	0.352*** (0.0867)
GIS*PCOMP	−0.822 (0.716)		
GIS*SHAREDM		−0.880* (0.493)	
GIS*EXPIRY			0.0493*** (0.0106)
EXPIRY	0.0174*** (0.00526)	0.0172*** (0.00524)	−0.00694 (0.00787)
SHAREDM	−0.866*** (0.294)	−0.483 (0.366)	−0.861*** (0.296)
PCOMP	0.538 (0.971)	0.272 (0.942)	0.459 (0.933)
DENSITY	0.000960* (0.000512)	0.000958* (0.000512)	0.000966* (0.000514)
INTER-AUTHORITY	0.237*** (0.0633)	0.234*** (0.0635)	0.235*** (0.0633)
AUTARCHY	0.451*** (0.0974)	0.451*** (0.0975)	0.450*** (0.0978)
OPERATOR 1	0.186** (0.0865)	0.183** (0.0867)	0.208** (0.0876)
OPERATOR 2	−0.0897 (0.0896)	−0.0955 (0.0901)	−0.0783 (0.0903)
OPERATOR 3	−0.00400 (0.0896)	−0.00533 (0.0898)	0.0110 (0.0900)
Constant	−0.732 (0.824)	−0.512 (0.798)	−0.498 (0.791)
Pseudo R²	0.119	0.119	0.122
Observations	4,351	4,351	4,351

Note: OLS regressions with city-clustered robust standard errors in parentheses with
***p<0.01 **p<0.05 *p<0.1

PPP contract expires in the municipality i, and X_{it} is a set of controls for a given municipality i at time t. The model is estimated using a standard probit procedure. The estimation results are presented in Table 9.3, where the dependent variable is the information transmitted to the municipalities in the form of updates to network maps. As such, the dependent variable measures the extent of reputational concerns by the incumbents and the estimated coefficients indicate the effects of innovation investments and other factors on the probability of reputational behaviour by incumbents.

The results in Table 9.3 indicate that investment in specific innovation capital input (*GIS*) has a positive and significant effect on the probability of reputational behaviour measured as network information transmitted to the municipality. This result contradicts the 'lock-in' thesis put forward by Williamson (1975). According to Williamson, investment in specific assets such the GIS leak detection system creates a 'lock-in' situation that makes it difficult for the public authority to switch to another supplier. Hence, investment in innovation enables the incumbent to enjoy a 'first mover' advantage. This dynamic is expected to foster opportunistic behaviour – i.e., withholding network information. Our results indicate that investment in GIS leak detection systems increases the probability of information disclosure. We explain this result by the fact that innovative investment in itself is a signal for reputational concerns and that information disclosure follows in tandem to reinforce the reputational signals. Furthermore, investment in GIS is costly, but it gives the innovative incumbents a competitive edge against other operators with manual or less sophisticated leak detection systems. Indeed, operators with GIS leak detection systems are able to provide more timely and detailed information at lower variable cost compared to rivals with older systems. In other words, once the investment is undertaken, an incumbent with GIS is better placed to meet the information demands of the municipality.

Turning to competition factors, we can see that the effect of potential competition between operators (*PCOMP*) on the probability of reputational behaviour is positive but insignificant. Therefore, the number of operators within a department does not affect the probability of reputational behaviour in our sample. However, the effect of the competition between public and private operators (*SHAREDM*) is negative and significant. This finding indicates that competition between organizational modes (i.e., between public and private provision) tends to reduce the probability of reputational behaviour. This result is confirmed in two of the three estimations (estimations 1 and 3). Therefore, the data suggest that the presence of several municipalities choosing in-house provision in the same geographical area seems to induce private firms operating in this area to conceal information. We explain this result by the possibility that competition between public and private provision may represent a more credible threat for private operators than competition captured by the number of firms. This explanation is in line with results reported by Chong et al. (2006). In other words, private firms may be more afraid of being evicted and replaced by a public provider than by another private firm, and therefore they behave more strategically when faced with public providers as competitors.

In our estimations, *EXPIRY* has a positive sign and it is significant in the specifications where it is not interacted with GIS. Therefore, the further away is the contract's expiry date, the higher the incentives to disclose information. In other words, the closeness of the contract's renewal reduces the probability of reputational behaviour and increases that of opportunistic behaviour. This is in contrast to predictions of the contract theory, which suggests that the incumbent's performance and reputational concerns increase towards the end of contract (Iossa and Rey, 2010; Yvrande-Billon and Gautier, 2008). Our finding indicates that the incumbents tend to disclose information early in the contract duration in order to induce the municipalities to carry out necessary repairs and thereby reduce the operating costs.

To interpret the results for the interaction term, we need to recall that the coefficient of *GIS* is positive. Given this, a positive sign for the coefficient of the interaction term implies that the factor interacted with *GIS* would have a complementary effect; whereas a negative sign would imply a substitution effect. The interaction term between investment in innovative capital (*GIS*) and competition (*PCOMP*) is negative but not significant. Hence *PCOMP* has neither substitution nor complementary effects. However, the interaction term *GIS*SHAREDM* is negative and significant. In other words, as the number of public-sector competitors increases, the probability of reputational behaviour decreases among incumbents that invest in GIS. Hence, we can conclude that *SHAREDM* has a substitution effect when interacted with innovation (*GIS*). Incumbents that invest in GIS tend to disclose less information when faced with competition from public-sector providers compared to other incumbents with the same level of investment in GIS but lower level of competition from public providers.

Finally, the coefficient on the interaction term *GIS*EXPIRY* is positive and significant, indicating that incumbents that invest in GIS tend to have a higher probability of disclosing network information (i.e., engaging in reputational behaviour) in early years of the contract compared to later years. Hence, the time to the end of the contract and investment in GIS are complements in their effects on the probability of reputational behaviour.

When *EXPIRY* gets closer to 0, the level of information transmitted by the incumbent to the municipality decreases. These results indicate that the probability of transmitting information to the municipality (i.e., the probability of reputational behaviour) decreases as the level of competition intensity increases. In other words, competition has an offsetting effect on the positive relationship between innovation investments and reputational behaviour.

To sum up, our preliminary results suggest that in France, investments in innovative capital are correlated with higher probabilities of reputational behaviour captured by network information transmitted to the municipality. Opportunistic behaviour is on average stronger when competitive intensity increases. Arguably, private firms may on average be all the more tempted to signal their reputational concerns during the contract by implementing innovative capital input; but they may decrease their commitment to reputational behaviour when competition between organizational modes increases or towards the end of the contract in order to lock-in the market.

DENSITY, INTER-AUTHORITY and *AUTARCHY* have significant and positive effects. The positive effects of *DENSITY* and *AUTARCHY* on the probability of reputational behaviour as measured by the transmitted network information can be due to higher bargaining power of the municipalities with dense populations (i.e., deeper markets) and richer water resources. Municipalities that organize water distribution in cooperation with other local authorities (*INTER-AUTHORITY*) also have a positive effect on the probability of reputational behaviour for the same reason.

Finally, operators' fixed effects show no significant impact except for one of the main operators (*OPERATOR1*). Independent operators are the reference variable. It seems that only the main operator has a clear strategy to provide more information and invest in reputational behaviour.

CONCLUSION AND POLICY RECOMMENDATIONS

In this chapter, we intended to contribute to the debate about the determinants of reputational versus opportunistic behaviour of incumbents in water services governed by PPP contracts. We particularly focused on two factors that could influence the firms' behaviours: investments in innovative capital and competition intensity at the regional or at the contractual level. Our results show that innovative capital input has a positive effect on firms' reputational behaviour measured by network information disclosure. The opposite result is found for competition at the regional level or at the contractual level, thus demonstrating that firms behave opportunistically when competition is higher. The interaction between innovation investment and competition shows that competition mitigates the impact of investments in innovative capital on the probability of reputational behaviour.

Of course, our work has some limitations. The most important one lies in the fact that we do not take into account the possibility that some PPP contracts may include provisions stipulating some performance obligations that have to be fulfilled by the firm with regards to information disclosure. We intend to address this shortcoming in the near future.

Nevertheless, our work raises an important point for policymakers. We showed that firms involved in PPP contracts in the water sector may strategically react to the competitive environment by concealing network information in order to raise rivals' entry costs. Therefore, some policies that aim to foster competition in this industry may fail if they don't take into account the strategic behaviours that firms could adopt to protect their rents. This is especially true when specific investments in innovative capital have been undertaken. Arguably, regulatory policies that reinforce the obligation for incumbents to invest in innovative capital that would provide better quality network information to public authorities should be encouraged.

REFERENCES

Affuso, L. and D. Newberry (2002), 'The impact of structural and contractual arrangements on a vertically separated railway', *The Economic and Social Review*, 33 (1), 83–92.

Branco, M.C. and L.L. Rodrigues (2006), 'Corporate social responsibility and resource-based perspectives', *Journal of Business Ethics*, 69 (2), 111–132.

Chong, E., Huet, F. and S. Saussier (2006), 'Auctions, ex-post competition and prices: the efficiency of public-private partnerships', *Annals of Public and Cooperative Economics*, 77 (4), 521–554.

Chong, E., Saussier, S. and B.S. Silverman (2012), 'Water under the bridge: when and how do municipalities change organizational forms in the provision of water?', Chaire EPPP working paper.

Crocker, K. and S. Masten (1996), 'Regulation and administered contracts revisited: lessons from transaction costs economics for public utility regulation', *Journal of Regulatory Economics*, 9 (1), 5–39.

Demsetz, H. (1968), 'Why regulate utilities', *Journal of Law and Economics*, 11 (1), 55–66.

Dowling, G.R. (2004), *Corporate Reputation: Strategies for Developing The Corporate Brand*, London: Kogan Page.

Fombrun, C.J. and M. Shanley (1990), 'What's in a name? Reputation building and corporate strategy', *Academy of Management Journal*, 33 (2), 233–258.

Gulati, R. (1998), 'Alliances and networks', *Strategic Management Journal*, 19 (4), 293–317.

Hoppe, E., Kusterer, D. and P. Schmitz (2012), 'Public-private partnerships versus traditional procurement: an experimental investigation', *Journal of Economic Behaviour and Organization*, forthcoming.

Iossa, E. and P. Rey (2010), 'Building reputation for contract renewal: implications for performance dynamics and contract duration', SSRN CEIS Working Paper no. 155.

Kim, I.G. (1998), 'A model of selective tendering: does bidding competition deter opportunism by contractor?', *The Quarterly Review of Economics and Finance*, 77 (1), 168–185.

Klein, M. (1998), 'Rebidding for concessions', *Public Policy for the Private Sector*, no.161, The World Bank.

Posner, R.A. (1972), *Economic Analysis of Law*, Boston: Little Brown.

Prager, R. (1990), 'Firm behaviour in franchise monopoly markets', *RAND Journal of Economics*, 21 (2), 211–225.

Rao, H. (1994), 'The social construction of reputation: certification contest, legitimating, and survival of organizations in the American automobile industry: 1895–1912', *Strategic Management Journal*, 15(S1), 29–44.

Williamson, O. (1975), *Market and Hierarchies: Analysis and Antitrust Implications*, New York: Free Press.

Williamson, O. (1976), 'Franchise bidding for natural monopolies – in general and with respect to CATV', *Bell Journal of Economics*, 7 (1), 73–104.

Wilson, W. (1967), 'Competitive bidding with asymmetric information', *Management Science*, 13 (11), 816–820.

Yvrande-Billon, A. and A. Gautier (2008), 'Contract renewal as an incentive device: an application to the French urban public transport sector', Working Paper, http://orbi.ulg.ac.be/handle/2268/122426.

Zupan, M. (1989), 'The efficacy of franchise bidding schemes in the case of cable television: some systematic evidence', *Journal of Law and Economics*, 32 (2), 401–456.

PART III

Governing innovation

10. Role of governance in national innovation systems: from intellectual property to intellectual capital

G. Scott Erickson

INTRODUCTION

This chapter brings together two distinct literature themes, from national innovation systems and intellectual capital. A growing scholarly and practitioner community views softer knowledge assets, those less defined by structured innovation mechanisms such as patents, as additional, alternative sources of competitive advantage for the firm. The growing recognition of intangible assets as a critical source of competitive advantage has important implications for corporate governance. The interplay between firm governance and its national environment raises further questions. By adding knowledge asset development and use to the perspective of national innovation systems, governing bodies have an opportunity to enact policies making their firms more competitive on international markets. Governance opportunities present themselves in the areas of strategy and investment, reporting, protection, and government stewardship.

National innovation system theory has proved valuable during the past two decades as a guide to creating the right national governance approach to generating innovation. Different nations have different circumstances, and optimal policies may vary by such circumstances; but the concept remains that systems can be designed to get government to encourage innovation (or at least get out of its way). An effective national system enables corporate leadership to better fulfill its own governance role of making the firm competitive and generating appropriate financial returns.

Over the past two decades, we have also seen a change in what is considered a valuable intellectual asset. While more formalized assets such as patents remain important, softer assets, termed intellectual capital, are also now considered critical to a lot of firms. Even the precursors of intellectual capital, raw data or information, have the potential for value as the advent of interest in big data shows. However, none are developed enough to be protected by traditional intellectual property. So a different set of national policies and procedures is needed if corporate managers are to be effective in developing, applying, and protecting valuable intellectual capital.

Hence, this chapter makes the case that national innovation system approaches would benefit from a broader consideration of what knowledge assets are valuable and how the national governance system might encourage the development and application of softer forms of knowledge. Specifically, by creating government programs to grow knowledge (education, infrastructure, etc.), by encouraging the establishment of common metrics and reporting standards, by creating protection mechanisms, and by forming procedures that would make government use of such assets predictable, governments have the potential to further the development of intellectual capital in their firms. In so doing, competitiveness can also be enhanced, as the best managers will be able to recognize the opportunities available and better manage these intangible assets. An understanding between government and corporate leadership about what the favorable conditions might be and how they will be maintained can be very helpful in establishing effective corporate governance relating to intangibles.

NATIONAL INNOVATION SYSTEMS

National innovation system (NIS) studies took root during the 1990s as it became clear that innovation was increasingly important to the competitiveness of nations and their businesses. The debate over different approaches to national competitiveness helped to drive interest in the topic, including the nature and the degree of government involvement in guiding or stimulating technological development. At the time, the Japanese model was in ascendance. Even though that model is now less credible, new examples such as Brazil, India and China (the BRICs), with more varied approaches, have risen to make the field even more relevant for today.

Growing out of the decades-old interest of economists in better explaining how innovation and change occur and a more recent, more practical focus on the competitiveness of nations, NIS studies focused attention on external environment conditions conducive to innovation. Although easily related to lower levels of analysis (e.g. regional innovation systems and/or local economic development), the issues at the national level were of particular interest to decision makers and had important implications for competitiveness policy. Nations with sub-optimal NIS structures could conceivably place their firms at a disadvantage when they compete in international markets (or with better-equipped foreign firms at home).

An exact definition of the NIS has been an elusive enterprise, leading to variations in the literature. Although the concept came out of pioneering work by scholars such as Freeman (1987), Lundvall (1988), and Dosi et al. (1988); the field really hit its stride with Nelson's (1993) *National Innovation Systems*. The edited volume featured studies, most written by major scholars in the field, of the major economies in the world, examining the 'national innovation system' behind each. From these studies, we began to get a more focused sense of what an NIS might be.

The basic concept, right out of Porter (1998), is that innovation by firms takes place within an environment, a national environment in this case, that can influence the results. The most obvious piece of this national environment is government support for innovation, whether through R&D funding, intellectual property protection, or other such direct mechanisms. Other government activities often noted in the literature include support for education (particularly science and engineering), tax policies, labour and employment policies, trade policies, antitrust policies, and similar conditions affecting industry. From a broader perspective, government participation in the economy (ownership, subsidies) can also have an impact, as can industrial policy or guidance. The perceived effectiveness of the Japanese Ministry of International Trade and Industry (MITI) in the early nineties was one of the precursors of interest in the NIS concept. Indeed, the MITI was credited with making Japanese firms more competitive by directing their efforts in targeted directions.

Other factors are also often discussed in NIS studies, including industry composition (nature of prominent industries), entrepreneurship and the role of small and medium-sized enterprises, and import/export levels. The latter is also used as a performance indicator. Some studies have included less well-defined environmental circumstances such as economic culture, characterized by matters such as whether there is a risk-taking, entrepreneurial spirit among the population, if the country is individualistic or group-oriented, or if attitudes are pro-business or not. So there is a tendency to look closely at policy factors as influencers in NIS studies, but these are not exclusive, as the economic culture aspect illustrates.

Given a particular national environment, there is also the question as to how resident firms react to the environment that delineates the NIS. As we shall see below, there are governance factors that shape the cost and incentive structures faced by corporate managers and affect the ways in which they employ organizational resources within a given environment. Indeed, one key aspect of governance work in this context is that the national framework for corporate governance affects the ways in which management performs its tasks (Weimer and Pape, 1999).

In comparing the different NIS philosophies and structures, there is, of course, a practical goal. If one NIS is superior, at least as a better fit for a given country, then it makes sense to continue to make policy decisions that support that preferred NIS. In order to compare, metrics are necessary. Typically, the overall impact of an NIS is judged by measures such as high-technology output and trade. More specifically, patent levels, sales of high-technology products, imports and exports of high-technology products, licensing flows, and similar outputs are routinely used to judge the effectiveness of the NIS in generating innovation and competitiveness. Sometimes this is evaluated against input levels (R&D expenditure, high-skilled labor) as well, providing a productivity comparison through input/output metrics.

So, essentially, the approach goes back to standard measures of national innovation, especially intellectual property or metrics incorporating intellectual property. One interesting change is the treatment of R&D expenditures as an input rather than an output. But what it boils down to is an approach looking at the results of a system and trying to figure out why those may be better or worse than another system. Further, could a change in NIS (more intellectual property protection, more spending on R&D, more education spending, etc.) engender better results? And is there a one-size-fits-all solution or does the optimal NIS for a given country vary by the conditions in that country?

One specific interest in this system of inputs, outputs, and influencing variables is intellectual property (IP) (Erickson, 1996). Typically, we define IP as more formalized intangible assets incorporating innovation, including patents, trademarks, and copyrights. Trade secrets are often added to the list though these are typically less formalized, less well-defined, and highly variable in terms of the laws protecting them. Aspects of IP such as the strength of protection (depth and breadth of innovation descriptions, length of protection, enforcement mechanisms, etc.) can be parsed, by nation, to try to determine what the appropriate policy structure might be. Different perspectives exist on whether there is a single 'optimal' patent system and other protection devices or, once again, whether customized types of systems might be best for specific nations. Generally, there is at least recognition that IP systems are an important part of how governments influence national innovation even if we still debate the details of what structure is best for a given country (Erickson, 1999).

The development of NIS theory and scholarship in the 1990s has led to continued discussion today. Major studies continue to contribute to the debate, as innovation becomes ever more important to national economies and interest has evolved beyond the major trading areas (USA, EU, Japan) covered in most of the early studies. We shall discuss some of these (e.g. Fillipetti and Archibuigi, 2011; Fagerberg and Srholec, 2008; Lundvall et. al., 2002) in more detail shortly, but they are notable for how they expand the field into new and more contemporary directions, including intangible organizational assets that may be even harder to define and manage.

As noted earlier, NIS theory also has important implications for corporate governance. As we'll discuss, the duty of managers to maintain competitiveness and generate appropriate returns from assets is highly influenced by the governance environment. NIS really brought the environment that dictates how innovation efforts are managed to the forefront of the conversation. We'll broaden the conversation even further as we look at the more contemporary view of critical organizational assets, management of them, and the environment within which it all takes place.

Indeed, at this point in time, we do have new research streams entering the conversation that could be an important extension of the NIS framework. Firms are increasingly seeing potential for competitive advantage from less formalized, often less high-tech types of knowledge assets. The trend could even be extended to include the current explosion of interest in business intelligence, big data, and related information processing applications. If firms are, indeed, finding competitive advantage on international markets from such knowledge and informational assets, what kind of formal and informal governance structures can shape an environment that fosters and supports the growth and exploitation of such assets? And what are the concerns of managers charged with stewardship of these assets under these conditions?

INTELLECTUAL CAPITAL: DEFINITION AND GOVERNANCE IMPLICATIONS

While IP constitutes the more easily identifiable, more formalized intangible assets of the firm, it is only a constituent part within a wider set of intangible assets. Although always recognized as an issue in conventional valuations of organizations, interest in how to evaluate intangible assets has increased throughout the technology boom of the 1990s, which made the intangible assets ever greater components of market capitalizations and perceived firm success. It became clear that the value of the firm and its physical assets may have very little to do with one another, engendering a rush to define the difference as the value of intangible assets. As only a small subset of the intangible assets could be explained by the traditional IP framework in a wide range of applications, parsing out the more specific nature of the intangibles and better managing the results became a pressing concern for both scholars and practitioners.

Consequently, the closely related fields of intellectual capital and knowledge management were born. Intellectual capital (IC) grew out of the accounting interest in identifying and measuring the intangible assets that were less formalized than traditional intellectual property (Bontis, 1999; Edvinsson and Malone, 1997; Stewart, 1997). From a strategic view (Wiig, 1997), IC breaks intangible assets into the pertinent categories with a view to give managers better information about the knowledge they are trying to grow and apply. Knowledge management (KM) was then the managerial interest in acquiring, growing, and leveraging softer knowledge assets to gain competitive advantage (Nonaka and Takeuchi, 1995; Grant, 1996). Characterized as more tactical, KM is all about understanding specific knowledge assets so as to combine them, share them, or in some other way make more effective use of them with the right tools (Wiig, 1997).

While the breadth of both fields cannot be fully covered in a short space like this, their basic tenets can be succinctly described. Both fields are based on the concept that firms possess data, information, and knowledge. In the terminology of the field, data are accumulated bits, information is organized data, and knowledge is information subjected to reflection and learning. Accumulated over time, this knowledge can have value (Gupta and Govindarajan, 2000; Zack, 1999; Grant, 1996). Indeed, some scholars informed by the resource-based theory of the firm have advanced the knowledge-based theory of the firm (Teece et al., 1997; Grant, 1996). There is also an increasing recognition that there is value in the knowledge precursors, data and information, because they can turn into knowledge with some purposeful study – hence the rise of phenomena such as business intelligence and data mining (Herschel and Jones, 2005).

In organizing what we know about KM and IC, scholars have found it useful to differentiate between knowledge assets in a number of ways. Initially, there is a distinction between tacit and explicit knowledge (Nonaka and Takeuchi, 1995), borrowed from earlier research in sociology and political economy (Polanyi, 1967). Tacit knowledge is individual, hard to express, and hard to codify or capture. Explicit knowledge can be more readily expressed, is more sharable, and can be codified by the organization and sometimes stored in information systems. The punchline to this differentiation, of course, is that firms will require very different systems for better managing and utilizing these types of knowledge. While more explicit knowledge can be managed with help from information technology, tacit knowledge often requires more relational approaches if the knowledge is to be leveraged and shared throughout the entity (Choi and Lee, 2003; Schulz and Jobe, 2001; Boisot, 1995).

Standard theory also distinguishes between human capital, structural capital, and relational capital (Bontis, 1999; Edvinsson and Malone, 1997). There are other versions, some adding categories, but most scholars stick with the three basic categories (and virtually all research includes the three in some form) (e.g. Andreou et al., 2007). Human capital relates to individuals and knowledge about their jobs, whether managing a corporation as CEO or operating a grinding machine. Structural capital has more to do with firm-specific knowledge including matters such as information technology and systems, corporate culture, firm organization, and other such matters that persist over time and are learned by newcomers. Relational capital includes knowledge about those outside the firm, including suppliers, customers, government, and others often referred to as stakeholders in other applications. Good customer relationships, including brand equity, as well as networks of partners and good relationships with regulators can all be important parts of relational capital. Interweaving all of these forms of IC is social capital (Nahapiet and Ghoshal, 1998), a separate and distinct concept referring to the individual relationships and trust, both inside and outside the firm, enabling sharing and growth of these valuable knowledge assets.

A variety of metrics have been created to try to evaluate levels of intellectual capital in firms, both bottom-up (assessing individual employee knowledge and adding it all up) and top-down (calculating intangible assets as a remainder from financial statements). Preferences vary, but just note that measurement is a topic that has been explored in some depth and that dozens of potential choices are available to firms looking to evaluate and then better manage their own IC (Sveiby, 2010).

If knowledge assets are the single most valuable asset available to a firm seeking to establish sustainable competitive advantage in the marketplace, per the resource-based/knowledge-based theory of the firm, there are clear implications for corporate governance. And, as would be expected, considerable theory has been developed concerning the intersections between the concepts of intellectual capital and governance.

Generally, corporate governance is characterized as the 'more or less country-specific framework of legal, institutional and cultural factors shaping the patterns of influence that stakeholders . . . exert on managerial decision-making' (Weimer and Pape, 1999: 152). Or, more specifically, corporate governance centers around the responsibility of the organization's leadership to generate growth and profit. The leadership is responsible for applying the capital at its disposal to increase value for stakeholders. Traditionally, tangible capital (financial, physical) has made up the assets of interest, but the increasing prominence of intangibles has brought them into the picture as well. Hence, corporate governance is also 'responsible for assuring, mobilizing and orienting human, culture, innovation, external-structure, and internal structure capitals oriented toward achieving the goals, and values of the firm' (Keenan and Aggestam, 2001: 269).

If the job of the leadership is to increase value, it has a responsibility to pursue all avenues that can lead there. Increasingly, that appears to mean application of less formal assets such as intellectual capital. This direction poses a number of difficulties. As we've discussed, intangible assets are bound up in intellectual capital and can be hard to define, let alone measure. Even when measurable, investments in IC are unlikely to produce an immediate payoff. The value of the investment will probably not be seen for a number of years (Cerbioni and Parbonetti, 2007). Further, as we've also discussed, developing IC is often a matter of managing a network of knowledge assets, not only within the firm but across boundaries. Consequently, governance structures become increasingly significant for managing relationships within and without the firm.

In governance scholarship, the agency problem that is due to separation of management and ownership continues to be a major issue. Generally, leadership needs to signal that it is taking appropriate steps to effectively manage the company. Often, the signal is accomplished through appropriate disclosure. With financial reporting, this is straightforward, as generally accepted accounting principles and reporting regulations dictate what is expected. For intangibles, the problem is more daunting, without standard reporting procedures or any particular requirement to disclose at all. Given the trend to more appreciation of the value of intangibles, there is at least some thought that financial reporting is no longer representative of the state of the firm (Bukh, 2003; Lev and Zarowin, 1999).

As a result, at the intersection of intellectual capital and corporate governance is an interest in disclosure. The art of managing knowledge assets is complex and, as previously noted, the payoff may be long in coming and difficult to tie directly to investment in knowledge. While the specifics of disclosure are still early in development (Abeysekera, 2006), there have been some moves toward standardization. Managers recognize the value of showing investment and interest in developing intangibles, and voluntary disclosure rectifies issues such as information asymmetry and agency (Li et al., 2008; Cerbioni and Parbonetti, 2007).

But good governance is also a matter of adapting to a particular national operating environment. Governance theory not only addresses appropriate structures and means for decision-making but also how the governance structure fits a particular national environment. Weimer and

Pape (1999), for example, specifically identify four national systems in their taxonomy: Anglo-Saxon, Germanic, Latin, and Japanese. We'll look at the interaction of corporate governance with national systems after a look at work that has been done on understanding IC at the national or regional level.

Intellectual Capital at the National Level

Interestingly, the field has also ventured into national accounts, tracking the intellectual capital of a number of countries or regions. This track has some differences in approach, as there are both different intentions behind the studies and different purposes for the outcomes (Andriessen and Stam, 2004; Bontis, 2004; Pulic, 2002; and Pasher, 1999). Even so, there are also similarities across the studies, with obvious connections to the more established micro-level work. There are also links to national innovation systems (Hervas-Oliver et al., 2011), allowing us to begin to draw together the different strains of this chapter.

Start with the approaches to IC on the national level. Table 10.1 shows the broad outlines of the categories and metrics of three seminal studies in the field, Pasher's (1999) work on Israel; Bontis's (2004) UN-financed analysis of the Arab countries; and Andriessen and Stam's (2004) paper on the European Union. One constraint faced by all the studies is availability of data, so there are some clear compromises in terms of using what exists as opposed to what might be an ideal metric. But that being said, there are some very clear tendencies and lessons.

Pasher's (1999) study was the first, and the groundbreaking one that defined the field. She used the standard IC framework of Human Capital, Structural/Process Capital, and Relational/Market Capital while adding the category of Renewal and Development Capital (from some of the early work in IC by Skandia and used in some firm- or industry-level studies). This addition was in recognition of the static qualities of the IC metrics, attempting to assess current investment in knowledge assets that should pay off in increased levels in the future. This became a regular practice in national IC studies, including the Bontis (2004) and Andriessen and Stam (2004) approaches in Table 10.1. What did not extend to future studies was an emphasis on some country-specific factors such as the state of agriculture, biotech, or services industries.

Bontis (2004) continued in much the same vein, with some differences in metrics as he found particular issues with data availability. He did, however, flesh out some of the concepts and details behind the metrics. Andriessen and Stam (2004), on the other hand, have introduced significant changes, particularly with respect to organization. Rather than

Table 10.1   Components of intellectual capital: evidence from three studies

Pasher (1999)	Bontis (2004)	Andriessen and Stam (2004) Assets (A) Investments (I) Effects (E)
Human Capital	**Human Capital**	**Human Capital**
Higher education	Organizational training	(A) Secondary education
Equal opportunities	Education spending	Computer training/use
Culture	Educational	Education and training
Health	participation	Researchers employed
	Educational quality	Employment
		Knowledge employment
		(I) Education spending
		Labor policy spending
		(E) Productivity
		Value-added services
Process Capital	**Process Capital**	**Structural Capital**
Communication	Computer literacy	(A) Household internet
and computer	Digital storage	Business internet
infrastructure	Library holdings	Patent apps (EPO)
Education (resources)	Transportation	Patent apps (USPTO)
Agriculture	Software	Scientific publications
(value-added)	Entrepreneurship	Enterprise indicator
Management	Venture capital	Entrepreneurial indicators
International		Startup time
experience		Venture capital
Entrepreneurship		EU directives
Venture capital		Government debt
Employment		R&D investment
Service sector		IT investment
Immigration		(E) e-commerce use
		Startup rate
		Income
		High-tech industry
		Life expectancy
Market Capital	**Market Capital**	**Relational Capital**
Market needs	Openness to different	(A) International meetings
International	cultures	hosted
connections	Foreign languages	SME's innovation
Openness to different	spoken	cooperation
cultures	Tourism (in and out)	Foreign students
Language skills	Business trust	Outgoing telecom

Table 10.1   (continued)

Pasher (1999)	Bontis (2004)	Andriessen and Stam (2004) Assets (A) Investments (I) Effects (E)
	International launch speeds Immigration and emigration Magazine exports International events Graduate students abroad	(E) Intl scientific cooperation Foreign patent co-inventors Royalty and license fee exports Services exports High-tech exports
Renewal and Development Capital R&D expenditures Scientific publications Patent applications R&D employment Startup companies Biotech companies	**Renewal Capital** Returning graduate students Foreign patents/ applications Foreign trademark registrations Intellectual aptitude of students	

a separate Renewal and Development Capital category, they break down each of the other IC groups between assets, investments, and effects. This approach is intuitively appealing as it provides a reading on the current stock of intellectual capital, its impact, and its potential for the future. It's interesting to note that the scholars don't see a source of investment in the relational capital category.

One important point to note about the studies is their provenance and intentions. Although scholarly work, there is very clearly a practical purpose to the studies, describing these countries and regions as attractive locations for knowledge-intensive industries. Pasher (1999) calls her study a 'balance sheet' of the IC of Israel, while Bontis (2004) was funded by the United Nations Development Programme and intended to show the 'invisible wealth' of the Arab countries. Andriessen and Stam (2004) track progress on the Lisbon Agenda, encouraging the development of the knowledge economies seen as the future of the EU.

One consequence of these approaches and their growth out of measuring the IC of companies is a more descriptive than prescriptive result. The same is seen in approaches that add up the IC of individual firms in order to capture the IC of a region or nation (Pulic, 2002). There are lessons to be learned in terms of governance, but they are not explicit. This is where the experience of NIS scholarship may add to the impact of the more recent national IC studies.

The link between NIS studies and national IC is becoming a topic of interest, with attempts being made to identify similarities and areas of convergence (Hervas-Oliver et al., 2011). The reasons are easily seen when comparing metrics. More contemporary NIS studies (Fillipetti and Archibuigi, 2011; Lundvall et al., 2002) can now include a human capital component, assessing the stocks of knowledge present in an economy. A recent study by prominent NIS scholar Jan Fagerberg (Fagerberg and Srholec, 2008), for example, includes science, research and innovation; openness; product quality standards; communication infrastructure; skills; finance; quality of governance; social values; type of political system. All of these have the potential to impact the firm's application of capital and the success of its leadership.

Much of this should be familiar from the national IC studies noted above, including science and R&D, openness, infrastructure, and skills. One difference that should be noted is in the environment surrounding innovation, including political system, economic system, social/cultural values, regulations, quality standards, and overall governance. This is more prescriptive than national IC, offering some judgments on the best environment within which to generate innovation or other forms of knowledge.

And this is the direction in which it would make sense for IC theory and practice, as well as governmental attention, to move. If knowledge assets, as argued in the knowledge-based theory of the firm, really are the competitive differentiator for modern firms, countries looking to put their own companies in the best position to succeed should consider IC-friendly national governance structures and practices. Indeed, Leif Edvinsson (2002: 29), one of the founding fathers of intellectual capital, suggested key areas for the political agenda to address, including: renewal (innovation capital), education (human capital), foreign trade (relationship capital), and industrial productivity (process capital).

Again, the main point is to identify the overlap between the two fields while also recognizing the potential for enriching the field by incorporating formal and informal governance mechanisms as an additional source of synergy. NIS studies were predicated on the idea of a national system primed to make the job of corporate leadership easier in terms of producing innovation from given assets. A national approach to intellectual capital can help in much the same way. By better defining the environment within which the management of knowledge assets takes place, corporate leadership can do a better job of governance in relation to developing critical intangibles. The interrelationship between national governance and corporate governance in this field can be seen in a number of areas.

GOVERNANCE OF INTELLECTUAL CAPITAL: INCENTIVES, DISCLOSURE AND PROTECTION MECHANISMS

Drawing back to a more focused perspective, what are the implications for intellectual capital, as opposed to intellectual property and other NIS concerns, from a governance perspective? Just as IP and innovation go together and can be influenced by other parts of the NIS environment, so IC and competitiveness go together. Should our view of the NIS be adjusted to include considerations for its impact on IC development within a country? In particular, should the governance aspects of the NIS be rethought so that they also include a national intellectual capital strategy and/or more explicit support for corporate governance regarding IC strategies?

This is probably appropriate from a number of perspectives. Considering each in turn, we'll look at how formal governance rules and structures can create the conditions to help corporate leadership grow IC, create reporting standards for IC, protect IC, and address the implications of sharing IC with governments. In each case, formal governance can influence the incentives to innovate by means of intellectual capital. Let us consider these dimensions in some detail.

The relevance of governance to *growing IC* is most obvious and easiest to explain. Within traditional NIS frameworks, there are always concerns about related government spending, laws, and regulations supporting innovation. Hence the governance of education (including science, math, and engineering), R&D spending, infrastructure (including telecom and internet), patent protection, and international trade are common areas of concern. That extends to the national IC system. In our discussion, we've seen that human capital, structural or process capital, and relational capital contain aspects of governmental participation. Regarding human capital, this would include support for basic education, more advanced education, employee training, and similar efforts to grow the base of employees and managers while also making them more knowledgeable. In terms of structural capital, governance areas of attention could be telecommunications, the internet, the formal knowledge base (as contained in patents), and support for entrepreneurship (venture capital, ease of starting a business, etc.).

Relational capital is a less clear-cut issue though. In the national accounts we have discussed, relational capital is portrayed by openness to cross-border trade, ideas, students, and other exchanges. This is considerably different than how resident firms view their own relational capital. For them it is more about market capital (relations with customers, including their brand value) as well as other external relationships, such as those with regulators, business partners up and down the value chain, local communities, and others. So governance rules and policies for brand equity, interfirm linkages and trust, and regulation, etc., will be important for corporate leadership.

As a result, in the context we are discussing here, the bigger concern for supporting firm-level relational capital would be how a government treats these issues. Can a firm create and protect a brand? Can it form and maintain close, data-driven relationships with customers? Do regulators work with business or against it? How easy or hard is it to form horizontal business partnerships? As little work has been done in this area, these factors will take more time to tease out. But they are important questions to ask and resolve from a governance viewpoint, in terms of both government policy and corporate managers' reactions to it.

The relevance of a governance perspective to *disclosure of IC* has already been recognized in the effort to devise reporting standards. Public firms do financial reporting, of course, and the required statements in that regard strongly influence non-public firms as well. With the required, agreed-upon standard in place, everyone knows what to measure and how to do it, and gains a metric that can be compared across different firms. Given the potential importance for corporate leadership to disclose IC development activities, as discussed earlier, an agreed-upon or recommended national metric would be of great help in convincing investors that governance is effective. While an overhaul of the reporting standards for public companies is unlikely, support is growing for voluntary disclosure to reassure investors, decrease the cost of capital, increase analyst coverage and reduce agency and information asymmetry costs (Li et al., 2008; Cerbioni and Parbonetti, 2007).

For intellectual capital at the firm level, there is some agreement about the general elements of intellectual capital or knowledge assets, but a variety of choices exist for actually measuring them. Sveiby (2010) lists 42 separate IC measurement methodologies used over the past twenty years or so. For a firm looking to assess its intangibles, compare them to other firms or to an industry standard, which is appropriate? While some are better known than others (e.g. Balanced Scorecard, Skandia Navigator), there is no one, settled standard for reporting on IC.

One important way in which governance can support greater development of knowledge assets is by creating such a standard. No state requires IC reporting, but there are examples of governing organizations looking to establish a framework and getting resident firms on the same page. If governance rules can be introduced to encourage firms to apply the same structure to IC statements voluntarily, the potential exists for more attention paid to the metrics, a greater ability to compare across firms and industries, and more information for managers looking to better manage their knowledge assets; with better potential for more innovation at both the firm and national/regional levels.

Two of the best-known national governance initiatives are the MERITUM project and the Danish Intellectual Capital Guidelines. Measuring Intangibles to Understand and Improve Innovation Management (MERITUM) was a European Union research project designed, among other things, 'to produce a classification of intangibles' and 'a set of guidelines for the measurement and disclosure of intangibles' (European Commission 2011; MERITUM 2001). The end product relies on the standard human, structural, and relational capital structure and is more a series of suggested indicators than formal guidelines. Yet, it still provides government-assisted direction in terms of what to look for if management wants to better evaluate its own IC. Details are noted in Table 10.2.

The Danish guidelines are somewhat related, with some of the same scholars involved, but are more widely used and had more significant participation from private sector firms (DMST, 2003). The work was backed by the Danish Ministry of Science & Technology. The result is much more detailed than the MERITUM or some other frameworks. The structure includes many familiar items (and some less familiar), and sorts indicators into the categories of resources, activities, and effects for each item – similar to the national accounts we saw in Andriessen and Stam (2004). A condensed version of the guidelines is presented in Table 10.2.

Even without getting further into the details, there are obvious advantages to having an environment such as that found in Denmark, where there is clear governmental guidance for any firm thinking about paying closer attention to its intangible assets and how it can measure and manage them better. This type of support could be an important addition to the conversation between governance and intangibles management perspectives.

A related but different governance concern is how a government helps to *protect the knowledge assets* that firms work hard to create and leverage. If intellectual capital is valuable to a firm, it would almost certainly be valuable to its competitors as well, perhaps more so. Indeed, the field of competitive intelligence (CI) is predicated upon the idea that valuable competitive insights can be gained from monitoring a competitor and

Table 10.2   Government-supported IC reporting guidelines

MERITUM Intangibles (MERITUM 2001)	Danish Guidelines (DMST 2003)
Highly trained people	Marketing of company to potential employees
Training activities	Hiring of experienced employees
Employee surveys (satisfaction)	Employee satisfaction surveys
Patents	Performance reviews
R&D activities	Training plans
Analysis of R&D rate of return	Flexible and transparent working conditions
Flexibility – structural capital	Creation of common identity and spirit
Increase codified routines	Mentor or introduction scheme for new employees
Use of codified routines	Good physical surroundings
Flexibility—relational capital	Competency recording
Select and act on key customers	Competency development plans
Loyal customers	Formal supplementary training
Direct marketing	Exchange of professional advice through daily work
Customer survey	Exchange of knowledge
Flexibility – human capital	Process optimization
Job rotation	Operating efficiency
	Develop proficiency in process control
	IT support of work processes
	Resource control
	Customer-oriented processes
	Quality assurance of processes
	Quality assurance of case handling
	Quality assurance of processes
	Knowledge exchange across the organization
	IT support of knowledge flow
	Marketing and profiting with respect to customers
	Diffusion of company's image
	Visibility in political system
	Dialogue with customer on cooperative process
	Customer satisfaction survey
	Compiling knowledge of users' needs
	Match users' needs through development of new products
	User surveys
	Partnership with external resources
	Contact with research and educational institutions

information about that competitor. Where knowledge management opens up opportunities for firms to compete on a higher level, so it also leaves them open to CI incursions and the risk of competitors obtaining valuable intellectual capital without going to the trouble or expense of developing it themselves (Rothberg and Erickson, 2005). From a governance perspective, both stakeholders and managers would want to protect valuable intangible assets. Just as good governance shows effective use of all assets, including knowledge, so it would show a concern to protect those same assets from misappropriation by a competitor.

Within an NIS analysis, protection of intellectual property (IP) through patents and other mechanisms is often an important component of the system. Basic IP theory suggests that companies and individuals will not undertake risky innovation without the protection that comes from patents and other devices. As asked in the previous section, what happens when we extend this concept to the broader category of intellectual capital? We've already discussed how IC encompasses intangible assets that often aren't patentable. And less developed phenomena such as data and information, which can be valuable to competitive intelligence efforts, are obviously lacking such protection.

As with intellectual capital reporting guidelines, there are indications that governments are starting to recognize opportunities to support innovation and knowledge asset development by reacting to these challenges. In this case, the most prominent example is in the United States, where the Economic Espionage Act (EEA) firmed up trade secret protection in such a manner as to cover many of these softer knowledge assets if corporate leaders take steps to properly qualify them. Trade secret law in the USA had always been somewhat fuzzy and varied by state. The EEA was enacted in 1997, establishing a federal standard, criminalizing trade secret misappropriation and adding enforcement with federal backing. The FBI has been known to get involved with EEA cases, up to and including sting operations. The Department of Justice (DOJ) prosecutes EEA cases. The specific statute reads:

> The term 'trade secret' means all forms and types of financial, business, scientific, technological, economic or engineering information, including patterns, plans, compilations, programme devices, formulae, designs, prototypes, methods, techniques, processes, procedures, programmes or codes, whether tangible or intangible, and whether or how stored, compiled or memorized physically, electronically, graphically, photographically, or in writing, if:
> - the owner thereof has taken reasonable measures to keep such information secret; and
> - the information derives independent economic value, actual or potential, from not being generally known to, and not being generally ascertainable

through proper means, by the public (18 United States Code §1839 (Supp. IV 1998)

What this establishes is a standard of protection for almost anything of business value, including data, information, and knowledge. The requirement on the user is to take steps to try to keep it secret and protect that secrecy. This has changed the game in terms of trade secrets and their application. One study we have conducted on DOJ cases pursued under the act found that a substantial number of the actions involved matter such as customer lists or product use/application knowledge rather than product inputs and production details that typically made up trade secrets in the past (Erickson and Carr, 2010). While enforcement and court interpretation of the law (O'Grady, 2006) will influence the impact of the law in coming years, there is little doubt that it is a major change in terms of protecting intellectual capital. Such protection can be another important environmental factor in encouraging effective corporate governance and both development and protection of knowledge assets.

One final area where governance can have an impact on a more expansive view of national knowledge assets is in *stewardship of intellectual capital*. One important aspect of the current thinking about IC that we haven't discussed in depth is the network concept. As firms, their supply chains, and distribution channels become ever more intertwined, including in how they share data, information, and knowledge, the knowledge assets flowing between them have grown exponentially. For many firms, it's not a matter of their own IC that they use, grow, and protect, but the IC of their entire network of business partners. Stewardship of the IC of others is an important topic. Are you protecting the critical knowledge assets of your business partners?

This again becomes a governance issue because corporate leadership would be expected to take care in deciding with whom to share valuable proprietary assets. Good decisions can be made, resulting in sharing with network partners who are good stewards of the intangibles and help to leverage and grow them. Poor decisions can result in sharing assets with untrustworthy partners. When you add the complication that governments are often one of those network partners, the decisions of corporate leadership get more complicated. Governments can be customers, purchasing data, information and knowledge, and they also may have access as a regulator or collector of the same. When this happens, firms may have concerns about what the government is doing with the IC. One area of concern is privacy. Another is, once again, protection.

On the privacy side, personal privacy is a concern with much of the knowledge asset base built and held by private businesses. Good governance suggests setting and administering a consistent privacy policy for information entrusted by customers. From a national governance point of view, there are very different standards for individual privacy around the world. The EU is probably in the forefront of protection, with recent and substantive regulation (European Commission, 2011) regarding the privacy of personal data. In the USA, on the other hand, privacy is a fuzzy right, somewhat established in case law ('the right to be left alone') but really protected legislatively only in specific circumstances (e.g. video store rental records, children) and only from the government – not necessarily from private companies. The ability of companies to acquire individual, private information based on promises can be compromised if shared with a government that doesn't protect the data or that applies it in unanticipated ways. TomTom, for example, was highly embarrassed when it was revealed it sold users' data to the Dutch and Australian governments that was then used to issue speeding tickets (Ramli, 2011). Government standards on personal privacy and government actions regarding personal privacy can affect some of the intellectual capital of firms, especially those serving consumers.

An even trickier circumstance is government protection of firms' proprietary intellectual capital. In an environment with increasing pressure for open governance, Freedom of Information (FOI) laws have the potential to require firms to hand over data, information, or knowledge that could be considered a valuable, secret asset of the firm (Erickson, 2009). FOI statute and practice vary radically across the world. There is the statute itself, but there is also the presumption of an executive branch (in the USA, Bush administration: deny FOI requests when in doubt; Obama administration: grant FOI requests when in doubt) and the specific agencies. Again, in the USA, a denial on the basis of 'confidential business information' or privacy can lead to continuous appeals and even court challenges. It can be easier to just grant the request and release the record.

The situation for business is that it may turn knowledge assets, including proprietary data and information, over to a regulator or other government agency, then find them released due to an FOI request with no input into the decision and nothing they can do about it. Evidence exists of forum shopping by specific competitors (Rice, 2000; O'Reilly, 1982) (Suzuki allegedly follows Toyota around the world, filing FOI requests to gain confidential information through governments) as well as of widely varying procedures and differences in decision-making (Guy and Oberlin, 2009; Kilgore, 2004). If the government is a partner with access to your proprietary knowledge assets, it helps to know what FOI policies and procedures are in place. If in doubt, firms may be better off minimizing interaction with government (and government contracts) if a connection puts proprietary IC at risk.

Once again, national governments can support effective corporate governance by establishing clear standards and enforcing good practices. Leadership at firms can effectively perform their duties if they weigh the positives and negatives of dealing with governments in relation to knowledge assets. In the case of regulators, corporate management may have little choice, but it does have options when it comes to doing business with the government and/or selling information to it. Effective stewardship by the government will aid corporate managers to make appropriate decisions on sharing intangible assets. In some cases, the right decision will undoubtedly be not to interact at all unless privacy and ownership concerns are properly addressed.

CONCLUSIONS

Changes in the range and nature of important intangible assets have created new opportunities and challenges for corporate governance. Although harder to identify and define, intellectual capital, which includes various permutations of data, information, and knowledge, could be drawn upon to conceptualize the change in the breadth and nature of innovative activity. Intellectual capital has the capability of creating competitive advantage for the firm and strategic management of such knowledge assets can be taken as a sign of enhanced governance.

But effective governance in this realm is not easy to develop and implement, as returns on intellectual capital are often not accruing until some years in the future. A number of complications exist which leaders need to overcome. Initially, growing knowledge assets in-house involves different types of assets (human, structural, relational) at different levels of development. Establishing investment in these assets, their stock levels, and their potential for future growth and contribution to profit is an unsettled area of management. But incorporating a system to do so and reporting out its results can reassure investors and does help provide insight into effective governance. To the extent that national bodies can help to create and standardize such reporting, the road to effective corporate governance is easier to navigate.

Similarly, corporate leaders should also be able to show they have taken steps to protect such valuable proprietary assets, both from prying competitors and from sloppy collaborators, including government. In the past, this has been done mainly through mechanisms such as patents and copyrights, but these new classes of knowledge assets often fail to meet patenting criteria and may not be as readily identifiable. But tools and techniques are available, from trade secrets to higher levels of information technology security. In some cases, the answer may simply be using care in deciding what knowledge or information to share with outside entities (again including government). Effective governance is shown in the proper care and stewardship of these knowledge assets and, once again, national governments can make this task easier with appropriate protection mechanisms written into law (and enforced) and attention paid to how corporate knowledge is handled when regulatory bodies are privy to it.

In short, effective corporate governance faces a number of new concerns that were not even on the radar two decades ago. Forward-looking managers are recognizing these threats and opportunities and acting upon them. But just as national innovation systems have been viewed as an effective approach to encouraging innovation, so national governments can now look to how they might help companies to also develop and protect these less well-defined intangibles that constitute a significant part of intellectual capital.

REFERENCES

Abeysekera, I. (2006), 'The project of intellectual capital disclosure: researching the research', *Journal of Intellectual Capital*, 7(1), 61–77.

Andreou, A., A. Green and M. Stankosky (2007), 'A framework of intangible valuation areas and antecedents', *Journal of Intellectual Capital*, 8(1), 52–75.

Andriessen, D.G. and C.D. Stam (2004), *The Intellectual Capital of the European Union*, Diemen, Netherlands: Centre for Research in Intellectual Capital.

Boisot, M. (1995), 'Is your firm a creative destroyer? Competitive learning and knowledge flows in the technological strategies of firms', *Research Policy*, 24(4), 489–506.

Bontis, N. (1999), 'Managing organizational knowledge by diagnosing intellectual capital: framing and advancing the state of the field', *International Journal of Technology Management*, 18(5–8), 433–462.

Bontis, N. (2004), 'National intellectual capital index: a United Nations initiative for the Arab region', *Journal of Intellectual Capital*, 5(1), 13–39.

Bukh, P.N. (2003), 'Commentary: The relevance of intellectual capital disclosure: a paradox?', *Accounting, Auditing & Accountability Journal*, 16(1), 49–56.

Cerbioni, F. and A. Parbonetti (2007), 'Exploring the effects of corporate governance on intellectual capital disclosure: an analysis of European biotechnology companies', *European Accounting Review*, 16(4), 791–826.

Choi, B. and H. Lee (2003), 'An empirical investigation of KM styles and their effect on corporate performance', *Information & Management*, 40(5), 403–417.

DMST (Danish Ministry of Science, Technology & Innovation) (2003), 'Intellectual capital statements – the new guideline', available at http://en.vtu.dk/publications/2003/intellectual-capital-statements-the-new-guideline.

Dosi, G., C. Freeman, R.R. Nelson, G. Silverberg and L. Soete (eds) (1988), *Technological Change and Economic Theory*, London: Pinter.

Edvinsson, L. (2002), 'The knowledge capital of nations', *Knowledge Management*, (April), 27–30.

Edvinsson, L. and M. Malone (1997), *Intellectual Capital: Realizing Your Company's True Value by Finding its Hidden Roots*, New York: Harper Business.

Erickson, G.S. (1996), 'Environment and innovation: the case of the small entity', *Industrial Marketing Management*, 25(6), 577–587.

Erickson, G.S. (1999), 'Patent law and new product development: does priority claim basis make a difference?', *American Business Law Journal*, 36(2), 327–347.

Erickson, G.S. (2009), 'Government stewardship of online information: FOIA requirements and other considerations', in K. Chen and A. Fadlalla (eds), *Online Consumer Protection: Theories of Human Relativism*, Hershey, PA: Information Science Reference/IGI Global, pp. 310–325.

Erickson, G.S. and C.A. Carr (2010), 'The changing face of intellectual assets: trade secrets and the Economic Espionage Act', in B.A. Everett and N.L. Trijillo (eds), *Technology Transfer and Intellectual Property Issues*, Hauppage, NY: Nova Science Publishers, pp. 197–211.

European Commission (2011), 'MERITUM – intellectual capital guidelines for firms', accessed at http://ec.europa.eu/research/social-sciences/projects/073_en.html

Fagerberg, J. and M. Srholec (2008), 'National innovation systems, capabilities and economic development', *Research Policy*, 37(9), 1417–1435.

Fillipetti, A. and D. Archibuigi (2011), 'Innovation in times of crisis: national systems of innovation, structure and demand', *Research Policy*, 40(2), 179–192.

Freeman, C. (1987), *Technology Policy and Economic Performance: Lessons from Japan*, London: Pinter.

Grant, R.M. (1996), 'Toward a knowledge-based theory of the firm', *Strategic Management Journal*, 17 (Winter), 109–122.

Gupta, A.K. and V. Govindarajan (2000), 'Knowledge flows within multinational corporations', *Strategic Management Journal*, 21(4), 473–496.

Guy, M. and M. Oberlin (2009), 'Assessing the health of FOIA after 2000 through the lens of national security archive and federal government audits', *Law Library Journal*, 101(3), 331–353.

Herschel, R.T. and N.E. Jones (2005), 'Knowledge management and business intelligence: the importance of integration', *Journal of Knowledge Management*, 9(4), 45–55.

Hervas-Oliver, J.-L., R. Rojas, B.-M. Martins and R. Cervello-Royo (2011), 'The overlapping of national IC and innovation systems,' *Journal of Intellectual Capital*, 12(1), 111–130.

Keenan, J. and M. Aggestam (2001), 'Corporate governance and intellectual capital: some conceptualisations', *Corporate Governance: An International Review*, 9(4), 259–275.

Kilgore, H.E. (2004), 'Signed, sealed, protected: solutions to agency handling of confidential business information in informal rulemaking', *Administrative Law Review*, 56(2), 519–534.

Lev, B. and P. Zarowin (1999), 'The boundaries of financial reporting and how to extend them', *Journal of Accounting Research*, 37(2), 353–386.

Li, J., R. Pike and R. Haniffa (2008), 'Intellectual capital disclosure and corporate governance structure in UK firms', *Accounting and Business Research*, 38(2), 137–159.

Lundvall, B.-A. (1988), 'Innovation as an interactive process: from user-producer interaction to the national innovation systems', in G. Dosi, C. Freeman, R.R. Nelson, G. Silverberg and L. Soete (eds), *Technological Change and Economic Theory*, London: Pinter.

Lundvall, B.-A., B. Johnson, E.S. Andersen and B. Dalum (2002), 'National systems of production, innovation and competence building', *Research Policy*, 31(2), 213–231.

MERITUM (2001), 'Final report MERITUM project', accessed at http://www.pnbukh.com/site/files/pdf_filer/FINAL_REPORT_MERITUM.pdf.

Nahapiet, J. and S. Ghoshal (1998), 'Social capital, intellectual capital, and the organizational advantage', *Academy of Management Review*, 23(2), 242–266.

Nelson, R.R. (ed.) (1993), *National Innovation Systems*, New York: Oxford University Press.

Nonaka, I. and H. Takeuchi (1995), *The Knowledge-Creating Company: How Japanese Companies Create the Dynamics of Innovation*, New York: Oxford University Press.

Pasher, E. (1999), *The Intellectual Capital of the State of Israel*, Herzlia Pituach: Kal Press, Israel.

Polanyi, M. (1967), *The Tacit Dimension*, New York: Doubleday.

Porter, M. (1998), *The Competitive Advantage of Nations*, New York: The Free Press.

Pulic, A. (2002), *The Intellectual Capital of the State of Croatia*, Zagreb, Croatia: International Business Efficiency Consulting.

O'Grady, et. al. v. Superior Court (2006), 139 Cal. App. 4Th 1423.

O'Reilly, J.T. (1982), 'Regaining a confidence: protection of business confidential data through reform of the freedom of information act', *Administrative Law Review*, 34(2), 263–313.

Ramli, D. (2011), 'Peeping TomTom sells your every move', *The Australian Financial Review* (6 May).

Rice, S. (2000), 'Public environmental records – a treasure chest of competitive information', *Competitive Intelligence Magazine*, 3(3), 13–19.

Rothberg, H.N. and G.S. Erickson (2005), *From Knowledge to Intelligence: Creating Competitive Advantage in the Next Economy*, Woburn, MA: Elsevier Butterworth-Heinemann.

Schulz, M. and L.A. Jobe (2001), 'Codification and tacitness as knowledge management strategies: an empirical exploration', *Journal of High Technology Management Research*, 12(1), 139–165.

Stewart, T.A. (1997), *Intellectual Capital: The New Wealth of Organizations*, New York: Doubleday.

Sveiby, K.-E. (2010), 'Methods for measuring intangible assets', accessed at http://www.sveiby.com/articles/IntangibleMethods.htm.

Teece, D.J., G. Pisano and A. Shuen (1997), 'Dynamic capabilities and strategic management', *Strategic Management Journal*, 18(7), 509–533.

Weimer, J. and J. Pape (1999), 'A taxonomy of systems of corporate governance', *Corporate Governance: An International Review*, 7(2), 152–166.

Wiig, K.M. (1997), 'Integrating intellectual capital and knowledge management', *Long Range Planning*, 30(3), 399–405.

Zack, M.H. (1999), 'Developing a knowledge strategy', *California Management Review*, 41(3), 125–145.

11. Concluding remarks on governance, regulation and innovation

Mehmet Ugur

In this book, we aimed to demonstrate that governance and regulatory quality matters for innovation on its own and through interactions with market structure as well as distance to the technology/efficiency frontier. Two observations have informed this aim. First, the received wisdom reflected in the policy debate tends to establish shortcuts between competition, product-market deregulation and globalization on the one hand and innovation on the other. Secondly, the existing literature, despite its richness and long history, tends to analyse the determinants of innovation separately rather than jointly. Yet, innovation is costly and associated with uncertain returns, externalities, indivisibilities and information asymmetries. Although most of these aspects are central to the analysis in the existing literature, the ways in which governance and regulation impact on these characteristics and hence on the innovation outcomes are not investigated adequately.

The contributors to the book demonstrate that incorporating governance, regulation and market structure and their interactions into the analysis is both necessary and rewarding. They have produced a wide range of results that indicate that governance and regulation matter for innovation and that one needs to be aware of complementary as well as offsetting effects that may result from interaction between governance, regulation, the market structure, and distance to the technology/efficiency frontier. The findings may not be helpful for articulating catchy shortcuts between innovation and its determinants, but they are highly informative about the costs and benefits of innovation even though the latter is a major determinant of long-term productivity and growth. They are also highly informative about the range of complementarities and trade-offs between policy choices. The general conclusions we derive from the analysis in this book and the implications for policy and research are summarized below.

One general conclusion is that country-level economic governance institutions matter for innovation. Specifically, rule of law, accountability, efficiency of the bureaucracy, control of corruption, and creditor protection are positively related to innovation – either in terms of R&D expenditures during the crisis period or in terms of patents granted by different patenting authorities over a longer time period. Furthermore, country-level governance quality has both complementary and offsetting effects on the relationship between market power and innovation. When market power is initially low (i.e., when competition is initially high), an increase in market power (i.e., a decrease in competition) tends to have a negative effect on innovation by inducing managerial slack or reducing the pressure on firms to innovate. In this case, better governance quality puts this negative effect into sharper relief – i.e., it reinforces the negative effects of increased market power (reduced competition). Stated differently, good governance quality combined with higher levels of competition is a strong driver of innovation – if the initial level of competition is already high.

Similarly, good governance also plays a welfare-enhancing role when the initial level of market power is high – i.e., when the initial level of competition is low. In this case, a further increase in market power has a Schumpeterian effect of increasing innovation. In other words, at initially high levels of market power innovation is driven by monopoly rents and causes welfare loss. Here, good governance has an offsetting effect that mitigates the welfare loss by weakening the positive relationship between market power (i.e., monopoly rents) and innovation.

Although governance quality has a positive effect on patenting activity, this effect is mitigated by market power. As the latter increases, the marginal effect of governance on innovation declines. Hence, governance quality is good for innovation, but it will not be good enough if it co-exists with high levels of market power.

Similar results have been obtained with respect to the relationship between corporate governance and innovation. We have demonstrated that corporate governance dimensions such as board independence and diversity, anti-merger defences, ownership type and shareholder rights are related to firms' innovation effort. Furthermore, these corporate governance dimensions interact with market concentration and produce offsetting effects with the exception of board independence.

We have also established that country-level governance institutions do interact with firm-level corporate governance. Specifically, we report that a regime with strong creditor rights is a significant institution that contributes to maintaining the R&D effort during crisis times. More interestingly, however, we also report that the interaction between institutional ownership of equity and a market-based financial system tends to have a large and negative effect on the R&D effort by European firms.

Remaining on the theme of governance and innovation, we have also addressed the question as to how past innovation effort may affect policy reforms aimed at enhancing the governance of innovation. We have addressed this question in the context of the European Union's Lisbon Agenda for innovation. Our findings indicate that the effect depends on whether innovation is measured in terms of effort (i.e., R&D or higher education expenditures) or in terms of outcomes (i.e., patenting intensity, technology transfer or intellectual property). We report that past innovation effort tends to induce policy reforms that would reduce the disparity between EU Member States in the long run. However, past performance in terms of innovation outcomes (i.e., in terms of innovative stock) tend to increase the disparity. Hence, it is important to study not only the effect of governance on innovation but also the effect of the latter on policy reform aimed at strengthening the governance of innovation.

Along a similar line, we have also addressed the question as to how innovation affects the behaviour of private suppliers in regulated industries. Specifically, we have asked the question as to whether investment in innovative technology increases the probability of reputational or opportunistic behaviour by private suppliers engaged in public-private partnerships in the French water industry. Our findings indicate that investment in innovative technology generates incentives that increase the probability of reputational behaviour (i.e., the probability of better service provision). However, we have also checked whether competition emerges as a substitute or complement to investment in innovation. Our results indicate that competition from public-sector providers tend to have a substitution effect on the probability of reputational behaviour whereas private supplier competition has no significant effect. Indeed, on its own, competition from private suppliers is found to have a negative effect on the probability of reputational behaviour. These results cast doubt about the extent to which competition between private suppliers of water can be relied upon as a disciplining mechanism that would deliver services of general interest effectively or efficiently.

Our findings are equally informative when we addressed the relationship between regulation and innovation from the opposite end of the telescope – i.e., when asked whether regulation increases or decreases innovation performance. First of all, and in contrast to received wisdom, we have established that prescriptive regulatory rules tend to have a positive effect on the probability of eco-innovation among UK firms at both ends of the innovation spectrum: the low-impact end-of-pipeline pollution control technologies and the high-impact environmental R&D investments. Indeed, we have also established that this positive effect remains significant under three scenarios: (i) the overall effect on the probability of innovation; (ii) the marginal effect on the probability of decision to embark on innovation; and (iii) the marginal effect on the probability of innovation by existing innovators. In other words, prescriptive innovation does not pick up winners only (i.e., induce only existing innovators), but also it encourages non-innovators to innovate. In contrast, incentive-based measures (which are the preferred option in the current policy debate) tend to be insignificant, with the exception of picking up winners in the medium-impact innovation in integrated technology.

In the case of information and communications technology (ICT), we report that two indicators of country-level regulation (i.e., regulation of network industries and effects of network industry regulation on other sectors) have negative partial effects on the level of investment in ICT technologies. However, product-market regulation and the size of the public sector in product markets have no significant effects. Although the negative relationship between network industry regulation and ICT intensity is in line with the received wisdom in the policy debate, this is by no means a universal finding – as indicated by the insignificant effects from product-market regulation and the size of the public sector. More importantly, however, when regulation is interacted with closeness to the technology frontier, the marginal effects differ. When industries are at the technology frontier, three types of regulation (regulation of network industries, effect of the latter on other sectors, and product-market regulation) tend to have a positive effect on ICT intensity. In other words, regulation tends to reinforce ICT absorption at the technology frontier. Regulation tends to have no significant effect on ICT intensity when industries are below the technology frontier – except when closeness to the technology frontier is minimum (i.e., when distance to technology frontier is maximum). These findings indicate that regulation may be deterring the laggard industries from catching up; but this effect may be due to the possibility that regulation may be inducing industries to undertake drastic innovation and this type of innovation may not be suitable for industries very far away from the technology frontier.

We have also examined the effect of regulation on innovation as well as distance to the efficiency frontier in the pharmaceutical industry, taking into account the level of market concentration. Our findings indicate that the R&D effort is not related systematically either to the level of market concentration or to the stringency of price regulation in 11 countries that are major players in the pharmaceutical industry. Similarly, the distance to the efficiency frontier is not related systematically either to the level of market concentration or to the stringency of price regulation in the same set of countries. Hence, we fail to find any support for industry claims that price regulation is harmful for innovation by pharmaceutical firms.

Finally, we have also explored the scope for extending the range of innovation activities to include less easy-to-measure intangible assets that are increasingly considered as potential determinants of firm value and performance; and the extent to which corporate governance regimes can be adopted to manage and protect these assets. Although normative, this question is pertinent because firms possess data, information and knowledge – which accumulate over time and create value. Yet the rules and metrics for measuring the value of these intangible assets and the corporate governance rules that would guide managers for managing and protecting them are under developed. We report that the governance perspective, by pointing out the importance of appropriate governance structures for innovation, can provide new insights into how corporate governance regimes can be adapted to ensure better management and support for creation, valuation and protection of intangible assets.

One policy implication of our findings is that innovation is not always driven by competition. Competition can drive innovation when its initial level is high. This is the case at both the firm and country levels – and in the case of both R&D expenditures and patenting activity. Policy reforms aiming to encourage innovation in environments characterized with high market power or concentration are likely to reduce innovation effort because innovation in such environments is driven by monopoly rents. At the country level, governance quality mitigates the positive relationship between market power and innovation when the initial level of market power is high. Therefore, policy reforms aimed at increasing competition in product markets will be more effective in stimulating innovation if they are accompanied with policy reform aimed at enhancing economic governance institutions such as accountability, rule of law, control of corruption etc. The role of corporate governance rules are less clear-cut as firms may be choosing the board type, the ownership structure or the openness to the market for corporate control endogenously.

Another policy implication is that the policy preference for deregulation as a means of stimulating innovation is not supported by the evidence we have analysed. Indeed, we have found that prescriptive regulation is good for eco-innovation by firms and different types of regulation do not reduce ICT intensity in industries close to the technical efficiency frontier. In the pharmaceutical industry case, regulation is not related either to innovation or to the distance to the efficiency frontier at the firm level. These findings are not surprising because deregulation induces competition in industries or sectors where the initial level of competition is high. As such, it sets in a reverse Schumpeterian effect whereby lower monopoly rents reduce innovation effort. Therefore, in such environments, it is preferable to combine product-market deregulation with innovation-related regulatory requirements when the latter can be justified on welfare grounds.

We acknowledge the fact that the existing research on innovation and its determinants is very rich and sophisticated. However, our findings in this book indicate that the existing tendency to focus on one set of drivers at a time is likely to yield biased results. The bias has both theoretical and empirical reasons. Given that governance, regulation and market structure all affect the costs and incentives faced by innovators, it is theoretically necessary to estimate not only partial effects from a particular driver but also marginal effects that take account of other drivers and their interaction with the driver of interest. This requirement also has an empirical basis: models that do not take account of interaction and/or non-linear effects are likely to be misspecified and would produce biased estimates.

Index